Robert B. Marchesani
E. Mark Stern
Editors

Saints and Rogues: Conflicts and Convergence in Psychotherapy

Saints and Rogues: Conflicts and Convergence in Psychotherapy has been co-published simultaneously as *The Psychotherapy Patient*, Volume 13, Numbers 1/2 2004.

Pre-publication REVIEWS, COMMENTARIES, EVALUATIONS . . .

"A SERIES OF STRONG ESSAYS BY PIERCING THINKERS who refuse to cloak themselves in collectively acceptable generalities. . . . Provides resources and road signs for independent-minded therapists of all persuasions."

Jeffrey K. Zeig, PhD
Director, The Milton H. Erickson Foundation

More pre-publication
REVIEWS, COMMENTARIES, EVALUATIONS . . .

"THIS BOOK CAPTIVATES THE READER with its almost dazzling variety of material. Untreated elsewhere, the subject matter begs for attention. Hendrika Van de Kamp's blend of a high level of historical scholarship and obvious delight in her exploration leaves us with a better understanding of the personhood and influence of Harry Stack Sullivan, one of the great psychiatric healers of the last century. Elizabeth A. Rock's creative approach to the 'easily aroused child' allows us to lift the mask of the bully; her description of one bullying prevention project is especially useful. E. Mark Stern's composite verbal portrait of an apparently schizophrenic homeless individual is, by turns, abstruse and appealing, fascinating and frustrating–and thus vividly reproduces the experience of the therapist in encountering this type of client."

Mary Anne Siderits, PhD
Director, Marquette University Center for Psychological Services

Routledge
Taylor & Francis Group
LONDON AND NEW YORK

Saints and Rogues: Conflicts and Convergence in Psychotherapy

Saints and Rogues: Conflicts and Convergence in Psychotherapy has been co-published simultaneously as *The Psychotherapy Patient*, Volume 13, Numbers 1/2 2004.

Psychosocial Approaches to Deeply Disturbed Persons, edited by Peter R. Breggin, MD, and E. Mark Stern, EdD (Vol. 9, No. 3/4, 1996). *"This book creatively describes the dedicated work of those who try to understand disturbed people rather than condemn them by labeling them as hopeless." (Revella Levin, PhD, Director, Center for the Study of Psychiatry and Psychology-East, New York City)*

Psychotherapy and the Dangerous Patient, edited by Jerome A. Travers, PhD (Vol. 9, No. 1/2, 1995). *"I cannot imagine that there is a psychiatrist, psychotherapist, or any other mental health clinician, or indeed, manager who would not find this volume of value. . . . Its inclusion of the raw and frankly alarming only adds to its value as a text." (British Journal of Psychiatry)*

Betrayal in Psychotherapy and Its Antidotes: Challenges for Patient and Therapist, edited by E. Mark Stern, EdD (Vol. 8, No. 3/4, 1993). *Contributing authors present various faces of betrayal as may be encountered by therapists in the office or in the profession.*

Psychotherapy and the Promiscuous Patient, edited by E. Mark Stern, EdD (Vol. 8, No. 1/2, 1992). *"A guide for clinical psychotherapists who treat sexual promiscuity." (SciTech Book News)*

Psychotherapy and the Self-Righteous Patient, edited by Jerome A. Travers (Vol. 7, No. 3/4, 1991). *"Penetrating, multidisciplinary analyses and illuminating case histories combine to advance treatment of those for whom 'love is never enough.'" (W. Stephen Sabom, STD, Psychotherapist, Houston)*

Psychotherapy and the Poverty Patient, edited by E. Mark Stern, EdD (Vol. 7, No. 1/2, 1991). *"Address[es] not only pscyhotherapy with patients of limited financial means, but psychotherapy with 'psychologically' impoverished clients. . . . Most chapters consist of case vignettes with the clinician's reflections of relevant issues." (Contemporary Psychology)*

Psychotherapy and the Widowed Patient, edited by E. Mark Stern, EdD (Vol. 6, No. 3/4, 1990). *"Contains much useful information for the members of the disciplines–such as psychology, social work, psychiatry, family practice, and the ministry–dealing with bereavement." (The Journal of Clinical Psychiatry)*

Psychotherapy and the Remote Patient, edited by Jerome A. Travers, PhD (Vol. 6, No. 1/2, 1990). *"Reminds readers that there are numerous perspectives from which to view problems that patients bring to the therapy setting. . . . This book is a must for any clinician wishing to maintain a sense of professional curiosity and growth." (Naomi James, PhD, private practice, Venice, California; President Elect, American Academy of Psychotherapists)*

Psychotherapy and the Grandiose Patient, edited by E. Mark Stern, EdD (Vol. 5, No. 3/4, 1989). *A practical book for any mental health professional who is working with grandiose clients.*

Psychotherapy and the Remorseful Patient, edited by E. Mark Stern, EdD (Vol. 5, No. 1/2, 1989). *"It is easily read as a combination of theory and practical applications–which, together with its extensive bibliography, rounds it out as a comprehensive treatment of a pivotal consideration." (Journal of the American Association of Psychiatric Administrators)*

Psychotherapy and the Self-Contained Patient, edited by E. Mark Stern, EdD (Vol. 4, No. 3/4, 1989). *Addresses the intricacies of working with the self-contained person.*

Psychotherapy and the Somatizing Patient, edited by E. Mark Stern, EdD, and Virginia Fraser Stern, PhD (cand.) (Vol. 4, No. 2, 1989). *"This book will stretch your mind. . . . If you want to appreciate the rich complexity of the somatizing patient, this book is for you." (David Kirkpatrick, MD, psychotherapist and psychiatrist, Ashland, Oregon)*

Psychotherapy and the Creative Patient, edited by E. Mark Stern, EdD (Vol. 4, No. 1, 1988). *Valuable insights into using psychotherapy as a means of stimulating a patient's creativity.*

Psychotherapy and the Bored Patient, edited by E. Mark Stern, EdD (Vol. 3, No. 3/4, 1988). *Here are important theories and therapies that shed light on boredom–why it is a necessity and an obstacle in a person's development.*

Psychotherapy and the Obsessed Patient, edited by E. Mark Stern, EdD (Vol. 3, No. 2, 1987). *A wealth of theoretical insights and suggestions for therapy with obsessed patients–those suffering from bulimia, monomania, love obsessions, and more.*

Psychotherapy and the Interminable Patient, edited by Jerome A. Travers, PhD, and E. Mark Stern, EdD (Vol. 3, No. 1, 1986). *Experts discuss the issues psychotherapists face in the treatment of long-term patients, including separation and autonomy.*

Psychotherapy and the Memorable Patient, edited by William Kir-Stimon, PhD, and E. Mark Stern, EdD (Vol. 2, No. 4, 1986). *"A joy to read. . . . For the experienced therapist, this book offers an opportunity to view the work of others. . . . For the therapist-in-training, it can help to reduce anxiety and provide reassurance." (Joseph Lassner, PhD, ACSW, Associate Professor of Social Work, Loyola University of Chicago)*

Psychotherapy and the Lonely Patient, edited by Samuel M. Natale, PhD (Vol. 2, No. 3, 1986). *"A beautifully written and sensitive book . . . covers a wide range of populations that need to cope with and confront loneliness on a daily basis." (Herbert J. Freudenberger, PhD, Psychoanalyst in New York City; Author,* Women's Burnout*)*

Psychotherapy and the Selfless Patient, edited by Jerome A. Travers, PhD (Vol. 2, No. 2, 1986). *A wealth of theoretical and clinical material on the developmental and philosophical issues regarding the origin and loss of self.*

Psychotherapy and the Grieving Patient, edited by E. Mark Stern, EdD (Vol. 2, No. 1, 1986). *"Of substantial assistance to the practitioner and an excellent review of the multitudinous aspects of grieving. An important contribution to the literature." (S. R. Graham, PhD, Fellow, American Psychological Association, Diplomate in Clinical Psychology)*

Psychotherapy and the Terrorized Patient, edited by E. Mark Stern, EdD (Vol. 1, No. 4, 1985). *Successful interventions for helping terrorized patients cope with and overcome the pangs of uncertainty and dread which they experience constantly.*

Psychotherapy and the Religiously Committed Patient, edited by E. Mark Stern, EdD (Vol. 1, No. 3, 1985). *"Enticing entré into fascinating clinical and conceptual material. . . . Provides . . . thought-provoking leads into a domain of growing importance." (Contemporary Psychology)*

Psychotherapy and the Uncommitted Patient, edited by Jerome A. Travers, Phd, and E. Mark Stern, EdD (Vol. 1, No. 2, 1985). *Provides keys to successful therapy with patients who are not committed to psychological treatment.*

Psychotherapy and the Abrasive Patient, edited by E. Mark Stern, EdD (Vol. 1, No. 1, 1984). *"A fascinating and relevant collection of essays by a group of senior psychotherapists from the various mental health disciplines." (Psychosomatics)*

Saints and Rogues: Conflicts and Convergence in Psychotherapy

Robert B. Marchesani
E. Mark Stern
Editors

Saints and Rogues: Conflicts and Convergence in Psychotherapy has been co-published simultaneously as *The Psychotherapy Patient*, Volume 13, Numbers 1/2 2004.

Routledge
Taylor & Francis Group
LONDON AND NEW YORK

First published 2004 by The Haworth Press, Inc.

2 Park Square, Milton Park, Abingdon, Oxfordshire OX14 4RN
605 Third Avenue, New York, NY 10017

Routledge is an imprint of the Taylor & Francis Group, an informa business

First issued in hardback 2020

Saints and Rogues: Conflicts and Convergence in Psychotherapy has been co-published simultaneously as *The Psychotherapy Patient*™, Volume 13, Numbers 1/2 2004.

Cover art, *Travelogues* and *The Pilgrim*, by Tobi Zausner.

Cover design by Lora Wiggins

Library of Congress Cataloging-in-Publication Data

Saints and rogues : conflicts and convergence in psychotherapy / E. Mark Stern, Robert B. Marchesani, editors.
p. cm.
"Co-published simultaneously as The psychotherapy patient, volume 13, numbers 1/2 2004."
Includes bibliographical references and index.
ISBN 0-7890-2552-3 (hard cover : alk. paper) – ISBN 0-7890-2553-1 (soft cover : alk. paper)
1. Psychotherapy. I. Stern, E. Mark, 1929- II. Marchesani, Robert B.
RC480.S213 2004
616.89'14–dc22

2004006248

ISBN 978-0-7890-2552-4 (hbk)

Indexing, Abstracting & Website/Internet Coverage

The Psychotherapy Patient

This section provides you with a list of major indexing & abstracting services. That is to say, each service began covering this periodical during the year noted in the right column. Most Websites which are listed below have indicated that they will either post, disseminate, compile, archive, cite or alert their own Website users with research-based content from this work. (This list is as current as the copyright date of this publication.)

Abstracting, Website/Indexing Coverage	Year When Coverage Began
• *CNPIEC Reference Guide: Chinese National Directory of Foreign Periodicals*	1984
• *e-psyche, LLC <http://www.e-psyche.net>*	2001
• *Family & Society Studies Worldwide <http://www.nisc.com>*	1991
• *Family Index Database <http://www.familyscholar.com>*	2003
• *Family Violence & Sexual Assault Bulletin*	1999
• *Psychiatric Rehabilitation Journal*	1999
• *Social Services Abstracts <http://www.csa.com>*	2000
• *Social Work Abstracts <http://www.silverplatter.com/catalog/swab.htm>*	1984
• *SocIndex (EBSCO)*	2003
• *Sociological Abstracts (SA) <http://www.csa.com>*	2001
• *Special Educational Needs Abstracts*	1989
• *Studies on Women Abstracts <http://www.tandf.co.uk>*	1993

(continued)

Special Bibliographic Notes related to special journal issues (separates) and indexing/abstracting:

- indexing/abstracting services in this list will also cover material in any "separate" that is co-published simultaneously with Haworth's special thematic journal issue or DocuSerial. Indexing/abstracting usually covers material at the article/chapter level.
- monographic co-editions are intended for either non-subscribers or libraries which intend to purchase a second copy for their circulating collections.
- monographic co-editions are reported to all jobbers/wholesalers/approval plans. The source journal is listed as the "series" to assist the prevention of duplicate purchasing in the same manner utilized for books-in-series.
- to facilitate user/access services all indexing/abstracting services are encouraged to utilize the co-indexing entry note indicated at the bottom of the first page of each article/chapter/contribution.
- this is intended to assist a library user of any reference tool (whether print, electronic, online, or CD-ROM) to locate the monographic version if the library has purchased this version but not a subscription to the source journal.
- individual articles/chapters in any Haworth publication are also available through the Haworth Document Delivery Service (HDDS).

ABOUT THE EDITORS

Robert B. Marchesani, MSSc, is Executive Editor of *The Psychotherapy Patient* journal and book series for The Haworth Press, Inc. He received his degree in psychoanalytic studies at the New School for Social Research in New York and trained at the Philadelphia School of Psychoanalysis. He maintains a private practice in New York City.

E. Mark Stern, EdD, ABPP, is Editor of *The Psychotherapy Patient* and Professor Emeritus in the Graduate School of Arts and Sciences at Iona College in New Rochelle, New York. He is a Diplomate in Clinical Psychology of the American Board of Professional Psychology and a Fellow of the American Psychological Association and the American Psychological Society. Dr. Stern has served as President of the Divisions of Humanistic Psychology and the Psychology of Religion of the American Psychological Association. He is currently practicing psychotherapy as a licensed psychologist with offices in New York City and Dutchess County, New York.

ALL HAWORTH BOOKS AND JOURNALS
ARE PRINTED ON CERTIFIED
ACID-FREE PAPER

Saints and Rogues: Conflicts and Convergence in Psychotherapy

CONTENTS

Rogue Roaming (A Final Preface)

Psychotherapists are estimable rogues, wonder-working sorcerers whose archetypes handily move into and beyond the tempests and zigzag patterns of the perplexed, even as they hold these now confidences in sacred trust. Riverboat gamblers; foretellers of the unseen and unexpected; wary exemplars sporting disarming guises, the psychotherapist somehow begs the demons welcome. Trained in daunting pragmatics, the therapists act more the role of transcendental redeemers.

Psychotherapists, social mavericks that they be, in the best of their circumstances, learn to stand just far enough away from the herd in order to hear what the lone outlander has not said, seen, and again witnesses, with visual acuity what remains concealed from the eyes. Roguelike, psychotherapists weave for each of their patients/clients coats of unexpected but well-fitted fabrics. These offerings and other extended options run counter to the endless pitch to solve one's woes with the vast storehouse of commercial vacuities.

The wilder therapists, visceral in their excitement to waken those clients who slumber in a passive acceptance of self-destructive processes, but as rogue doctors on the frontier, continue to maintain a deep reverence for all experience, even the tempests of disordered worlds.

Yes, there are the adventurers who plod and join into the schizophrenic sphere even as the biomedics warn away with powerful potions of their own. And those clients who travel at top speeds through mood cycles would, by far, remain lost and not found ever again, were it not for the rogue therapist who calmly, though often without known remedy, accompanies the lone traveler through cave and mountaintop.

[Haworth co-indexing entry note]: "Rogue Roaming (A Final Preface)." Stern, E. Mark. Co-published simultaneously in *The Psychotherapy Patient* (The Haworth Press, Inc.) Vol. 13, No. 1/2, 2004, pp. xv-xxiii; and: *Saints and Rogues: Conflicts and Convergence in Psychotherapy* (ed: Robert B. Marchesani, and E. Mark Stern) The Haworth Press, Inc., 2004, pp. xiii-xxi. Single or multiple copies of this article are available for a fee from The Haworth Document Delivery Service [1-800-HAWORTH, 9:00 a.m. - 5:00 p.m. (EST). E-mail address: docdelivery@haworthpress.com].

Therapists work in many settings: in private and group practices, in schools, prisons, hospitals for the physically ill and the mentally tarnished. They have found working spaces in houses of worship, in the courtroom and in the military barricade. Some misappropriate their roles, seeing themselves as forensic experts, judges of who is sane and who is insane. Others are tempted to identify with the power of the medical white coat. There are soldier-therapists, some who see, rediscovered in the battle fatigued enlistee, a courage to suffer as much the now as life's latter footprints. Schools have set psychologists to separate wheat from chaff, those capable of easy lessons and the distracted, the dull-witted, the bullied and the bully. Strangely, for many, the engagement of men and women by the field of psychology has left a certain amazement at how they can help the lost child better walk through incomprehensibility and primordial darkness.

It is to the emotionally needy and the wantonly bewildered that the wilderness guides may, here and there, cast bread crumb paths along tangling forest floors. Rogues launch unwitting travelers to make perhaps the one try that will confirm a life. And all the time, it is a special sort of intuition which not all therapists equally have, but when present, such intuitiveness provides unusual fields of vision, flickering lanterns capable of penetrating invisible walls of fear.

The Psychotherapy Patient has usually kept company with the rogue therapists. Some are in search of a guidebook, a dream book, a weathered atlas, while others search for little more than confirmation of what they have always done. *The Psychotherapy Patient* series is as much a printing of mistakes and rain-lashed best attempts as it is of Falstaffian-like boastings. Of claimed skills, failed attempts, the strength to be a loggerhead, and in all of this, a slight peek behind the Persian blinds. To future generations, this series may well prove to be a refreshing find in the past, a dead sea scroll of all but forgotten procedures, boundary definitions and purifying rituals.

With this very last printing, *The Psychotherapy Patient* begins to orient its place in history. Weighing in its many wandering excursions, its experimental conservatories, and its willingness to salute the magnum opus still waiting birth, this publication grimaces as it falls into sleep.

The series owes its fertilization and birth to The Haworth Press, Inc., publisher Bill Cohen. Both prophet and entrepreneur, Bill proposed his strong interest in hosting and distributing a procession of theme-centered volumes, claiming that each would illumine through attributes focused into a continuum that would appeal to psychotherapists of whatever leanings and predispositions and perhaps just to those who consume the psychotherapy largess. In that initial meeting with Bill Cohen, I visualized a potpourri, but nonetheless an animated anthropology of idiosyncratic practices alongside nonastringent investigations. The books would serve as a nonparochial addition to the venues of the time.

Bill Cohen knew me as the editor of *Voices: The Art and Science of Psychotherapy*, the journal of the American Academy of Psychotherapists. As a lay, but no less sophisticated, spectator, he was among those quick to appreciate the qualitative advantage of the pithy quality *Voices* had pioneered. He saw in its contents the sharpened wit of a distinctively experiential American psychotherapy.

There was more and different room for what *Voices* had groomed. He envisioned additional frontiers to further address the rapid questioning of issues raised in the psychotherapy enterprise. And so he offered to print and publish this then new publication. The Haworth Press, Inc., has since taken aboard many new and exhilarating publications. In all, it has, with rare exception, retained faith in its dynamic relationship to the underlying axioms of experiential and related psychotherapies.

The Psychotherapy Patient came to be a series of journals/books, each one, however loosely, thematically based, but always inviting its contributors to challenge tradition and parade their new modes of expression. *The Psychotherapy Patient* was from its launching, a rogue publication. With this volume, *The Psychotherapy Patient* comes to an end, even as its sometime discolored pages will remain an oasis for those who refuse to be lured into an increasingly robotically inclined mental health system. Were these volumes to continue, they would undoubtedly participate in the newer cultural wars. But these battles now call on new enterprises to strike the notes of this ever unfinished polyphony. Remaining iconoclastic to its end, the charge to wrestle down sacred idols remains the perduring enjoinder.

And now to hallow all those, living and dead, who helped create the radiance of this publication. Each has been a unique presence, each a rogue marker: enthusiastic, loyal, devoted.

At the beginning there was Marie Coleman Nelson, late honorary editor of this series. Gifted with the an inimitable genius for new and unique paradigms for psychotherapy and for the psychotherapist, Marie made do as necessary double agent, rare mediator and distinguished honest broker. Her pursuits into what is appropriately dubbed transpersonal psychology, along with her desire to elude fame, places her well among the accompanying spirits and candidates for sainthood.

Also among the dead: Genevieve Izinicki, an intrepid soul whose role in creating an editorial office crossover from *Voices* to *The Psychother-*

apy Patient ranks high in the life of both publications. Her life's journey from the encroaching gates of convent life to her insistent insurgency as first, a pastoral counselor, and later as an adventuresome psychotherapist, blended in well with the launching of *The Psychotherapy Patient* editorial office.

The editorial board–a fluctuating consortium of heroes, hermits and compadres–offered, as time and occasion demanded, a many flavored critical lucidity. Then, of course, my daughter Cailean, who, while struggling with her own creations but who in turn with her husband Darren Press helped at a crucial juncture in the life of the publication, gathered and sorted through manuscripts as they passed along that neverending flow of publisher's directives.

Recalling associate editors, I call up memories of many collaborative conversations with Jerome Travers. Dr. Travers's eminence in being guest editor of several key issues of *The Psychotherapy Patient* series dubs him a lasting notability in the tradition of this publication.

The recently deceased Lawrence Tirnauer, though not as active a force in the series, had, nevertheless, been a cultivator of ever-emerging constructs in psychotherapy, a fete which has deserved him a lasting place on the masthead.

And, as well, associate editor and inspiration/inspired companion, ally, contributor, partner in dialogue and spouse, Virginia Fraser Stern, has engaged and been engaged both in the issue-to-issue process of making *The Psychotherapy Patient* a salient project and in always affirming the less obvious but critical importance of artistic groundings in stretching the range of what it means to do psychotherapy.

Late on board, but no less major helmsman and well-earned heir to that visionary province of Marie Nelson: Robert B. Marchesani. For the several past years, Robert has been the creative majordomo of this publishing venture. Generationally younger than most of the early forces in this publication, Rob has gifted us with brilliant intellect and his keen artistic apprehensions. He has, in the past few years, become the equal partner and central collaborator with this editor.

Wandering, as I have over nearly half a century, I never stop feeling pride and being amazed as I look over the lives of some of the luminaries in the field of psychotherapy. In editing this series and the two editorships of other related publications, these observations along with others as a member of several editorial boards and as a program chair for the Division of Psychotherapy of the American Psychological Association and another stint as program chair for an annual Institute and Conference of the American Academy of Psychotherapists, I have been afforded that rarest of opportunities to look at close range at some of the most notable shamans of psychotherapy.

Having wandered the meteoric trail of gatherings, workshops, conferences, caucuses and councils of psychotherapists who were sharing their working worlds; demonstrating their unique approaches to otherwise intractable enigmas; honoring colleagues with their revelations; their incomparable gnosis, this has been a marvelous journey. I have met members of the Freud family and waved birthday greetings to Carl Jung as we gathered along the side of a tour boat on Lake Zurich. I count among my memories conversations with Alexandra, a psychiatrist in her own right, and proud daughter of Alfred Adler. I was, early in my career, part of the active team of the Society for the Treatment of Psychiatric Offenders, led in New York City by Mellita Schmideberg, daughter of Melanie Klein. I took walks with Edward Glover and counted as dear friends John Wakentin and Carl Whitaker, two main players in the development of both experiential and family therapy. I am pleased to have known Albert Ellis and Rollo May, again two major figures in the struggle for a unique American psychotherapy. In Europe, and before he had made an impression on American psychotherapy, I heard Ludwig Binswanger speak to a small audience in Zurich on existential psychotherapy. I spent many hours with the launching forces of Gestalt Therapy, Laura Perls and her husband Fritz. And I performed in the psychodrama theatre in New York under the directorship of its founder and genius, Jacob Moreno. Most gratefully, I was supervised by some of the keenist thinkers in psychoanalysis, including Thedor Reik and Silvano Arieti. I consider myself a man of great fortune to have had Martin Grotjahn and Andras Angyal as my two dearest mentors.

My vagabond roamings have inspired where inspiration has since been standardized in manuals. The joy of doing the psychotherapy I have engaged in over the last half of the 20th and on into the 21st century has from its start been radically exploratory, though never without its risks.

In the wake of risk-taking, I was both interested and in no small way baffled by a recently published article by Thomas Szasz (Szasz, 2003). Tom Szasz, a giant in the field, both as a theorist and ethicist, has intrigued me by his insistence that psychotherapy is, when practiced fittingly, a confession and a moral dialogue involving an expert listener and a willing client.

A bit more history: I first set eyes on Thomas Szasz during an unlikely Palm Sunday blizzard. It was in Boston at a meeting of the American Society of Psychosomatic Medicine. Timing: just past the mid-

1950s. My late dear friend Louis Heyn, who was Thomas Szasz's classmate at the Chicago Psychoanalytic Institute, introduced me to the dapper young Hungarian-American who would ultimately have much value to contribute to the ethics of psychotherapy. Dr. Szasz has remained a heroic presence in a climate where the mental health field has too often drifted into policing.

This having been said, rogues we therapists have been, and with even the best intentions at heart, rogues we will continue to be. Note, however, that it is often the rogue who rates consideration for beatification. One need hardly look to the more traditional arc from sinner to saint than Augustine of Hippo, the Quaker George Fox and theologian Paul Tillich. Clearest about their lives is that desecration is hardly ever eradicated, but rarely stands in the way of good works.

Spiritual comrade though I sense Thomas Szasz to be, I shyly edge away from his too swift condemnations of the reprehensible actions taken by no small number of the glowing pillars of the psychotherapy movement. Szasz's (2003) article that I recently read in the *Psychoanalytic Review* convicts and adjudges some of psychotherapy's greatest with no sign whatever of Szasz's own humility in conducting this onerous task.

Some historical wanderings are in order: While taking others to task for treating involuntary patients, did the young Thomas Szasz ever treat an involuntary patient while serving his psychiatric residency at the University of Chicago? That would have been in and around the mid- to late-1940s. Being in the company of Freud's spiritual heirs, Szasz seems less inclined to set their humane achievements against the background of the menacing prison warden. Ronald D. Laing was, most would agree, a reckless soul. Professor Szasz finds Laing no heir assumptive to the antipsychiatry movement. Laing himself rejected such an inscription. Yet Szasz is all too willing to retell the story of Laing's failure to protect his own daughter from a series of electric convulsive therapy. When affliction hits home, it is no easy matter to stay the course. Laing was, by all admission, hardly the successful father. But then again, how to define success? Are the arrows Szasz aims at Dr. Laing meant to enrage the reader even before considering that the bad dad was the founder and prime promoter of Kingsley Hall–a several-year experiment in psychiatrists and schizophrenic people living in an egalitarian setting. Was Laing not making a play for anti-institutionalization as an alternative to the traditional mental asylum? Why not one word of appreciation by Szasz of Laing's capacity to dare enter into the existent world of schizophrenia?

Nor is Laing the only rogue cited for his sinful ways. Forgotten, but for the fact that a psychoanalytic institute was named after him, psychiatrist William Alanson White is taken to task by Dr. Szasz for his pernicious role as the gatekeeper of a mental hospital. I've reviewed a little of White's life, and what would make him a near notable are his pioneering attempts at bringing psychotherapy services to those who might have otherwise been banished to an otherwise repressive institution for years.

And while Harry Stack Sullivan may well have treated involuntarily hospitalized psychiatric patients early in his career, I doubt that this would rank him, as Szasz seems to suggest, as little more than an unconcerned prison guard. As Hendrika Vande Kemp so well attests to elsewhere in this volume, Sullivan envisioned his interpersonal theories as possible models for the ways and means of mediating between warring powers–hardly the archetype of the jailer.

Erik Erikson, art teacher by training and humanist by tradition, is similarly accused by Dr. Szasz for encouraging the psychoanalytic treatment of involuntary hospitalized patients. Certainly Mr. Erikson, a significant voice in the humanistic sector of psychodynamics, was one of the important forces behind the establishment of the Austin Riggs Foundation in Stockbridge, Massachusetts. Riggs, known for its open-door policy, is indeed a psychoanalytically oriented residential and day treatment facility. What Szasz does not advert to is that those who founded Austin Riggs were pioneers in the possibilities of engaging deeply troubled youths in the process of intensive introspective treatment.

Likewise, Professor Szasz fails to credit Erikson with biographical studies into the roots of fanaticism. The fanatic, usually a sometime adolescent idealist, negates that idealism for an all too easy a black-and-white picture. Erik Erikson's classic psycho-biographical studies of Martin Luther and Gandhi have provided learned accounts of rare exuberance highlighting how genius operates within particular social contexts.

Karl Menninger, certainly a rare American icon, is brought to task as well for involuntary treatment. But again, there is no mention of Karl Menninger's diatribes against the use of psychiatric diagnosis within the criminal justice system. Nor does Dr. Szasz give Karl Menninger any credit for his pioneering efforts in the establishment of safe haven communities for homeless and abused children. Karl Menninger, author, among many other titles, of *Whatever Happened to Sin?*, thoughtfully addresses the need for personal responsibility in all self-healing. Dr. Szasz appears to have forgotten his own words. In a letter Szasz wrote dated October 12, 1988, he offers Karl Menninger his "deepest respect for (his) sincerity . . . integrity" by holding fast "to the values of free will and responsibility."

Later Dr. Szasz cites Frieda-Fromm Reichman as still one more handy target. She, more than Sullivan, probably treated more hospitalized patients at the celebrated Chestnut Lodge in Maryland. Dr. Szasz notes little of what is humane in her incredible interactions with otherwise hopeless patients and the fact that she facilitated an important moral interaction between herself and the author/patient Hannah Green (aka Joanne Greenberg) in the thinly fictionalized *I Never Promised You a Rose Garden*. What makes the account so special was the protective context in which the client could engage in a life-affirming battle to secure her own capacity to thrive.

Jacques Lacan, hardly a favorite of mechanistic psychiatry, may in 1945 have indeed ordered, as reported by Szasz, a series of electric convulsive therapy for Pablo Picasso's jilted companion Francoise Gilot. Here again, Dr. Szasz chooses to pass over Lacan's attempt at creating a phenomenology of the psychosis. To a hospitalized patient, Lacan poses a paradox: "The drama of being ill, for you, is the electroshock" (Schneiderman, 1980, p. 40). Lacan hardly ignores the potential for freedom while recognizing the prevailing confining ethos acting as the central governing force for individual psychotic persons.

Finally, and to my most personal dismay, Dr. Szasz accuses the body of humanistic psychologists of unwarranted self-congratulations in his citing my friend, Duquense Psychology Professor Constance Fischer's fine-tuned exploration (in a special issue of the *Humanistic Psychologist*) of several "compassionate, caring, deeply respectful" approaches to personality assessment as merely self-congratulatory, "concealing personal and professional self-aggrandizement" (Szasz, 2003, p. 55). In his dismissal of Dr. Fischer's exploration, one finds little worth in Szasz's accusations of exploiting a vulnerable population.

How very sad that in his late years, Thomas Szasz fails to distinguish between friend and foe of the humanistic model. How sad is his own miscarriage of his lifelong mission in not allowing any degree of sainthood to his vast gallery of rogues.

With these lines, and in solidarity with rogues from Laing to Fischer, I take final leave of my editor's perch. Within half a century of practice and commentary, I have been privileged to experience a most gracious calling. I depart as your editor, forever one in union with a diverse crowd of rogue humanists: each one with pimples and scars, yet each one a personal testament to the art and theory of psychotherapy. So I, a rogue, take my leave. To where? To the hiding.

> They were only a thin slice among contiguous impressions which formed our life at the time; the memory of a certain image; moments; and houses, roads, avenues areas fleeting, alas as the years.
>
> –Marcel Proust
> *Swann's Way*

E. Mark Stern

REFERENCES

Schneiderman, S. (Ed.) (1980) Returning to Freud: Clinical psychoanalysis in the school of Lacan. New Haven, CN: Yale University Press.

Szasz, T. (2003) The cure of souls in the therapeutic state. The Psychoanalytic Review 90/1, 45-62.

Off the Top of My Head, or My Two Shoulders: An Introduction to Saints and Rogues

Robert B. Marchesani

> God is not a saint, strange to say. There is much to object to in him, and many attempts have been made to improve him. Much that the Bible says about him is rarely preached from the pulpit because, examined too closely, it becomes a scandal.
>
> –*GOD: A Biography*, Jack Miles, winner of the Pulitzer Prize

> The great consolation in life is to say what one thinks.
>
> –Voltaire

I'd like to make this final introduction to *The Psychotherapy Patient* a personal one. It is an aftersession with my own analyst. A reflection of an experience of psychotherapy as both patient and therapist, something that is not just unique to those of us who decide to follow our analysts/therapists into the woods of this process we call psychotherapy. Children who grow up to have children are also still children of their parents and walk similar tightropes as those of us who decide to do this work for a living.

[Haworth co-indexing entry note]: "Off the Top of My Head, or My Two Shoulders: An Introduction to Saints and Rogues." Marchesani, Robert B. Co-published simultaneously in *The Psychotherapy Patient* (The Haworth Press, Inc.) Vol. 13, No. 1/2, 2004, pp. 1-6; and: *Saints and Rogues: Conflicts and Convergence in Psychotherapy* (ed: Robert B. Marchesani, and E. Mark Stern) The Haworth Press, Inc., 2004, pp. 1-6. Single or multiple copies of this article are available for a fee from The Haworth Document Delivery Service [1-800-HAWORTH, 9:00 a.m. - 5:00 p.m. (EST). E-mail address: docdelivery@haworthpress.com].

http://www.haworthpress.com/web/TPP

Digital Object Identifier: 10.1300/J358v13n01_01

In Herman Hesse's novel *Siddhartha*, after many adventures in a monastery, in business and with a lover/teacher, Siddhartha settles down with his old childhood friend Govinda to become a simple ferryman, taking passengers across the river, just talking, and listening to the river and to each other. Siddhartha has a son who will not listen to him, and so he suffers letting go of this son. In a temple on the Lower East Side in Manhattan is a Buddhist temple within which are pictures of the life experiences of Siddhartha as a young man lining the walls of the temple on the way to the altar where there sits a gigantic golden Buddha, Siddhartha's destiny, so the legend goes.

In psychotherapy, we sit, much as one sits in meditation practices. We sit and we practice listening and thinking about our experience. Transference is an experience. Behavior is an experience. As much as debates continue about "behaviorism" and psychodynamics, I see the picture a little differently. What can be more behavioral than telling someone to just sit or lay down and say everything? Or to talk about acting out which can be become a kind of sin? The meditation teacher tells the practitioner to sit still and just let everything that comes to mind be. One of the hardest things in psychotherapy, as in meditation, is to do nothing. And one of the hardest things to accept is doing nothing, maybe being nothing. Ah, there's a fear! But doing nothing can be its own liberation. If the first rule of the ethics of treating people is do no harm, our world and our lives might be better if less were done. Abuse is a matter of someone doing something that should not have been done to the Other. So if one is doing nothing but listening and letting the Other be, maybe something therapeutic can happen.

When one sits and thinks, all sorts of things come to mind, and one can become as startled by thoughts of destruction as one can become happy with more creative thoughts. Human potential becomes a matter of consequence. Rogues may be more capable of destructive actions and saints of creative ones. In the Passolini film *Teorema* (1968) (Italian for Theorem), a stranger visits a household and affects every person in the family in an unusual way. He sleeps with the wife, the daughter falls in love with him, the son takes up painting and the father leaves his job and goes screaming into the desert. The daughter begins to sit outside eating nothing but thistle. She soon begins to levitate, and people come and bring her flowers. She was becoming a saint, one who was giving up the world's temptations.

Temptations abound in therapy, but where do they not abound? The teacher who falls in love with a student, the married Senator who takes a page boy, the preacher who fondles children. These are but a handful.

Others exist as well and begin early in life between mother and father and baby and between siblings, then classmates and friends, coworkers and colleagues.

In the last volume, we dealt with things vulgar and grotesque in everyday life. The Italians have two phrases, *Faccia Bella* and *Faccia Brutta*, to describe "beautiful face" and "ugly face." On a book stand in New York is a novel by Mary Monroe, *God Still Don't Like Ugly.*

"You're cute when you're mad," a girlfriend once said to her boyfriend. "He gets ugly when he drinks," another said of her husband. Like the two faces of comedy and tragedy, saints and rogues may represent things that are ugly and things that are beautiful.

Each morning the world awakens. Each morning we wake up having to relieve ourselves and clean ourselves of the night's productions, internal and external. Our bodies are much like the day we entered the world, only we are alone, whether or not someone else lies next to us. We get ourselves up and cleaned off to face the day.

But unlike the first day of our infancy when we were almost wholly unconscious, as adults we must also face cleaning up our psyches, dreams, nightmares, depressions, anxieties–those too we are faced with and face each other with. However, our job of recognizing that isn't always easy, and so tensions begin in silences first around the bed, then around the kitchen table, and off with us to the office, classroom or studio all the while with the saint and rogue on our shoulders. One may whisper a temptation, the other a caution. One says, "Go this way. . . ," the other, "That way!"

This last and final volume of *The Psychotherapy Patient* journal and book series may sum up the whole of the work of psychotherapy where two or more people meet to find out what's going on in their lives and why. It is a talk therapy but also one of another kind. It is a kind of talk that allows for everything to be put into words, to be verbalized, to be imagined, and to be communicated to another. If a tree falls in the woods and no one is around to hear it, does it make a sound? So goes the old adage. But if a tree falls and someone does hear it, there is a desire to tell it to another. An Other who will listen.

Some go to therapy and find it hard to say what is on their minds. A thought occurs that makes the thinker secretly say, "Should I say it or not?" In a preliminary conversation about this, Susan Barsky, whom I interviewed in the last volume about her work as a playwright, talked about a film she had made for a school project entitled *What To Do* in which she was a character who had to make the all-too-common decision: Do I go to the party or do I stay home and study? But each time she considered which to do, there was an angel on one shoulder telling her one way to go and the devil on the other telling her the opposite. It is these two opposing forces that *Saints and Rogues* takes up. Some patients come into psychotherapy already with the pressures to be a saint, ridden with guilt, pained by anxiety. Others come in as rogues, scoundrels, dishonest, vagrant. Saints may be the angels but also the ones with the greatest burden to behave, the opposite of the rogue who can be the epitome of *mis*behavior. When opposites attract, all hell, and hopefully heaven, can break loose. But what happens when saints and rogues are indistinguishable? Jesus Christ himself was called the devil by some, the messiah by others. The old whore/Madonna complex is another way of looking at the saint/rogue complex, for the two are not always clearly defined and separate.

The title of my introduction may be precarious at best. It is a common phrase. *Off the top of my head* connotes the first thing that comes to mind. But what if one heard from a parent or some other authority, "How can you even think that?" How do we reach the frontier of our thinking that allows a freedom of speech? If we have been editing our thinking, and maybe at times necessarily so, how can we know that we have a green light to speak? Must we suspend all morality to allow such a freedom? In *Liar Liar* (1997), Jim Carrey plays a lawyer who cannot tell the truth until his son makes a wish one day. While at a meeting of his partners and other associates, Carrey's character can no longer lie and out comes the most outlandish thoughts about each person in the room. Maybe for the sake of humor, they are all "negative" thoughts we might say, criticisms, mockery even, yet each one brings a great laugh from each of the victims of his honesty, for everything he says about them seems to be true.

One psychotherapy patient says, "I feel hostility but another voice tells me not to be hostile . . . " The voice of civility speaks into one ear, the voice of the uncivil into the other. Sanity on one shoulder, insanity on the other.

Now, if a rogue is a dishonest person and if being honest means saying things that might hurt someone or their feelings, where does that leave us? We encourage our patients to let their thoughts and feelings be expressed, but what happens when the rogues come marching in? One can experience oneself as becoming more *and* less human, and this goes for both the therapist and the psychotherapy patient, for what is said and thought is heard and taken in and changes us both.

If Voltaire was right, that "The great consolation in life is to say what one thinks," then the great desolation in life may be to withhold what one thinks, leaving such a one lost in the forest with no one to tell about the tree that fell.

Mothers can be saints or rogues. From pregnancy on, the mother begins to suffer for the child. But the child can also begin suffering for the mother. Both experience growing pains. But children are often born into the messes of the parents and their strained relations and become as soldiers on the battlegrounds of the household. Some suffer silently, others fight back to survive. We might say the saint is one who suffers while the rogue is one who inflicts suffering. Saints, then, may suffer the sins of the rogues. The very freedoms the rogues take, the saints give up in their service. The psychotherapist practices a form of self-denial in keeping otherwise expressed actions in fantasy. So does the mother or father who does not swing at their child when the child misbehaves, or for no reason at all except to vent their own frustrations, making the child pay for other sins. For the rogue child, the parent may become the saint, enduring abuses and mistreatments. Likewise, for the rogue parent, the child suffers, whether it be nights of alcoholic stupors and rages, messes and other confusing scenes polluting memory, becoming someone who suffers for the sins of the fathers and mothers who are suffering other sins passed down in the blood of family experience.

Every church, temple and mosque, every religion, organization and school has its saints and each has its rogues with plenty to shuffle being both.

If Jack Miles's book on God is any consolation, even God himself, or herself, has had a history of destructiveness and otherwise less than saintly behavior. Unless of course, Miles himself misunderstands the creator from "the good book." But we who are less godlike and mere mortals can wrestle with our own grand notions of our selves and of each other in attempting to live this ordinary life. A life in which time is of many essences–one minute of suffering becomes like an hour of waiting as one hour of pleasure is like the flash of a passing minute. Hopefully, the painstaking efforts of parenting and therapy, art and love are worth it in the end. Our tiny explorations of men and women great and small in this volume might leave behind something worth at least wondering about. The enigmatic third gender, the intolerable bully, the ethnic outcast, the composite psychotherapist, and the lost soul all share a glimpse of what is possible and what should not be.

I am grateful to E. Mark Stern for inviting me to strain at the borders with the last four issues of *The Psychotherapy Patient*, the last four books in the series he gave birth to and invited me to try my hand as his coeditor, beginning with *Awe and Trembling* (1999), *Frightful Stages*

(2001), and most recently, *Inhabitants of the Unconscious* (2003). But things in this world must be profitable to survive, and so we hang up our hats at least for now and make our departure from this stage, hopefully taking with us a few morsels of wisdom, and leaving behind one or two for other stages, maybe even other profits. Adieu!

Harry Stack Sullivan (1892-1949): Hero, Ghost, and Muse

Hendrika Vande Kemp

SUMMARY. The author summarizes major contributions of Harry Stack Sullivan (1892-1949) that lie outside his well-known contributions to the interpersonal school of psychoanalysis. She describes him first as a tragic hero who tried to depathologize homosexuality in psychiatry and in Selective Service screening procedures–a role immortalized in John Fisher's 1996 play, *Combat!* She also interprets features of his "personality" in light of his "theorem of reciprocal emotion." She then explores ways that he haunts the family psychology and therapy literature as a "ghost" who influenced Nathan Ackerman, Carl Whitaker, Don Bloch, Don Jackson, Robin Skynner, Salvador Minuchin, and R. D. Laing; and as a "buried ancestor" whose ideas pervade the family therapy literature. Finally, she summarizes his role as "muse" to pastoral theologians, emphasizing Sullivan's reciprocal influence on Anton T. Boisen in their explorations of the role of concealment and cosmic dramas in psychosis; his life-changing effect on O. H. Mowrer, who incorporated Sullivanian ideas into his integrity

---

Hendrika Vande Kemp, PhD, is a clinical psychologist, family therapist, and historian of psychology. She was for 25 years on the faculty of the Graduate School of Psychology at Fuller Theological Seminary. She is now in private psychotherapy practice in Annandale, Virginia.

Address correspondence to: Hendrika Vande Kemp, 7815 Rebel Drive, Annandale, VA 22003-1429 (E-mail: hendrika@earthlink.net).

[Haworth co-indexing entry note]: "Harry Stack Sullivan (1892-1949): Hero, Ghost, and Muse." Vande Kemp, Hendrika. Co-published simultaneously in *The Psychotherapy Patient* (The Haworth Press, Inc.) Vol. 13, No. 1/2, 2004, pp. 7-61; and: *Saints and Rogues: Conflicts and Convergence in Psychotherapy* (ed: Robert B. Marchesani, and E. Mark Stern) The Haworth Press, Inc., 2004, pp. 7-61. Single or multiple copies of this article are available for a fee from The Haworth Document Delivery Service [1-800-HAWORTH, 9:00 a.m. - 5:00 p.m. (EST). E-mail address: docdelivery@haworthpress.com].

http://www.haworthpress.com/web/TPP

Digital Object Identifier: 10.1300/J358v13n01_02

therapy; and the centrality of Sullivan for the dimension of the "we" in Paul E. Johnson's "dynamic interpersonalism."

KEYWORDS. Harry Stack Sullivan, Anton Boisen, O. H. Mowrer, Paul E. Johnson, community, psychological homicide, living in love, homosexuals in WWII, theorem of reciprocal emotion, family psychology, interpersonal principles, psychosis

HARRY STACK SULLIVAN, THE MAN: A TRAGIC HERO?

Harry Stack Sullivan, the founder of the interpersonal school of psychiatry, would have little patience with an effort to classify him as saint or rogue, as such attributions reify personality whereas Sullivan believed so-called personality is merely a function of the interpersonal situations in which we find ourselves. In "The Illusion of Personal Individuality," Sullivan wrote:

> For all I know every human being has as many personalities as he has interpersonal relations; and as a great many of our interpersonal relations are actually operations with imaginary people–that is, in-no-sense-materially-embodied people–and as they may have the same or greater validity in life as have our operations with materially-embodied people like the clerks in the corner store, you can see that even though "the illusion of personal individuality" sounds quite lunatic when first heard, there is at least food for thought in it. (Sullivan, 1964, p. 221)

It is regrettable that Sullivan's major biographers–Arthur H. Chapman (1976) and Helen Swick Perry (1982)–failed to apply this critical observation in their efforts to understand Sullivan as a person. Kenneth Chatelaine (1978), in his biographical dissertation, grants that Sullivan "was the perfect example of the different selves he writes about that we present to different people" (p. 429), and he states:

> I believe the real Sullivan was in his books and especially his recorded lectures and talks (if you have ever heard his recorded lectures something more like Sullivan the man comes across), which contained his ideas and theories, many of which had, I believe, their origin in his own life experiences. I also believe the real Sullivan was present when he was with his patients–especially his schizophrenic patients, and when, at times, he was alone with his adopted son. (pp. 429-430)

Like Chatelaine, I have found the man Sullivan revealed more clearly in his writings than in the published biographies. I have since the early 1980s been interested in Sullivan's work, and "live and breathe" the contemporary interpersonal psychology based in part on his seminal ideas (see especially Benjamin, 1996, 2003). But my interest in Sullivan's personal story began only after I heard hints about his possible schizophrenia, and increased when I heard about his homosexuality. I will not attempt here to paint a complete picture of Sullivan, the man. I will discuss several aspects of his "personality" as Sullivan (1953) himself defined that term: "the relatively enduring pattern of recurrent interpersonal situations which characterize a human life" (p. 111). For Sullivanian interpersonal theorists, personality manifests itself "only in interpersonal relationships, whether real or illusory" (Carson, 1969, p. 26). Similarly, they define character as "the durable, multiple-level pattern of interpersonal tendencies organized into stable or unstable equilibria" (Leary, 1957, p. 24). I will reflect on ways that Sullivan's "theorem of reciprocal emotion" sheds light on his apparently multifaceted characters.

Sullivan, the Closet Homosexual Uncloseted in His Work

Swick Perry's (1982) biography is primarily sociological rather than psychological in nature and suffers from her "selective inattention" to Sullivan's homosexuality which had already been publicly documented by Chapman (1976), who confidently declared "Sullivan was a homosexual, and this fact was well known to, or strongly suspected by, most of his contemporaries" (p. 12). Chapman felt that this accounted for the slow acceptance of Sullivan's ideas, as "many psychiatrists and behavioral scientists [would] hesitate to admit their indebtedness to a psychiatrist whose homosexuality was commonly known" (p. 12). Chapman believed that Sullivan's juvenile chumship with Clarence Bellinger (whom he does not name) was "homosexual in the full genital sense of the word" (p. 23), and that "his homosexual urges jabbed him intermittently until his final disease-ridden years" (p. 38). Chapman felt Sullivan revealed too much of his shadow side in *Personal Psychopathology* (Sullivan, 1972), a book which Chapman (1976) thought "shows Sullivan as a passionate, immature, emotionally confused person. It reveals his homosexuality, and it discloses weird concepts and prejudices" (p. 50). Chapman dismissed Sullivan's ideas about the role of the chum relationship, because Sullivan "generalized his own emotional maldevelopment into a universal law of personality formation" (p. 181). Chapman, who apparently would not have endorsed the 1973 decision of the Board of Trustees of the American Psychiatric Association to remove homosexuality from the *Diagnostic and Statistical Manual of Mental Disorders*,[1] chose not to name any of Sullivan's sexual partners, claiming that "further discussion of Sullivan's sexual life would harm the families of persons recently dead" (p. 62),[2] but he does explicitly mention Sullivan's homosexuality in his 1990 sketch for *American National Biography*. We do know that in later years Bellinger was consistently negative about Sullivan, dismissing him as "a homosexual son-of-a-bitch" (Swick Perry, 1982, p. 313). Sullivan in turn "never told anyone about his early friendship with Clarence Bellinger, or gossiped about him," which Swick Perry took as evidence that "Sullivan remained clearly indebted to Bellinger for what friendship Clarence offered in the loneliest years" (p. 147). She avoided labeling Sullivan explicitly as homosexual or bisexual, despite recounting that friends and colleagues "report that he had some sexual experiences with women as well as with men" (p. 334) and opined that "there is no ready label for how he lived and thought and yearned" (p. 334). What he did, in fact, was live for 22 years with his male partner James Inscoe Sullivan (Jimmie) who was 20 years his junior and known to most of Sullivan's friends and colleagues as his adopted son or foster son, which was one of the convenient fictions that kept Harry's homosexuality in the closet (Chapman, 1976, p. 66; Swick Perry, 1982, p. 209). Swick Perry later confessed to Michael Allen (1995) that Jimmie had purportedly been a "former male hustler" (p. 9). Sullivan (1942) described Jimmie as "a former patient," a description to which Jimmie (who typed the manuscript) objected but which Sullivan refused to change (Swick Perry, 1982, p. 209). In 1927, when Sullivan met him, Jimmie was 15 or 16 and had been standing in front of the psychiatrist Ernest Hadley's Washington, DC, office building in a catatonic pose. Hadley took him to Sullivan at Sheppard & Enoch Pratt Hospital.[3] We do not know what motivated Sullivan to take Jimmie in at a time when "by several accounts he was mute" (p. 338), but Jimmie soon became what Swick Perry described as "family, household staff, and office staff . . . a competent cook, a skilled secretary, a devoted companion" (p. 209). But she was not able to write the words "sexual partner."[4]

Nor was this conclusion one that Chatelaine (1978) could accept, despite the fact that he reports virtually overwhelming evidence regarding Sullivan's sexuality and that of the attendants who worked on the special ward at Sheppard & Enoch Pratt. Chatelaine interviewed William Elliott, who did relief work on the ward and "was convinced that Sullivan and most of his attendants were homosexual," although "he saw no overt homosexual genital contact between patients and attendants, or between patients themselves" (p. 399). He recalled "a common belief that a homosexual relationship existed between Sullivan and his secretary, Mr. Munson" (p. 400), who briefly lived with Sullivan and Jimmie. Chatelaine also interviewed Arthur Linton, a supervisor at the hospital, who claimed that "Sullivan himself was 'gay' but had it under control," that "all his hand-picked attendants were 'gay' or were latent homosexuals, except the chief attendant," and "all of Sullivan's patients were young male homosexuals who he personally picked from the general hospital population" (p. 404). Swick Perry, in her introduction to *Schizophrenia as a Human Process* (Sullivan, 1962) dismissed the description of the ward as a "homosexual society" as "idle and pseudopsychoanalytic speculation" (p. xxi). Sullivan himself shed some light on this in *A Harry Stack Sullivan Case Seminar* (Kvarnes & Parloff, 1976) which features transcripts of a seminar conducted by Sullivan in 1946-1947 for the residents at Sheppard & Enoch Pratt, with commentary by John C. Dillingham, Robert G. Kvarnes, Stanley Jacobson, and Irving M. Ryckoff. Someone poses a question concerning the role of a permissive environment "as well as the role of homosexually oriented attendants in handling these patients" (p. 208). Sullivan says, regarding the attendants:

> If you very carefully eliminate therefrom the psychopathic personalities, you have people who are at least amenable to a calm discussion of the worries of people who fear they are homosexual. To that extent it is not so much a permissive environment as an educable environment. They do not have loathing or dread or fear of this, or paranoid ideas about the doctor when the doctor tries to tell them what might be done, and certainly they do not suffer from appalling disgust reactions when they see certain performance of patients which often call out such reactions in the most benevolently

> disposed of the other sort. So that so far as I am concerned, what is probably meant by "homosexually oriented" attendants has been very helpful indeed in building up a hospital organization.
>
> A thing you might not immediately realize is that in this environment, which I finally felt worthy of being tried, there was extraordinarily little and brief concern with homosexual cravings. (p. 209)

Of himself, Sullivan said:

> Due to certain idiosyncrasies of personality, I feel at no particular disadvantage in dealing with homosexuals. I have, in fact, discovered that homosexuals have one of thirty-two different types of problems. It always carries a great many quotation marks. Some of those thirty-two seem to be entirely resistive to any technique which I have invented. Many of them are quite easily handable. (p. 209)

As Kvarnes, Ryckoff, Jacobson, and Dillingham discuss these comments in light of what they call the "myth" of Sullivan's homosexuality, Kvarnes tells the others, "I don't know of any instances of acknowledged homosexual relationships" (Kvarnes & Parloff, 1976, p. 224). Ryckoff declares:

> I think that no one knows, but it does seem more like a myth, since you would assume there would be some evidence. I think what he is alluding to there is the fact that he found himself one of the few people who was genuinely at home in this area–that is, he was not put off by homosexuality. He could stay with it and share the experience of what homosexual existence was like, I think to a greater extent than many other people at that time. Or even now, for that matter–it's not easy to stay with that kind of thing. I think he was sort of bragging about that. (pp. 224-225)

Ironically, the editors dedicate the book to James Inscoe Sullivan who as Sullivan's "foster son . . . self-effacingly but efficiently maintained for Sullivan a supportive environment that helped this somewhat irascible, rather temperamental genius to engage productively in a wide range of productive activities" (dedication page). It would have been a much greater gift to both Jimmie and Harry had these men in their discussion acknowledged Jimmie for the homosexual partner he really was. Their own judgment about homosexuality is implicit in Ruckoff's statement "it's not easy to stay with that."

Sullivan on Depathologizing Homosexuality

Sullivan himself, at least in his later years, was adamant about his conviction that homosexuality should not be a focus for treatment. Instead, the psychoanalyst should focus on the other "dynamics of difficulty" (Sullivan, 1956, p. 5) in the person's life. Sullivan (1953) described extensive "patterns of manifestation of the integrating tendencies of the intimacy need and lust" (p. 290). In a summary statement, he writes:

> Since I have set up three classifications of intimacy, four classifications of the general interpersonal objective of the integration of lust, and six classifications of genital relationship, this results in seventy-two theoretical patterns of sexual behavior in situations involving two real partners. As a matter of fact, there are only forty-five patterns of sexual behavior that are reasonably probable; six very highly improbable; and the rest just aren't possible. From this statement I would like you to realize, if you realize anything else, how fatuous it is to toss out the adjectives "heterosexual," "homosexual," or "narcissistic" to classify a person as to his sexual and friendly integrations with others. Such classifications are not anywhere near refined enough for intelligent thought; they are much too gross to do anything except mislead both the observer and the victim. For example, to talk about homosexuality's being a problem really means about as much as to talk about humanity's being a problem. (p. 294)

Whatever else may be said about the strengths and weaknesses in Sullivan's *Personal Psychopathology* (1972), it reveals an extensive effort to classify the range of intimacy problems in both heterosexual and homosexual relationships. Sullivan proclaims with the insight of a seasoned marital therapist that

> marriage and other relatively durable interpersonal relations involving sexual adjustment are the test of personality evolution. Their psychopathology is the psychopathology of personality. Every deviation which has thus far concerned us has its exemplification in the mating and mismatings of the person and the spouse.

> Nearly every type of interpersonal situation can be set up in these legal or extralegal affiliations. (p. 322)

In addition to discussing the normal homosexual phase of adolescence, Sullivan described a variety of mother-son patterns that might lead to later homosexual behavior.[5] Echoing the opinions of a number of other psychiatrists whose views led to the 1973 decision to remove homosexuality from the DSM, in *Conceptions of Modern Psychiatry*, Sullivan (1940/1945) succinctly stated what he believed to be true of homosexual partnerships: "Some of these are relations of love, and are stable and durable. Some of them are devoid of love and are very transient. Some of them are relations of hatred, durable or otherwise as the determining circumstances dictate" (p. 41). There was no need for him to add that the same patterns can be described in heterosexual relationships, although his lengthy descriptions of relationships in *Personal Psychopathology* (1972) embody Sullivan's considerable insight into a potential classification system of interpersonal pathologies in relationships between persons who have achieved heterosexual genitality. Sullivan (1940/1945) included homosexuality in his list of "actual syndromes" or "disorders of personality" which reflect "a blend of developmental factors with the vicissitudes of the person in his communal existence with others" (p. 37). In recent years, Lorna Benjamin (1996, 2003) has followed Sullivan's lead in describing all of the DSM-IV personality disorders in interpersonal terms, viewing them as predictable disorders of communal existence.

Sullivan's homosexuality is thoroughly explored by Allen (1995),[6] who argues that the young Sullivan "was neither the largely asexual bachelor of Helen [Swick] Perry's dreams nor was he the closeted, repressed, and self-loathing homosexual of my imaginings" (p. 8). Instead, "Sullivan was actively–and courageously–engaged with his sexuality" (p. 8). Allen maintains that Sullivan

> found a way to integrate his sexuality into his professional and intellectual concerns, and, in the process, took these rather remarkable risks: Between 1925 and 1930, Sullivan wrote a review of a very controversial book, took as his life-long companion a 16-year-old youth, conducted a daring, 5-year clinical experiment at Baltimore's Sheppard-Pratt psychiatric hospital, and took his first trip to Europe where he read a startling paper to the World League for Sexual Reform and spent almost eight weeks in Berlin with two homosexual friends–all actions that bring into sharper focus what may have been, I believe, uppermost in his mind. (p. 8)

Sullivan reviewed the anonymously authored *The Invert and His Social Adjustment* (Anomaly, 1927) in 1927 (Sullivan, 1927d) and spoke of it at the 1929 Second Colloquium on Personality Investigation,[7] where Sullivan described the book as "a remarkable document by a homosexual man of refinement; intended primarily as a guide to the unfortunate sufferers of sexual inversion, and much less open to criticism than anything else of the kind so far published. An interesting psychopathological document" (quoted in Swick Perry, 1982, p. 338).[8] Allen (1995) described this book as

> an extraordinary document for its time [which made] a case for compassion, tolerance, and understanding for homosexuals. The book was (again, for its time) quite audacious, and Sullivan's seeking it out and penning a respectful and serious review, was, by drawing attention to himself on such a taboo issue, itself audacious–especially in light of what else Sullivan was up to that year. (p. 9)

That was the year Sullivan began his relationship with Jimmie, while he was also attaining national prominence with his experimental treatment program at Sheppard-Pratt. When that experimented ended with his resignation in 1929, Sullivan and Jimmie moved to New York City. But before their move, he took an eight-week trip to Europe with the political scientist Harold Lasswell, and the two of them spent a great deal of time in Berlin with William V. Silverberg, a young American psychiatrist who later assumed control of Sullivan's ward at Sheppard-Pratt. Both men were, according to Allen, homosexual, and Allen suggests all three were attracted to Berlin because it "was a relatively open city for homosexuals, drawing people from all over Europe who wished to explore their sexuality" (p. 11). On the way home from this trip, Sullivan delivered his paper on "Archaic Sexual Culture and Schizophrenia" to the Third Congress of the World League for Sexual Reform in London. Here, he spelled out explicitly his belief that schizophrenia and homosexuality are intertwined (Sullivan, 1929). "He argued that a homosexual phase in adolescence is a necessary prelude to achieving heterosexual intimacy and that the failure to explore one's sexuality in adolescence can result in schizophrenia" (Allen, 1995, p. 12). Sullivan recommended that "sexual experience be provided for all youths in the homosexual phase of personality genesis in order that they might not become hopelessly lost in the welter of dream-thinking and cosmic fantasy making up mental illness" (p. 12). After speculating on Sullivan's reasons for establishing the experimental ward at Sheppard-Pratt, Allen suggests that

> what obsessed Sullivan in the early years of his career, what led him to passionately choose psychiatry as a career, and what motivated him to create a gay *and* schizophrenic treatment ward in 1925 was his own experience with what we now call homosexual panic. . . . Sullivan's experience with what he loosely called "schizophrenic" states is therefore quite relevant to understanding his life. I suspect that throughout his life, Sullivan used the expression "schizophrenia" euphemistically; . . . that was, perhaps, as close as Sullivan could get to speaking frankly with his prim, heterosexual secretary about his sexuality. (pp. 13-14)

Sullivan as "Tragic Hero." Sullivan made a final, valiant effort to depathologize homosexuality when he served as psychiatric consultant to Selective Service Director Clarence A. Dykstra, beginning on December 5, 1940. Sullivan's efforts began earlier, when he served as a member of the American Psychiatric Association's Military Mobilization committee which "developed the military's wartime program for psychiatric screening" (Bérubé, 1990, p. 9). In May of 1940, Sullivan and his colleagues at the William Alanson White Foundation began work on a screening plan, as well as efforts to convince President Roosevelt and his Selective Service advisors of the need for screening, which would reduce the costs of post-war veteran psychiatric care by "weeding out potential psychiatric casualties before they became military responsibilities" (p. 10). On November 7, 1940, the Selective Service issued *Medical Circular No. 1* to "more than 30,000 volunteer physicians at local draft boards" (p. 11). This circular "explained in lay terms five psychiatric 'categories of handicap'–expanded to eight in later versions–and concluded with a list of miscellaneous 'deviations' examining physicians should watch for. Homosexuality was not mentioned in the first screening circular" (p. 12). This situation had changed by May 1941, when the circular issued by the Army Surgeon General's Office and the revised version of *Circular No. 1* included "homosexual proclivities" in the list of disqualifying "deviations" (p. 12).

Allan Bérubé (1990), in *Coming Out Under Fire: The History of Gay Men and Women in World War Two*, summarizes how the official process quickly sabotaged Sullivan's position:

> Sullivan's initial plan for psychiatric screening, consistent with his own psychiatric theory, included no references to homosexuality. But his belief in the relative unimportance of "sexual aberrations" in determining mental illness was undermined as his plan passed through Washington bureaucratic channels. To each revision of Sullivan's initial plan, other psychiatrists added fragments of the more-dominant psychiatric theory that homosexuality was a mental disorder that should disqualify a man for military service. Throughout the war, whenever psychiatrists tried to reform the military's policies on homosexuals, their proposals were subject to this same process of compromise and modification. (p. 11)

As these revisions were taking place, "the Navy Surgeon General's Office, Bellevue Hospital in New York, and the Menninger Clinic in Topeka, Kansas, also held seminars on military psychiatric screening for their personnel" (p. 14). These lecturers "described gay men exclusively within the context of mental illness" and

> spoke of latency, tendencies, proclivities, and personality types. They discussed homosexuality not as a distinct phenomenon but as an aspect of three personality disorders: psychopaths who were sexual perverts, paranoid personalities who suffered from homosexual panic, and schizoid personalities who displayed homosexual symptoms. (p. 15)

Any hopes Sullivan might have to counter such trends in thinking were totally derailed when Major General Lewis B. Hershey replaced Dykstra in the spring of 1941: "Hershey was hostile to psychiatry and represented to Sullivan the kind of hard-line military official who thought that the psychiatrically unfit were whiners who needed to be toughened up" (p. 18). Sullivan bitterly resigned his post in November 1941. In 1942, a paragraph on sexual perversions was incorporated into the army mobilization regulations, establishing "the Army's antihomosexual screening procedures for the rest of the war" (p. 19). Only a small minority of his colleagues shared Sullivan's belief "that sexuality played a minimal role in causing mental disorders and that adult homosexuals should be accepted and left alone" (p. 11). Sullivan was deeply concerned about the long-term consequences of being rejected by draft boards for homosexuality, whether real or falsely claimed in men whom the Army and Navy psychiatrists labeled "reverse malingers" (p. 20). Examination records had virtually no confidentiality protection, and "the psychiatric diagnoses written on draft records were explicit, often humiliating, and seemed punitive" (p. 21). Sullivan feared that those rejected for the draft might find that their past employers turned them down for future employment because of the diagnoses listed on draft records, leading to "much pointless embarrassment, misunderstanding, and aggravation of handicap" (p. 21).

World War II and its aftermath eventually led Sullivan in the direction of international peacekeeping, but his effort to address the plight of homosexuals in the military has not gone unnoticed. His contributions were recognized not only by Bérubé (1990), but also by the gay playwright John Fisher, who made Sullivan a hero in his World War II play *Combat! An American Melodrama* (Fisher, 1996) which ran first at Berkeley's Zellerbach Playhouse in 1996 and in a shorter version at the Victoria Theatre in San Francisco's Mission District early in 1998.[9] The shorter play earned Fisher the 1998 Will Glickman Playwright Award for the best new play to receive its world premiere in the San Francisco Bay Area each year (*Examiner* staff, 1999). In *Combat!* Fisher interweaves the stories of the War, a gay soldier trying to understand his personal story and the story of his gay minority group, and the story of Sullivan's "campaign to destigmatize homosexuality in the military" (Winn, 1998/2003). A central character in the play is the "Mysterious Stranger," modeled on Mark Twain's *The Mysterious Stranger* which Sullivan (1953) summarized in *The Interpersonal Theory of Psychiatry* as an example of "the evils of transcendental power at the disposal of man" (p. 342).[10] Fisher (1996) portrays with great sensitivity Sullivan's growing dismay as military personnel revise his screening tool, the growing tension created by his desire to enhance the profession of psychiatry through its role in military personnel screening which would require him to assent to the prevailing view on the pathology of homosexuality and to betray his personal conviction that homosexuality was not psychopathological, and his painful decision to resign his position. Fisher's Sullivan fears that the revised screening tool will force homosexuals to lie to the military and to continue living that lie, and "it will also introduce certain ideas and attitudes towards homosexuality into the lives of every American who comes in contact with that examination" (Act I).[11] He continues, "Write into the psychiatric examination that homosexuals must be unfit to serve and you will have written it into the Bill of Rights that gays do not have rights as surely as Jefferson and Adams and Franklin and all the rest wrote it into the charter for this nation that blacks shall not be free" (Act I). He feared that homosexuals would "never turn to a psychiatrist except to have their proclivities invalidated as surely as a priest would have invalidated them in the dark ages" (Act I). He asserted that "I cannot accept any definition of homosexuality which does not presuppose that gays are capable of attaining the very best in any profession" (Act I). Winn (1998/2003) ends his review with a lament: "In looking back on the first, staggering steps of gays in the military, Fisher reminds us that a half century later, a new day still hasn't come." Harry Stack Sullivan would share his grief.

Sullivan the Man in Light of the Interpersonal Principle of Complementarity

In this section, I will reflect on ways that Sullivan's "theorem of reciprocal emotion" sheds light on his apparently multifaceted character. In doing so, I speak as an interpersonal *psychologist* in the neo-Sullivanian interpersonal tradition, and not as an interpersonal psychoanalyst or a representative of the cognitive-behavioral school which brazenly calls itself "interpersonal psychotherapy."

Sullivan's influence on psychoanalysis has been widely documented by such writers as Burton (1971), Chapman and Chapman-Santana (1980), Evans (1996), Havens (1977), Levenson (1992), Mullahy (1952, 1970), Mullahy and Melinek (1983), Pearce (1985), Shainess (1978), Silverman (1975), Witenberg (1973), and a variety of contributors to *Contemporary Psychoanalysis*, the journal of the William Alanson White Institute, and *Psychiatry*, the journal founded by Sullivan. As Fiscalini (1995) noted, "All contemporary interpersonal analysts, however they may differ from one another, have been profoundly influenced by Sullivan's seminal ideas" (p. 1).

Sullivan's concept of "interpersonal psychotherapy" has also been usurped by Gerald Klerman and Myrna Weissman and their colleagues to describe a form of cognitive-behavioral therapy with a relational focus (see Klerman & Weissman, 1993; Klerman, Weissman, Rounsaville, & Chevron, 1984; Markowitz, 1997; Marziali & Monroe-Blum, 1994; Mufson, Moreau, Weissman et al., 1993; Stuart & Robertson, 2002; Weissman, Markowitz, & Klerman, 2000; Wilfley, Mackenzie, Welch, Ayres, & Weissman, 2000). In May 2000 Klerman and Weissman founded the International Society for Interpersonal Psychotherapy to propound this form of cognitive-behavioral psychotherapy which is Sullivanian only in name (Weissman, 2000).

The Theorem of Reciprocal Emotion. There is a third school of interpersonal psychology and psychotherapy that is very much neo-Sullivanian but which focuses, not on the psychoanalytic remnants of

Sullivan's theory, but on the observable implications of Sullivan's (1953) theorem of reciprocal emotion:

> Integration in an interpersonal situation is a reciprocal process in which (1) complementary needs are resolved, or aggravated; (2) reciprocal patterns of activity are developed, or disintegrated; and (3) foresight of satisfaction, or rebuff, of similar needs is facilitated. (p. 198; see also Sullivan, 1954, pp. 128-132)

In this tradition, which applies operationalized interpersonal principles to individual psychotherapy and to a variety of interpersonal contexts, the classic texts are Sullivan's (1953) *Interpersonal Theory of Psychiatry* and two groundbreaking reports of Sullivan-inspired research: Timothy Leary's (1957) *Interpersonal Diagnosis of Personality* and Robert Carson's (1969) *Interaction Concepts of Personality*. A later text in that tradition is Anchin and Kiesler's (1982) *Handbook of Interpersonal Psychotherapy* (see also Kiesler, 1996). In the research program described by Leary (1957), the theorem or reciprocal emotion becomes the principle of reciprocal interpersonal relations. In later interpersonal theories it is articulated as the principle of complementarity (see Carson, 1969), which is based in part on Foa's (1961) observation that "an interpersonal act is an attempt to establish the emotional relationship of the actor toward himself and toward the other, as well as to establish the social relationship of the self and the other with respect to a larger reference group" (p. 350), and "each behavior serves the purpose of giving or denying love *and* status to the self and to the other" (p. 351). Thus, in every interpersonal interaction the persons involved are seeking to define the relationship in a way that maintains their personal self-esteem. If the other person gives us what we are seeking in the transaction, it is categorized as complementary: The other responds to the emotional component of our action with a matching degree of love or hate, and to the "intentionality" component of the action by submitting to our effort to dominate, agreeing to dominate when we want to be submissive, by granting the autonomy we seek, or by taking the autonomy we offer. When the other fails to give us what we are seeking, the response may be categorized as anticomplementary or noncomplementary. Kiesler (1983) noted that in relationships three kinds of interactions can occur: *Complementary* interactions evoke approach behaviors from both participants, as both feel enhanced security; *anticomplementary* interactions lead to avoidance or escape actions, as the participants experience increased anxiety (Benjamin [1996] uses the label *antithetical* for such interactions); *acomplementary* interactions evoke a mixture of approach and avoidant responses. The clinical implications of this part of Sullivan's theory have been worked out in exquisite clinical detail by Edward Teyber (1997) and by Lorna Benjamin (1996, 2003). Benjamin's approach is exceedingly complex, as it incorporates aspects of Sullivan, George Herbert Mead (1934), object relations theory, Leary, and various other interpersonal and social-psychological research models. Most interesting for this discussion is the way she incorporates interpersonal theory at multiple levels in her textbook on interpersonal diagnosis and treatment (Benjamin, 1996). She first translates the DSM symptoms of pathology into interpersonal terms. She then articulates a set of pathogenic hypotheses based on interpersonal history (thus incorporating Sullivan's developmental emphasis). She next connects the interpersonal history and the contemporary symptoms. She also examines characteristic wishes and fears associated with each personality disorder, thus incorporating a Sullivanian understanding of anxiety as an exclusively *interpersonal* phenomenon.[12] Benjamin makes very specific use of the interpersonal principles of complementarity and anticomplementarity, or antithesis, as she outlines specific therapeutic strategies for each of the personality disorders, focusing on the best ways to facilitate collaboration, to recognize and block maladaptive patterns, to strengthen the will to give up maladaptive patterns, and to facilitate new learning. Benjamin's approach is a clinical application of Sullivan's thinking that brings to fruition the ideas outlined in "The Data of Psychiatry" (1938), where Sullivan discussed in detail the interpersonal processes surrounding a man motivated by resentment who must learn to become aware of the interpersonal stimuli impinging on him, and whose complex behavior remains unavailable to the psychiatrist for scientific analysis because of the lack of recording equipment and direct observation.

Sullivan as Responder to His Interpersonal Context. Sullivan ended his essay on "The Data of Psychiatry" with the sentence: "The psychiatrist of all people knows the relative character of his formulation of the other person, even if he has gained such skill that he is often quite correct" (Sullivan, 1964, p. 55). Sullivan knew that his conclusions could only be based on his own interpersonal experience of the patient, and on his interpretations of interpersonal encounters, fantasies, and dreams reported by the patient. He knew that his patients might behave entirely differently with someone else. And he believed enough in the power of changing the interpersonal environment as a way of changing so-called "personality" to design his treatment ward as an experiment in changing personality through a controlled interpersonal environment. Sullivan's friends, colleagues, and biographers for the most part seem not to have grasped the implications of this formulation for understanding Sullivan himself.

Swick Perry (1982), in summarizing Sullivan's "personality," claimed that

> Many of Sullivan's colleagues described him as being exclusively one or another of these three kinds of characters: a withdrawn and cantankerous drunk; a somewhat pretentious high stepper and sophisticate; the kindest, most considerate man who ever lived. Seldom did he show all three sides to the same person. Such reports seem puzzling and mutually exclusive until one examines the paucity of his early relationships with men and the sharp differences between them, so that the growing child found it difficult to pattern his own life after such dissimilar people. (p. 73)

Swick Perry hoped to understand Sullivan by examining his interpersonal history and the discrepant influences of Sullivan's shy, taciturn father, his glamorous and successful Uncle Ed, and his "modest, friendly, and scholarly" teacher, Herbert Betts (p. 73). She also suggested that Sullivan relied heavily on the defense mechanism of provoking envy, quoting his own words: "I suppose that provoking envy in others is one way of sparing oneself the most acute development of it" (Sullivan, 1956, p. 138n). But Sullivan's own definition of envy suggested nothing more than covetousness or greed, and Sullivan regarded envy as a mild emotion, much less potent than jealousy, which he said might be construed as "envy of others' capacity for intimacy" (p. 138n). He acknowledged that "it is possible that I underrate the extent to which one can suffer envy, for I recall few instances in which I felt intensely envious" (p. 138n). I suspect Sullivan would have eagerly embraced Melanie Klein's distinctions in this regard: "Jealousy is based on love and aims at the possession of the loved object and the removal of the rival. It pertains to a triangular relationship and therefore to a time of life when objects are clearly recognized and differentiated from one another" (Segal, 1973, p. 40). "Envy aims at being as good as the object, but, when this is felt as impossible, it aims at spoiling the goodness of the object, to remove the source of envious feelings" (p. 40). Even Klein, with her considerable insights into the process of envy, focused primarily on envy in infants who envied the goodness of the mother and clients who envied the goodness of the therapist. She did not speak directly to the experience of being the object of envy, but implicit in Kleinian theory is the notion that envy is provoked simply by being, and not by any particular doing. I suspect that those who experienced Sullivan negatively were those who did not possess either his intellectual prowess or his clinical sensitivity, and who thus brought into their interactions with him their hostile spoiling maneuvers, which became the stimulus for Sullivan's hostile responses. There is a hint of this in the case seminar discussion reported in Kvarnes and Parloff (1976). Kvarnes suggests that some of the rumors about Sullivan's alleged alcoholism, schizophrenia, and homosexuality constituted efforts to "discount the person and his work" (p. 225). Kvarnes felt that some people had a "need to cut [Sullivan] down. Goodness knows he was irascible and cutting enough to have hurt a number of his colleagues' feelings" (p. 226). I have no doubt that Sullivan could be sarcastic and cantankerous (although there is little evidence for "drunk"). As Chapman (1976) reported, Sullivan at times "verbally flailed some of his fellow conferees" (p. 76), and "he usually won his verbal battles" (p. 56). Chapman also remarks that "impartial examination of the records of some of these professional meetings indicates that on many occasions his opponents chose to abandon the field rather than to descend to Sullivan's level of rudeness and insult" (p. 56). His rivals "found him crude and vituperative" (p. 56). But Chapman also notes that Sullivan had good reason to debate his colleagues, in that

> he was always the patient's advocate, and obvious insensitivity by a psychiatrist to a patient's problems, or tendencies to theorize about patients rather than to understand their suffering, brought tongue-lashings from Sullivan. It made no difference whether the offender was a distinguished psychiatrist presenting a paper before a full auditorium or a psychiatric resident in a small teaching conference. (pp. 55-56)

As the case seminar discussants examined this part of Sullivan's personality (Kvarnes & Parloff, 1976), Ryckoff commented on Sullivan's alleged competitiveness, saying of Sullivan that "the one thing he wasn't going to take was anybody presuming to occupy an equal position to him–that someone would presume to have a definition or make a judgment" (p. 131). He continued, "the stories I've heard are to the effect that as soon as somebody raised his head and presumed to spell something out on a more definitive level he would immediately counterattack" (p. 131). Kvarnes responded: "Well, I saw that happen a number of times later, but it seemed entirely justified because guys would overstate or pontificate" (p. 131). Kvarnes speculated further about Sullivan, "I think where he would come in sarcastically was with someone who was being somewhat smart-alecky or pompous or overknowing" (p. 131).

We can examine two incidents reported in Sullivan biographies from an interpersonal perspective to see how Sullivan's allegedly hostile behavior appears in fact simply to be a spontaneous response to hostile interpersonal behavior on the part of a colleague.

The first incident is reported in Chatelaine (1978), in what is on the surface a discussion of Sullivan's supposedly difficult writing style. Chatelaine recounts this incident after stating that "the difficulty and complexity of Sullivan's thinking and writing is well known" (p. 3). He then relates the following anecdote by David Rioch, who joined the staff at Chestnut Lodge in 1943: "Rioch and Sullivan were together one night at a cocktail party and after a few drinks, Rioch said to Sullivan: 'Harry, why the blazes can't you write so people can understand you?' At which Sullivan 'exploded' and forthwith left the party" (p. 3). This strange incident, which certainly offers no evidence one way or another as to the difficulty of reading Sullivan, does provide insight into the way colleagues may have on other occasions provoked Sullivan. At what is supposed to be a social event, in which Sullivan might have expected informal conversation about his dogs or Jimmie or the war or his failing health, Rioch instead greeted Sullivan with an unexpected and unnecessary hostile attack on an aspect of his personhood over which he has little control. Rioch apparently told this story with no awareness of his hostility, and he was apparently surprised by Sullivan's reaction, which arose from Sullivan's acute sensitivity to such hostility. Surely the interpersonal failing in this case was Rioch's and not Sullivan's.

A second incident is related by Swick Perry (1982) in the context of a discussion of Sullivan's proverbial impatience with psychoanalytic conjecture. William Silverberg, Sullivan's colleague at Sheppard-Pratt, "recalled an incident when he made the mistake of offering Sullivan that sort of off-the-cuff interpretation while a guest at Sullivan's house during the Sheppard years" (p. 182). Silverberg told Swick Perry:

> I do not recall how the subject arose, but Sullivan remarked to me one afternoon that as a child he had always hated and feared spiders. I commented quite naively–like the fool where angels fear to tread–that spiders generally symbolized the mother. "Oh, do they now?" said Sullivan in a sing-song, argumentative Hibernian into-

> nation. "And how do you know that?" he asked so challengingly that I felt warned not to pursue the subject. "Oh, I think I read it somewhere," was my reply, limping rather hastily away from the battlefield. So far as I know, the topic of spiders was never mentioned again by either of us. (p. 182)

This encounter begins with Sullivan revealing a highly vulnerable part of himself. Silverberg responds by distancing through the role of expert, as he suggests that Sullivan suffers from problems with his mother, thus putting Sullivan in a one-down position. Had Silverberg expressed a personal interest in Sullivan, he might have heard Sullivan's interesting dream of the spider and the web (Sullivan, 1953) and its crucial role in Sullivan's decision to study schizophrenia.[13] Thus, by presuming to know Sullivan, Silverberg forfeited the opportunity actually to know him, and inadvertently reinforced Sullivan's already strong tendency for concealment.

Harry Stack Sullivan Reaching into My Unconscious

I have, in my career as historian of psychology, immersed myself in the lives of a number of people. During the process of writing about G. Stanley Hall (Vande Kemp, 1992), I developed a thorough dislike for him as a person. While writing about Gordon Allport (Vande Kemp, 2000), there was one incident that left me with a bad taste in my mouth, and a greater awareness of his humanness. As I researched the life of Diana Baumrind, a living psychologist (Vande Kemp, 1999), I developed a deep respect for her as a person. As I read Sullivan's works, the Sullivan biographies, and interpretations of Sullivan, I repeatedly felt a deep empathy for him. I had no doubt that much of his empathy for his patients grew out of painful childhood experiences and out of his inability to find a true peer among his colleagues, one who might understand him both emotionally and intellectually. A few months after I had begun my intensive study of Sullivan, I found myself angry at Swick Perry (1982) for accusing Sullivan of denying Clara Thompson "the love of a man for a woman" (p. 214), as if this were a failing on Sullivan's part, and as if the friendship and close professional collaboration between Thompson and Sullivan wasn't enough. Why did Swick Perry feel compelled to write that "on every dimension, except probably one–sexual intimacy–this relationship became one of the most important in his life, as well as hers" (p. 200)? Then I dreamed that Sullivan had a wife and child. In the dream I was paging through a book that included glossy photos, one of which showed Sullivan with his wife and a child. The wife was wearing a blue and white dress. As I "journaled" the dream, I interpreted it first as fulfilling my wish for Sullivan (perhaps his own wish as well?) that he could have lived the life he publicly professed as healthy and mature (because of prevailing psychoanalytic ideas), rather than endure the tragedy of feeling that something was wrong with him, of not being free to pursue his preferred love interests, and having his ideas discounted because of his homosexuality. Later I took the dream as depicting Swick Perry's wish that Sullivan would have married Clara Thompson and thus provided her with more conventional photographs for her biography.[14] Readers can no doubt provide other interpretations for this dream, but they cannot deny what was also obvious to me: Sullivan's plight moved me enough to invade my unconscious as well as my conscious life. His pain touched me at a deep level. And I wished to know him well enough to own such a personal photograph, or perhaps to have taken it.

Chatelaine (1978) concluded that "if we asked, will the real Harry Stack Sullivan please stand up, three men at least would rise and they would be the 'real' Harry Stack Sullivan and represent beautifully his own conception of how the self is formed and the illusion of individual personality" (p. 437). Perhaps Chatelaine is correct. But certainly the "real" Harry Stack Sullivan was also a man who knew firsthand about the "interpersonal crime" he so eloquently described as committing when "I profoundly wound [a patient] by throwing out some verbal rattling of something that comes to my mind" (Sullivan, 1956, p. 111n3) and about the "psychological homicide" which is "unwittingly perpetrated by attendant, nurse, or the psychiatrist who forgets that his duty is to understand and assist, not to tinker and amuse himself" (Sullivan, 1962, p. 18). Regarding such psychiatric interpretations, Sullivan remarked that

> it is emphasized that interpretations and other suggestions thrust upon the patient without close regard to the life situations from which the psychosis resulted, and painstaking study of the indices to the actual conflicts which necessitated the upheaval, in themselves represent a destructive dillettanism which jeopardize any success which might otherwise result from the psychosis; and thus tend to determine an unfavorable outcome. (p. 18)

SULLIVAN AS A "GHOST" OF FAMILY PSYCHOLOGY AND THERAPY

The Concept of a Family Ghost

Family psychologists and family therapists speak of "ghosts" when they describe the presence of past generations and/or extended family members, actual or psychological, in the family's life or in the family therapy session. Carl Whitaker dealt with ghosts, in the form of the felt presence of absent family members, by bringing the absent family members into the therapy session, thus making the ghosts real (Haley & Hoffman, 1967). Norman Paul focused his process of "operational mourning" on exorcizing or disembodying the ghost of previously unmourned deceased family members who haunt the family's present life by functioning as members of the current family system (Paul, 1966, 1967a, 1967b; Paul & Grosser, 1965; see also Minuchin, 1974, p. 116). Salvador Minuchin often assigned homework so that processes initiated in the session might be facilitated at home by his "ghost" (Minuchin & Fishman, 1981, p. 154), and he emphasized that the family therapy process must move from a family system that included the therapist to one that included the family and the therapist's "ghost." In Sullivanian terms, such ghosts or psychological presences are among the fantastic or illusory "other ones" who are "exterior to sensual contact–effective by virtue only of the individual's faith in their past or present existence elsewhere" (Sullivan, 1972, p. 47). Sullivan's ghostly presence pervades the literature of family psychology and family therapy at various levels.

Pioneer Family Therapists and Family Psychologists Who Were Directly Influenced by Sullivan

Nathan Ward Ackerman (1908-1971). Nathan Ackerman (1971) acknowledged a Sullivanian influence in his work when he wrote that "the nature of my professional pursuits sensitized me to Sullivan's views on interpersonal relations and to the contributions of social science" (p. 148). Ackerman attended the New York Psychoanalytic Institute between 1937 and 1942, with Clara Thompson–who had been Sullivan's analyst and friend (Swick Perry, 1982)–serving as his training analyst (Bloch & Simon, 1982, p. 2). Ackerman (1958) credited Sullivan, Karen Horney, Frieda Fromm-Reichmann, Clara Thompson, Erich Fromm, Franz Alexander, and Abram Kardiner for the new perspective on psychotherapy in which "the therapist is a more real person, his personality plays a more definitive role, and the realities of the current interpersonal and wider social experience assume an expanded importance" (p. 277). Following Sullivan's lead, Ackerman conceived of "personality as an expression of a biopsychosocial continuum, in which behavior is influenced in a parallel way by inner physiological experience and by the processes of social participation" (p. 278). Lyman Wynne (1984) noted the similar experience of Ackerman and Sullivan:

> Much of his approach was adopted and elaborated by others, so well integrated into their methods that Ackerman soon became unrecognized as a distinctive source. Something of this sort surely happened with Harry Stack Sullivan, who also suffered relative oblivion until posthumous publications brought the recognition that he had earned during his tempestuous life. (p. 279)

Carl Whitaker (1912-1995). Carl Whitaker also reflected the influence of Sullivan, specifically in the emphasis on the therapist as a participant observer and the focus on interaction (Neill & Kniskern, 1982, pp. vii, xi, 81, 176). Neill (1982), in his biographical introduction to Whitaker's work, used Sullivan as a kind of foil to Whitaker, who was also raised on a New York farm. Neill stressed the differences between the two men:

> Sullivan's family, as described in Chapman's [1976] biography, was cold, distant, and reproachful. There was, in that Catholic ethos, little hope for escape from earthly suffering or eternal perdition. Sullivan became, and remained, isolated, defensive, and pessimistic. For Whitaker, on the other hand, raised in a Calvinist tradition, work could provide a sort of salvation; he could 'make' something of himself. He broke out of the shell of his loneliness and forced himself to make friends. (p. 2)

Don D. Jackson (1920-1968) and Donald A. Bloch (1922-). Two early leaders of the family therapy movement, Don Bloch and Don Jackson, were residents from 1950 to 1953 at Chestnut Lodge in Rockville, Maryland (Guerin, 1976, p. 5), where Sullivan had, beginning in 1942, delivered and recorded the 248 lectures that formed the core of his posthumously published works (Sullivan, 1940/1945, p. v).[15] Broderick and Schrader (1991) actually have Don Jackson "supervised by Sullivan" (p. 28), who would have been a ghostly presence indeed![16]

Don Jackson consistently acknowledged his indebtedness to Harry Stack Sullivan, Gregory Bateson, and Ludwig von Bertalanffy for focusing on interpersonal aspects of etiology and psychotherapy (Bodin, 1981). Jackson and Lederer (1969) placed Sullivan's definition of love at the center of their understanding of marriage. Quoting from *Conceptions of Modern Psychiatry,* they write: "When the satisfaction or the security of another person becomes as significant to one as is one's own satisfaction or security, then the state of love exists" (p. 42). This involves a kind of "living in love" rather than a "being in love": "love consists of a devotion and respect for the spouse that is equal to one's own self-love" (p. 55):

> Sullivan's definition of love *is* important. It describes not a unilateral process, but a two-way street, a bilateral process in which two individuals function in relation to each other as equals. Their shared behavior interlocks to form a compages[17] that represents *mutual* respect and devotion. One spouse alone cannot achieve this relationship. Both must participate to the same degree. The necessity for both spouses to "give" equally is one of the reasons that a marriage built upon mutual love is so rare. (p. 55)

Jackson and Gregory Bateson, two of the four authors of the seminal 1956 paper on the double bind in schizophrenia (Bateson, Jackson, Haley, & Weakland, 1956) both acknowledged a debt to Sullivan. Sullivan, as editor of *Psychiatry*, published Ruesch and Bateson's (1949) article on "Structure and Process in Social Relations" prior to the appearance of their 1951 book *Communication: The Social Matrix of Psychiatry.* Bateson's work, and the later communications research at the Mental Research Institute, embodied the ideals expressed by Sullivan in *The Fusion of Psychiatry and Social Science.* Miller and Sobelman write:

> 30 years before the paper on double bind, [Sullivan] anticipated the theme of conflicting communicational channels when he stated that there is a difference in what the schizophrenic thinks and what he feels called upon to say to others he feels he must accommodate (Sullivan, 1927[c]). These observations were noted later by Jackson (1961), one of the authors of the paper on the double bind. Sullivan's emphasis on anxiety as a primary, disjunctive influence is echoed in the many references to anxiety in the paper on the double bind; his postulate that, under the impact of anxiety, tenderness

> is replaced by malevolent behavior is virtually paraphrased in the description by Bateson et al. (1956) of the primary and secondary conflicting injunctions. (Miller & Sobelman, 1985, p. 28)

In a 1947 paper, Sullivan focused his interest in communication on international concerns. He wrote (in Sullivan, 1964), "All the semiotic or semantic perfection conceivable in a statement is of no moment if the hearer is motivated to refute or misunderstand it. The 'record' may look very well. What difference does that make in terms of understanding collaboration?" (p. 280). He would no doubt be pleased by the various answers to this question provided by the research of the Palo Alto School which owes so much to his inspiration (see Bodin, 1981).

A[ugustus] C[harles] R. "Robin" Skynner (1922-2000). The British family therapist, Robin Skynner (1976), integrated a variety of Sullivanian concepts into his psychodynamic family theory. Skynner wrote of Sullivan:

> His formulations anticipate and explain many of the later findings of family therapists concerning the transmission over generations of shared systems of denial and of family myths, as well as the manner in which psychotics become the members who cannot keep the family skeletons in the unconscious cupboard and so have to be split off and shut away in a cupboard (mental hospital) themselves. Sullivan's work with psychotics and obsessionals led him to recognize the necessity for more active support and concern for the therapeutic relationship in the former, and more active control of the evasive intellectualization of the latter, again heralding the more active, challenging approaches typical of family therapy. (p. 374) (p. 1)

According to Schlapobersky (2000), Skynner's mother "worried whether he would end up a genius or a lunatic. With hindsight, he realized that, lacking the resources for the first option, he spent much of his life trying to avoid the second. He ultimately compromised by entering a mental hospital through the staff entrance" (p. 1). The last sentence could certainly be applied to Sullivan. Skynner was valued for the deep spirituality he nurtured through "a long association with the Gurdjieff Society" (p. 3) whereas Sullivan appeared to believe the family myth that "one of his ancestors was the West Wind depicted as a horse who ran towards the sunrise to meet the future" (Thompson, 1949/1962, p. xxxiii), and he typically left his friends with the greeting "Gods keep you," a phrase through which "one got a glimpse of the Irish lad with the tradition of pagan gods. One could have no doubt that he meant, May the good forces in the world protect you" (p. xxxiv).

Skynner delighted in his long marriage and professional partnership with his wife Prudence. After her death he "enjoyed a relationship with Welsh landscape painter Josh Partridge, who provided inspired care after [Skynner] suffered a serious stroke in 1993" (Schlapobersky, 2000, p. 3). Sullivan also was nursed in his final years of ill health by his male partner of 22 years, James Inscoe Sullivan.

Salvador Minuchin (1923?-). Structural family therapy is a highly culture-sensitive approach that reflects the rich ethnic history of its founder, Salvador Minuchin: The child of Russian Jews who immigrated to Argentina, Minuchin was jailed as an anti-Peronist revolutionary; he fought in the Israeli war for independence, then was a physician to a multilingual Israeli army regiment; in New York, he developed a therapeutic milieu at a residential treatment center for children; in Israel, he directed residential institutions for displaced children of the Holocaust and participated in kibbutz life (Minuchin & Nichols, 1993). Like Sullivan, Minuchin felt like a cultural misfit. According to Richard Simon (1984), Carl Whitaker considered Minuchin's interest in society's outsiders to be a reflection of Minuchin's "own experiences as an immigrant and cultural outsider" (p. 22). Whitaker described Minuchin as a "stranger in a strange land" and a "psychosocial orphan" (p. 22)–both phrases that could easily be applied to the Irish Sullivan in upstate New York. Minuchin reports that, after his years in Israel, he trained at the William Alanson White Institute of Psychoanalysis in New York City because "I was attracted by the ideas of Harry Stack Sullivan, the creator of interpersonal psychoanalysis. He saw the psychoanalyst as a participant observer, and his ideas of human development and pathology included an understanding of the individual set in his circumstances" (p. 25). Minuchin frequently alludes to Sullivan's one-genus postulate, generally without citing a source. Sullivan would no doubt have been pleased with Minuchin's social interest, his early emphasis on family development (1974), and in his (1984) thoroughly interpersonal declaration that

> we live our lives like chips in a kaleidoscope, always part of patterns that are larger than ourselves and somehow more than the sum of their parts. Our individual epistemology usually blinds us to this kaleidoscopic self, and that is unfortunate because, when

> we look at human beings from this perspective, whole new possibilities open up for exploring behavior and alleviating pain. (p. 2)

Minuchin's ideas about family therapy, like Sullivan's interpersonal notions, threatened the psychiatric establishment. Minuchin reports that he made himself very unpopular with the Department of Psychiatry at the University of Pennsylvania "by insisting that child psychiatry was family psychiatry" (Minuchin & Nichols, 1998, p. 31). His insistence on family therapy for the middle class, and not just the poor, "stepped on many toes and, to the psychiatric establishment, felt like betrayal of the guild" (p. 31). When the Pennsylvania Council of Child Psychiatry launched an investigation "aimed at taking away from the [Philadelphia Child Guidance] clinic the right to train child psychiatrists," an internal committee concluded that "Dr. Minuchin's ideas are dangerous for the Department" (p. 31). Minuchin confesses that he provoked this response by "insisting on making my total nonacceptance of the usual way of working highly visible, forcing the establishment to challenge me" (p. 31). This style also sounds much like Sullivan's. The threatening truth that Minuchin has preached zealously for nearly four decades is that the concept of the 'single, unattached adult' is nonsensical: "nowhere among living organisms can one find 'unattachment,' yet it exists in our human typologies" (Minuchin & Fishman, 1981, p. 14).[18] Both Minuchin and Sullivan would agree with John Macmurray (1961/1979) that the true state of individuals is always as "selves-in-context," so that two or more individuals in relationship constantly influence each other in patterns that tend to maintain stable relationships, patterns that we tend to mislabel and reify as "traits" or "personality factors."

R[onald] D[avid] Laing (1927-1989). R. D. Laing, who was a strong voice for the antipsychiatry movement as well as a vocal critic of the family as a social structure, had deep respect for Sullivan, and the ghost of Sullivan no doubt freely roamed the corridors of Kingsley Hall. Laing (1963) praised Sullivan's *Schizophrenia as a Human Process,* and despaired about the fact that so few of Sullivan's ideas had taken root:[19]

> Reading these articles by Sullivan written thirty or forty years ago is a somewhat depressing experience. They are altogether more contemporary than they should be. What were brave and sometimes reckless dicta then should have become hypotheses, long since confirmed or disconfirmed. Instead, most of the issues are still open, most of the work that Sullivan's vision demanded is still not done. Perhaps there is still time. (p. 63)

Laing (1959/1965a) subscribed to Sullivan's "one genus" principle (p. 34) and spoke of an ontological insecurity that he recognized as being much like Sullivan's principle of interpersonal anxiety: "the ontologically insecure person is preserving rather than gratifying himself: the ordinary circumstances of living threaten his *low threshold* of security" (p. 42). In describing the person's response to ontological insecurity, Laing (1960/1969) wrote: "some engage in desperate 'security operations,' to use Sullivan's phrase; others engage in sincerity operations" (p. 36). Laing apparently was unaware of Sullivan's insightful discussion of sincerity operations. In *Personal Psychopathology*, written between 1927 and 1933 but not published until 1972, Sullivan was already well aware of the true function of human communication and how it might lead to what Laing described as "mystification" (1965b) and "untenable positions" (1960/1969):

> It thus comes about that the content of most verbal behavior in interpersonal relations is not due to inconsistencies inherent in the meaning of verbal symbols, but to the multiple integrations of the situations in which they both originated, and are put to ineffective use. Conversation, on which many throughout their life put the utmost of conscious faith, is only occasionally used to convey accurate or comprehensive information. It is chiefly used as a tool in producing satisfactory situations and in contributing to activity for satisfactory resolution of these. Moreover, in conversation, the words used and their grammatic ordering may be largely subordinate to inflectional and other devices used to create the "impressions" communicated. It is in large part as the result of this impressionistic "misuse" that there arises the vagueness of verbal symbols–so distressing to the compulsive thinker who often, *passim*, is a past master at casting a deceptive screen of words over concrete reality. One's verbal symbols, other than those carefully elaborated as *terms* in abstract formulations, are not inconsistent but generally vague and frequently overlapping. One's use of them may be extremely inconsistent and unconsciously or deliberately fraudulent. (Sullivan, 1972, p. 280)

In *The Interpersonal Theory of Psychiatry* Sullivan (1953) devotes special sections of the chapter on "Malevolence, Hatred, and Isolating Techniques" to "Required Behavior and the Necessity to Conceal and Deceive" and "Verbalisms and 'As If' Performances." He writes:

> A great many children quite early begin to develop the ability to conceal what is going on in them, what they have been doing behind someone's back, and thus to deceive the authoritative figure. Some of this ability to conceal and deceive is literally taught by the authority-carrying figures, and some of it represents trial-and-error learning from human example–that is, by observing and analyzing the performances, the successes and failures, of servants and the like. (pp. 207-208)

Children learn early on to conceal and to deceive, and in the process learn both to rationalize and to engage in "*as if* performances" (p. 208).[20] It is in this context that Sullivan discusses the multiple *personae* produced by the great variety of interpersonal situations in which we find ourselves. He writes:

> I long since set up the conception of me-you patterns, by which I mean the often grossly incongruent ways of behaving, or roles that one plays, in interpersonal situations with someone else. And all of them, or most of them, seem just as near the real thing–the personification of the self–as can be, although there is no more making sense of them from the standpoint of their representing different aspects of durable traits than there is of translating Sanskrit before you understand language. (p. 209)

In *Clinical Studies in Psychiatry*, Sullivan (1956) described in detail how these deceptive processes characterize the communication of hysterics, obsessional characters, and schizophrenics. For example, he wrote of the obsessional that "he is secure as long as he is engaged in some explicit or implicit verbal operation which is apparently communicative, but is actually uncommunicative because it is somewhat too autistic" (p. 147). In *Personal Psychopathology* Sullivan (1972) wrote of the *retrograde falsification* of experience that characterizes the psychopathic personality (p. 121). In a rather perceptive analysis of the psychopathic lie, Sullivan wrote:

> There is little or no conscious determination to deceive to be found behind his apparently fraudulent utterances . . . the statements of the psychopath are for the most part remarkably well adapted to the immediate interpersonal situation in which he happens to be . . . the intention to deceive is not as conspicuous as his inability to believe the facts that he has experienced. (p. 121)

R. D. Laing and Harry Stack Sullivan truly were kindred spirits who shared acute perceptions about "sincerity operations" and the speaker or writer's relation to the things said and written, whether she is "telling the truth, lying, pretending, equivocating" (Laing, 1960/1969, p. 111) and thus placing self and other in untenable positions. Sullivan's work on deception had a profound effect on both Anton Boisen and O. H. Mowrer, whose applications of Sullivan I will discuss below.

Sullivan as a Buried Ancestor in Family Psychology

In addition to the family therapists already discussed, a number of others acknowledged a debt to Sullivan or recognized his influence. Beavers (1977), for example, noted that "Sullivan was a systems theorist before Von Bertalanffy developed the science, describing the self as a 'unitary system' which cannot be separated from its necessary environmental milieu without ceasing to be a living organism" (p. 226). He also recognized the postmodernist element in Sullivan's thinking:

> No man has objective truth, scientific or otherwise, and the individual's subjective view of the world is as close to "reality" as anybody's alleged objectivity. Harry Stack Sullivan's beautiful term, "consensual validation," with which he replaced the Freudian concept of "reality testing," shows a profound understanding of science and of human development. (pp. 12-13)

Beavers included Sullivan with a group of therapists whose ideas he examined "from the standpoint of contributions to furthering the eight variables derived from family systems studies" (p. 238). Beavers (pp. 238-249) identified ways that Sullivan contributed in seven of these eight areas: a systems orientation, boundary issues, contextual clarity, power issues, encouragement of autonomy, negotiation and task performance, and transcendent values. He felt that "Sullivan, a rather austere intellectual and cognitive person, did not make significant improvements" in the area of affective issues (p. 246), a judgment which suggests that he should have read more of Sullivan than he actually did, as empathy was at the core of Sullivan's developmental theory and his therapeutic understanding.

Miller and Sobelman (1985) discussed in some detail how Sullivan and Kurt Lewin "served as the conduits, through the writings of Bateson and Jackson, of the holistic and teleological traditions to the field of family therapy" (p. 19). Broderick and Schrader (1991) credit Sullivan with three influences on the family therapy movement: First, he "was the most interpersonally oriented of all the American analysts" (p. 18). Second, "he was among the first to assert and to demonstrate that schizophrenia could be treated by psychotherapy" (p. 18), a notion that influenced the work of Murray Bowen and Don Jackson. Third, "he was foremost a clinician rather than a theorist," and "he refused to be impressed with any theory which could not be demonstrated in practical work with patients" (p. 18).

Ivan Boszormenyi-Nagy, the later founder of contextual family therapy, in 1957 became the program director of a family therapy research project at Eastern Pennsylvania Psychiatric Institute in Philadelphia that "explored intensive psychotherapy of hospitalized psychotic patients" which was influenced in part by the interpersonal theories of Frieda Fromm-Reichman, Harold Searles, and Sullivan (Boszormenyi-Nagy, Grunebaum, & Ulrich, 1991, p. 201). Sullivan would no doubt have recognized in the relational ethics of the contextual approach an antidote to interpersonal crime.

We also find clues to the pervasive influence of Sullivan on family therapy in the pages of *Family Process*, the premier family therapy journal launched in 1962. An electronic search of the journal's pages through 1999 reveals multiple references to Sullivan's works, with *The Interpersonal Theory of Psychiatry* (1953) cited 14 times; *Clinical Studies in Psychiatry* (1956) cited four times; *Conceptions of Modern Psychiatry* (1946) cited three times; and single references to two journal articles (1927b, 1927c).

I find it interesting also as a historian to see how much of family theory itself is latent in Sullivan's work. In *Clinical Studies in Psychiatry* (1956) Sullivan discussed family processes that mitigate against future paranoia and prejudice (pp. 343-344), including a brief discussion of the role of siblings. Here (p. 377) and elsewhere Sullivan described a technique that is very much like the strategic family therapist's reframing and that achieves at the same time Minuchin's emphasis on the positive (Minuchin & Fishman, 1981). He discussed explicitly the process of scapegoating later described in great detail by Ackerman (1966). Of the victims, Sullivan (1956) wrote:

> They have, perhaps, been excellent scapegoats for others, in that they were so bothered that they were not at all expert at returning the goat to the other person with thanks. They were people especially vulnerable to having blame transferred to them. And they have had the greatest difficulty finding scapegoats themselves; they just have not understood people, or how to deal with people,

> well enough to make others scapegoats. They are among the most handicapped at juggling blame around. (p. 336)

Of the family processes, Sullivan remarked that

> the extent to which explanatory doctrines which make other people responsible for one's own shortcomings are utilized varies from family to family. That is, the products of one family will have greater ingenuity at discovering how other people are to blame for their sins of omission and commission; and the products of another will be much less clever at discovering scapegoats. (p. 342)

Sullivan also commented extensively on family dynamics in *Personal Psychopathology* (1972), where he commented on various aspects of birth order and sibling position, noting specifically the role of first-born and youngest children, of only children, and of families having daughters only or sons only. His discussion of family history-taking in *The Psychiatric Interview* (1954) also shows considerable insight into the influence of sibling position. I suspect Sullivan would have been pleased to find his genogram included in the major textbook on genograms in family assessment (McGoldrick, Gerson, & Shellenberger, 1999, p. 116), where the authors highlight the significance of the early death of his older siblings (p. 41) and the fact that in his family there were "too many people for one particular role" (p. 116). Sullivan was a fine family psychologist, despite the fact that he never advanced to the role of family therapist, and family psychologists can benefit greatly from reading his work.

SULLIVAN AS MUSE FOR PASTORAL THEOLOGIANS

In *A History of Pastoral Care in America*, E. Brooks Holifield (1983) discussed the fact that pastoral theologians of the 1950s and 1960s–especially Carroll Wise, Albert Outler, Paul Johnson, and Wayne Oates–"were attracted to a psychology that accorded a significant place to an interpersonal 'context of relationships'" (p. 316). Holifield attributes this interest to the continuing influence of Anton Boisen and to the "social psychology of the neo-Freudians–like Fromm, Horney, and Harry Stack Sullivan–and the small-group movement that emerged out of Kurt Lewin's experimentation in group dynamics" (p. 316). Holifield remarked that Sullivan's "friendship with Anton Boisen and his support of Boisen's work had helped ensure that the pastoral writers would be among his early admirers" (p. 318). Seward Hiltner (who for many years served as a consultant to the Menninger Foundation on "theological dynamics" [Hiltner, 1972]) believed "that the idea of the 'social self' could 'prove to be the key to the relationship between psychology and religion'" (Holifield, 1983, p. 322), and Albert Outler believed

> that the theory of interpersonal relations held by such therapists as Harry Stack Sullivan contained "more points of contact with Christian notions than any other single perception in modern psychotherapy." An interpersonal psychology suggested possibilities of linkages with biblical themes such as "covenant," ethical notions such as "love," descriptions of the Church as an "organic body," and religious motifs such as "encounter" with the divine presence. It also provided a set of analogies for referring to God as the subject of an I/Thou relationship. (pp. 322-323)

Sullivan extensively influenced three men whose works are well-known among pastoral theologians: Anton T. Boisen, Paul E. Johnson, and O. Hobart Mowrer.

Anton Theophilus Boisen (1876-1965). Most historians of the pastoral psychology movement regard Anton T. Boisen (1936, 1955, 1958, 1960) as the father of Clinical Pastoral Education (CPE) and as one of the first modern pastoral theologians. Boisen had "five psychotic episodes in his lifetime, three of them severe enough to require hospitalization" (Aden, 1988, p. 3). The third hospitalization, in 1935, was at Sheppard & Enoch Pratt Hospital in Baltimore (Boisen, 1960, p. 177), where Sullivan's influence was still felt. Various scholars have summarized Boisen's contributions to the psychology of religion and pastoral theology, and some have explored his psychotic experiences (Aden, 1988; Bregman, 1979; Hall, 1967; Patton, 1988; Pruyser, 1967), and a few scholars have examined his contributions to psychiatry (Goldwert, 1995; Powell, 1977), but Boisen scholars generally say little or nothing of the relationship between Sullivan and Boisen. Holifield (1983) mentioned Sullivan's friendship with Boisen, and Patton (1988) actually claims that Boisen "unintentionally echoes the views of Harry Stack Sullivan who, like Bowen, was most influenced in the development of his views by his attempt to understand schizophrenia" (p. 44). Had Patton read Boisen more carefully, he would have noted that in the preface to *The Exploration of the Inner World*, Boisen (1936) acknowledges Sullivan, who "helped with certain portions of the manuscript" (p. xi).

Sullivan and Boisen in fact had both personal and professional connections and perhaps a mutual influence. In *Out of the Depths* Boisen described having just finished writing his paper "Personality Changes and Upheavals Arising out of the Sense of Personal Failure" (Boisen, 1926) when he read Sullivan's 1924 paper:

> I was deeply interested in this, for it gave needed support to my own views. I wrote to him, therefore, and a little later I went down to see him at the Sheppard and Enoch Pratt Hospital in Baltimore, where at that time he was clinical director. I saw him many times after that, always with increasing respect and affection. (Boisen, 1960, p. 156)

In 1928 Boisen and his colleagues spoke about clinical theological education at the section on religion of the American Sociological Society in Washington, DC. In the course of a discussion, Boisen (1960) wrote:

> I let slip the view that there was much to support the ancient theological doctrine that conviction of sin was a first step in the process of salvation. To many of those present such a view was heresy, and they were not slow in expressing themselves. I was greatly delighted when Dr. Harry Stack Sullivan, who had come to this meeting at my invitation, arose and defended my position in one of his characteristically keen and witty speeches. (p. 166)

In his 1931-1932 paper on "Modified Psychoanalytic Treatment of Schizophrenia," Sullivan wrote of Boisen:

> There are some ecclesiasts who find joy in tinkering with the mild mental disorders, in Church Healing Missions and the like. These folk might learn much from, for example, the Rev. Anton Boisen, Chaplain of the Worcester State Hospital, who has come by the tedious and often deeply disturbing road of observation and experimentation to a sane grasp of the relations of religious thoughts and techniques to the schizophrenia problem. (Sullivan, 1962, p. 290)

Boisen (1960) wrote that

> the purposive and constructive features of the acute disturbances which bear such a close resemblance to the experience of George

> Fox have in this country been recognized by Dr. Harry Stack Sullivan [1924] in a view which coincides closely with the findings of this inquiry. (p. 110)

He continues,

> In addition to his recognition of the constructive aspects of the acute disturbance, Dr. Sullivan has given much attention to the social factors and the social implications of mental illness. He has not however paid much attention to the religious implications of these experiences and it is doubtful whether he would be likely to help our patient through to the type of solution which Fox actually achieves unaided. (p. 111)

Despite Boisen's doubts, Swick Perry maintained that Sullivan apparently "partly identified" with George Fox, who, according to Sullivan, "had a lurid schizophrenic panic and a fairly prolonged schizophrenic illness. . . . Anyway, he was able to maintain, perhaps improving mental health, with recurrences of fairly serious personality disorder" (quoted in Swick Perry, 1982, p. 193). Boisen (1936) referred to Sullivan's (1931-1932) observation "that there seems to be nothing other than the purpose of the interpersonal situation which distinguishes the psychoanalytic transference relation from other situations of interpersonal intimacy" (p. 161n).

Boisen (1936) believed that some forms of psychosis (including the experiences of George Fox, which he explored in a chapter entitled "George Fox Among the Doctors") were "essentially problem-solving experiences which are closely related to certain types of religious experience" (p. 53), and he felt his own psychotic episodes "left me not worse but better" (1960, p. 202). Boisen also experienced "five major decisions which have been marked by deviation from the normal" (p. 202). He felt that all 10 abnormal episodes began under conditions he saw as characteristic of creative mental activity. Boisen noted that many cases of psychosis involve "ideas of world catastrophe, of death, of rebirth, of cosmic importance and of mission" (p. 53). One can hardly read Sullivan's (1956) description of "the feeling of urgency" in *Clinical Studies in Psychiatry* (pp. 316-320) without thinking of Boisen's tremendous sense of urgency in relation to his idea of "the group of four" (Boisen, 1960, pp. 77-142) and his extensive descriptions of cosmic drama and cosmic catastrophe (Boisen, 1936). Sounding very much like Sullivan, Boisen (1936) proclaimed that

> the examination of the causative factors in dementia praecox has led us to the conclusion that the primary evil lies in the realm of social relationships, particularly in life situations involving the sense of personal failure. We have found one characteristic common to the group as a whole: they are isolated from their fellows through a social judgment which either consciously or subconsciously they accept and pronounce upon themselves . . . the psychotic accepts the social judgments of the group in which he has been reared, and by the standards which his early guides have implanted he stands condemned. The result is an intolerable loss of self-respect. (p. 28)

Here, Boisen is very much in agreement with Sullivan, who claimed in his 1927 paper on "The Onset of Schizophrenia" that "there seems little reason to doubt that cultural distortions provided by the home are of primary importance" (Sullivan, 1962, p. 104). Sullivan recognized Boisen's work in the "Onset" paper, where he wrote in a footnote "See, for an interesting consideration not unharmonious with our views, Anton Boisen 'Personality Changes and Upheavals Arising out of the Sense of Personal Failure'" (Sullivan, 1962, 112n). In that paper Sullivan insisted that schizophrenic psychosis "seems never to occur in those who have achieved if only for a short time a definitely satisfying adjustment to a sex object" (p. 104). This is consistent with Boisen's (1936) observation that "with the doubtful exception of a few married men there were none in the group who had arrived at healthy adult sexual development with wholesome expression of the sex drive" (p. 27). Boisen described three chief methods by which these men dealt with their sense of personal failure: drifting, delusional misinterpretation (self-deception), and panic (pp. 28-29, 40). One suspects that the many conversations with Boisen influenced Sullivan's thoughts about the outcomes of schizophrenia. Sullivan, who had abnormal transformative experiences of his own, would not have been unduly concerned with what Boisen (1936) described as "the inevitable biases of the participant observer" (p. 11).

In 1944 Sullivan accepted Boisen's invitation to visit Elgin, Illinois, on his way to New Mexico. Boisen offered a delightful picture of Sullivan:

> As the time of his visit approached I wrote to him, asking him to let me know when he would arrive, and by what train. I received no reply and did not know what to do. Finally, on the morning of the appointed day, I received a telephone call. Dr. Sullivan was wait-

> ing in the Baltimore and Ohio Station in Chicago, 40 miles away. I hurried in and found him pacing nervously up and down, holding by the leash one of his favorite cocker spaniels, and with two heavy bags piled up on the side. I was certainly glad I had not suggested he take the interurban train! He gave two splendid lectures at our hospital and a superb demonstration of his technique of interviewing patients. (p. 184)

Boisen's respect and love for Sullivan were obviously reciprocated. The anonymous writer of the dust jacket text for Boisen's (1960) *Out of the Depths* writes that this book "intimately reveals the Anton Boisen of whom Harry Stack Sullivan, the brilliant psychiatrist, said: 'We are struck by the power, the courage, the depth, and tenderness of feeling, clear insight and intelligence.'" Sullivan published several of Boisen's papers in *Psychiatry*: "Types of Dementia Praecox" (1938), "Economic Distress and Religious Experience" (1939a), "Form and Content of Schizophrenic Thinking" (1942b), and "Religion and Personality Adjustment" (1942c); Boisen (1939b) also contributed a book review. Sullivan also invited Boisen to be one of eight reviewers of Erich Fromm's (1941) *Escape from Freedom* (Boisen, 1942a) in "a synoptic series of reviews" (Swick Perry, 1982, p. 388).

Sullivan and Boisen shared an interest in the process of concealment. Much of this is implicit rather than explicit in Sullivan, who spoke of it most explicitly in *The Interpersonal Theory of Psychiatry* (1953):

> People who have customarily low self-esteem may minimize their anxiety by concealments and social isolation, may channel their anxiety and disjunctive motivations in interpersonal relations by exploitative attitudes and substitutive processes, or may manifest them in dissociative processes. (p. 351)

Sullivan himself was often very secretive, concealing most of "the details of his life before he achieved prominence" (Allen, 1995, p. 3). Swick Perry (1982) wrote of his early professional years that "the job applications filled out by Sullivan himself show almost a clinical picture of confabulation" (p. 163) and that with his application to the Medical Reserve Corps in 1918 Sullivan "began a certain series of falsifications of his life and experience, as reported in subsequent documents, that are at best confusing when one is trying to reconstruct these years. The changes in names are themselves mystifying" (p. 170). Despite extensive efforts, Chapman (1976), Chatelaine (1978, 1981), Swick Perry

(1982), and Allen (1995) were unable to solve the mystery of Sullivan's whereabouts in 1910 and 1911, between the time he left Cornell and his resurfacing in Chicago. Sullivan's reticence extended to his early years. Swick Perry (1982) reports that "innumerable colleagues . . . were astounded to learn many years after Sullivan's death that he had grown up on a farm; they had always assumed he had urban background" (p. 203). Allen (1995) expressed what is most likely a common opinion about Sullivan's reticence: "It seems to me that when someone is extraordinarily secretive about a period in their life it means that they are hiding something–hiding activities they perceive as deeply embarrassing or activities, which, if disclosed, would, they believe, seriously threaten their current well-being" (p. 7). Swick Perry (1982) believed that Sullivan's secret was "that he had suffered a schizophrenic breakdown at Cornell and was hospitalized, perhaps for as long as two years. In addition she believed that he continued to have episodes of schizophrenia for many years afterward" (Allen, 1995, p. 7). Allen (1995) and Chapman (1976) assume the secret to be Sullivan's homosexuality. In my own reading of Sullivan, as he wrote about concealment and retrograde falsification and other types of deception leading to interpersonal alienation, I felt that he understood exactly why one might use these defenses, and other manifestations of selective inattention, in an effort to create an interpersonal world whose reflected appraisals would not be primarily of the "bad-me" variety.

Boisen (1936) wrote very explicitly about processes of concealment and their destructive effects for schizophrenics. He wrote: "the sense of guilt is essentially a social judgment which operates within the personality itself" (p. 156) and "*the real evil in mental disorder is not to be found in the conflict but in the sense of isolation or estrangement.* It is the fear and guilt which result from the presence in one's life of that which one is afraid to tell" (p. 268). Treatment for guilt involved in part "thoroughgoing honesty in the facing of the facts. There must be an abandonment of all subterfuges and disguises and the consequent finding of justification and satisfaction in the sense of inner peace and fellowship" (p. 211). In his later autobiography Boisen (1960) told of the important turning point when, after a period of anguished prayer, "Something seemed to say to me almost in words, 'Don't be afraid to tell'" (p. 47), and he followed this admonition by sharing his concerns openly with his mother. Sullivan too valued confession and the facing of facts. As early as 1929 he participated in a discussion in which he pushed Edward Sapir on a distinction Sapir made between "confession as a device to bring about social solidarity and as a device for discharging the feeling of guilt of the individual" (Sullivan, 1962, p. 231), ending the discussion by observing that "it is my perhaps overindividualized belief that these are identical" (p. 232). It is this common emphasis in Boisen and Sullivan on the negative effects of concealment and the positive effects of confession that profoundly influenced O. H. Mowrer.

O. Hobart Mowrer (1907-1982). O. Hobart Mowrer, a well-known "learning psychologist" who was president of the American Psychological Association in 1954,[21] reported having at least eight "more or less incapacitating depressions, two of sufficient severity to require hospitalization" (Hunt, 1984, p. 912; see also Mowrer, 1974). Out of this personal pain, Mowrer eventually developed integrity therapy (R. C. Johnson, Dokecki, & Mowrer, 1972; Mowrer, 1961, 1964, 1967; Mowrer & Vattano, 1974), a group approach which elevated Jourard's (1964) "principle of Honesty, Openness or Transparency" to a place of prime importance (Mowrer, 1974, p. 355). Mowrer added a second principle of "Responsibility, i.e., a willingness not only to confess but also to make restitution" (p. 355). Before Mowrer found this apparent solution to his problems, he engaged in four courses of psychoanalysis, including extensive work with Hanns Sachs. In the spring of 1944 Mowrer, who had been classified 4-F for his history of emotional instability, accepted an appointment with the Office of Strategic Services (OSS) in Washington, DC, where he stayed for about a year. He reported that his assessment work with OSS candidates for "special hazardous overseas assignments" (p. 15) exacerbated his psychological problems:

> I knew that if I were on the other end of the stick, I could not take it. We were subjecting these men to various tests and ordeals, including an attempt to break the "cover story" they were required to concoct during the assessment period–all of which positively terrified me. I knew, emotionally if not intellectually, that I too had a "cover story," and I wasn't about to take any chance at having *it* cracked. (Mowrer, 1966, p. 15)

Mowrer's anxiety grew so intense that he took a month's leave of absence to return to Boston for intensive work with Hanns Sachs. He returned to his OSS duties uncertain about his ability to handle them, but fairly certain about one thing: he was "*through with psychoanalysis*" (p. 16). His life began to change in the spring of 1945, when he had the opportunity to enroll in two courses at the Washington School of Psychiatry, one of which was a course with Harry Stack Sullivan. Mowrer reported:

> Beginning with the Sullivan seminar in the spring of 1945, I ceased blaming morality (as embodied in my conscience and embedded in society) for my difficulties, and began to look at my own interpersonal failures and fraudulence as the root of the problem . . . following my "season in Hell" in 1953, I began to think much more seriously about religion. . . . I felt that psychology had not "saved" me; and since I was still in a state of confusion and dismay I hoped that Christianity might. (pp. 33-34)

Sullivan's lectures awakened in Mowrer an awareness of the importance of honesty and openness in interpersonal relationships. He concluded that "no very close scrutiny of my life was necessary to show that my interpersonal relations were deeply 'unsound'" (p. 17), and that "there was deep dishonesty in *all* the more important interpersonal relationships in my life" (p. 18). Soon after his encounter with Sullivan, Mowrer reports that "I shared with my wife, contritely but as gently and considerately as I could, the secrets of my adolescence–and some additional ones I had acquired after marriage" (Mowrer, 1974, p. 353). He felt that he "was repudiating certain forms of deviant (secretive, dishonest) behavior" (p. 353). Soon thereafter he began to publish the ideas that crystallized into integrity therapy. In his early book on personality, Mowrer (1950) argued that there is a form of anxiety induced by guilt: "Anxiety comes, not from acts which the individual would commit but dares not, but from acts which he has committed and wishes that he had not. It is, in other words, a 'guilt theory' of anxiety rather than an 'impulse theory'" (p. 537). Despite his efforts to live a more honest life, Mowrer was hospitalized for a suicidal depression in August 1953, on the eve of his ascendence to the presidency of the American Psychological Association. After three and a half months of hospitalization he continued to see the Chicago psychiatrist who saw him through the acute crisis. In 1956 Mowrer was invited to respond to a paper presented by Boisen at an APA symposium on Religion and Mental Health. Mowrer had read Boisen's 1936 book, and after reading Boisen's (1958) paper, Mowrer (1966) concluded that his illness on the eve of his APA presidency served the functions of confession and penance:

> By not showing up in Cleveland I had "unconsciously" accomplished two things: (1) I had greatly extended my confession–now several thousand of my fellow psychologists knew there was something "wrong" with me, although they did not know precisely what; and (b) I had "done penance" in that I had declined the hon-

> ors and undergone the humiliation of hospitalization and the pain of a severe agitated depression. (p. 24)

Mowrer became increasingly convinced that in the neurotic individual "an identity crisis arises because of foolish, short-sighted *decisions* which the individual himself has made (to do deviant things and to hide them), for which no one but himself can be properly blamed. Such a person has had some freedom of choice and has exercised it badly" (p. 29). Mowrer's early papers on these topics were collected in *The Crisis in Psychiatry and Religion* (1961), where his central argument is that disingenuous amorality may be a cause of personality disorders. A second collection of papers was published as *The New Group Therapy*, a book in which Mowrer (1964) described the integrity therapy groups which were based on his understanding of the early church. Mowrer (1966) contended that "early Christianity was basically *a small-groups movement* in which alienated, sinful, 'neurotic' persons confessed before and did penance under the guidance of the particular 'congregation' (or 'house church') to which they belonged or wished to belong" (p. 35). He believed that Christianity, rather than being too "Puritanical, legalistic, rigid" suffered a different sin: "Is it not, rather, the church's claim that it has, in one form or another, special power–through the sacraments, preaching, or prayer–to 'forgive' sins, in the sense of pardoning them, getting the evil-doer off easy, 'cheap grace'?" (p. 36). Mowrer felt that we should "revitalize the ancient practice of living openly, in community and fully under the judgment of one's family, friends, and close associates" (p. 37). His integrity groups, which he led with his wife, emphasized the value of confession, restitution, and involvement (Mowrer, 1976). By the time Mowrer wrote his chapter for *A History of Psychology in Autobiography* (1974), he was less enthusiastic about integrity therapy, although he remained committed to an interpersonal model. To symbolize his commitment to his wife and family, he "requested and graciously received permission from the editor of this volume to reproduce, at the outset of this chapter, a family rather than an individual photograph" (p. 336). He was beginning to acknowledge that his emphasis on relational integrity, which had helped him to overcome characterological defects, had not cured his depression, which he described as a "thorn in my flesh" (p. 358) and categorized as "a type of depression that is largely constitutional, or 'endogenous'" (p. 359). He expressed gratitude "for relief obtained from medications during my most recent–I dare not say 'last'–depression" (p. 359). He also advocated a "widespread eugenic attack" on depression and similar problems (p. 359). When he wrote his final autobiographical statement, three years after the death of his wife Molly, Mowrer (1983)–who suffered from hypoglycemia–argued that orthomolecular biology might provide "the fourth psychiatric revolution" (p. 322). Despite his emphasis on interpersonal relationships and responsibility to significant others, Mowrer "considered the decision to live or not to live to be personal" (Hunt, 1984, p. 914). With Molly dead, his children established in their own homes, and an unsuccessful effort to start self-help groups for hypoglycemics, Mowrer committed suicide on June 20, 1982, not long after writing his final autobiographical statement. In a testimony to Mowrer's "valuation of self-disclosure," Hunt (1984) publicly revealed the cause of Mowrer's death in the *American Psychologist* obituary.

One wonders if things might have gone differently had Mowrer been a better psychopathologist: He failed to differentiate between neurosis and psychosis, and thus to separate issues of the mind/body relationship from interpersonal and social alienation. To his own detriment, he conflated two of the four dimensions of personality outlined later by Paul Johnson–the intrapersonal and the interpersonal–and failed to recognize the potential benefits of the transpersonal. He also might have been helped had he understood at an earlier point one of Sullivan's major emphases: that of the powerful effect of the interpersonal environment on the action of the individual. Mowrer's emphasis on responsibility in integrity therapy actually constituted a radical individualism that never grasped the essence of Sullivan's (1953) theorem of reciprocal emotion.

After Sullivan's death there were also rumors of suicide (Swick Perry, 1982, pp. 417-419), but Sullivan's death was "undoubtedly natural, caused by meningeal hemorrhage with lesions of the liver and kidneys" (p. 417). Sullivan died while he still had much for which to live, and as Thompson (1949/1962) attested at his funeral,

> His belief that a way could be found to bring lasting peace to the world was a fire within him which sustained his frail body in the last physically ill years of his life. Several times in the last few years he outwitted death in a way that seemed like a miracle. He wanted to live and he lived productively. He will go on living with us and through us who have known him. He died the death of a hero in the midst of carrying on the work dearest to his heart. (p. xxxv)

Paul E. Johnson (1898-1974). Paul E. Johnson was an American Methodist pastor, pastoral theologian, and psychologist of religion

(Holifield, 1990). Johnson introduced Clinical Pastoral Education at Boston University School of Theology in 1941; cofounded the Institute of Pastoral Care, with Rollin Fairbanks, in 1944; and from 1952 through 1963 directed the Danielsen Pastoral Counseling Service in Boston. In his early work, Johnson incorporated Rogerian client-centered therapy, but he soon judged that approach to be "unduly individualistic and self-centered." Drawing on personalist theology and the works of Fritz Künkel, Jacob Moreno, Gordon Allport, Victor Frankl, Martin Buber, Kurt Lewin, and Sullivan, he developed what he called "dynamic interpersonalism" (Johnson, 1957, 1967), taking the position that "the essential nature of persons was shaped in their encounter with other persons" (Holifield, 1990, p. 613). Johnson (1957) defined personality as "a developing integration of goal-seeking life processes, arising from multidimensional needs and persisting through interacting relationships to experience meaning and achieve a community of values with other persons" (p. 26). Johnson argued that the "I" at the center of personality interacts in four dimensions: the biological (me), the physical (it), the social (we), and the ideal (thou). An adequate theory of personality must take all four dimensions into account. Thus, Johnson's dynamic interpersonalism draws on Freudian psychoanalysis (me), Lewinian field theory (it), Sullivan's interpersonal psychology (we), and Allport's personalistic psychology (thou). In my history of psychology classes, and in several publications (Vande Kemp, 1981, 1996, 2001), I've addressed this problem by describing four dimensions or phases of reality: (a) the *im*personal or *non*personal (it); (b) the *inter*personal (we); (c) the *intra*personal (me); and (d) the *trans*personal or *super*personal (thou). Like Johnson, I believe that we must approach each of these realities with distinctive metaphysical and epistemological assumptions. Sullivan also was aware of these dimensions when he described the child's learning to differentiate "(a) things characterized by objective reality of the physical kind [it], (b) things characterized as purely personal subjective reality [me], and (c) things characterizable as socially valid [we]" (Sullivan, 1962, p. 191).

Johnson (1957) wove Sullivanian insights into his pastoral theology in numerous ways. In his discussion of the struggle for freedom, he noted that our view of ourselves "will be (as Sullivan would say) reflected appraisals of what other persons think of [us]. The stronger the ties of family affection, the more effort will be required to stand alone and be [a] self" (p. 153). In his discussion of the religious conscience, he remarked that "what Sullivan called consensual validation is needed by the conscientious person to check private visions with the careful observations of others" (p. 166), thus bringing consensual validation into the process of spiritual discernment. Johnson brought Sullivan's concept of "security operations" into his discussion of the personality under stress (p. 170). Johnson also accepted Sullivan's theory of malevolent transformations, stating that Sullivan was "unable to find support for the theory that man is essentially a devil, or possessed of some wonderful thing called sadism" (p. 184). Citing Ruesch and Bateson (1951), who were themselves indebted to Sullivan, Johnson (1957) asserted that "psychiatrists are increasingly viewing mental illness as disturbances of interpersonal relations, and particularly of communication" (p. 209). Johnson adopted Sullivan's view of the psychiatric interview as "a situation of vocal communication in a two-group to elucidate characteristic patterns of living" (p. 214). Following both Boisen and Sullivan, Johnson declared that "whatever separates me from another person causes alienation within myself" (p. 220).[22] Johnson also perceived Sullivan as moving in the direction of the understanding of community implicit in Martin Buber's description of I-Thou relationships. He wrote:

> Sullivan has not been vocal about these ultimate questions, as he was working within a naturalistic frame of reference. Yet he was evidently moving in the direction of *Community* as the ultimate consideration of his interpersonalism. Beginning as he did with the relation of person-to-person in a two-group, he moved out in the final period of his life to concern for the world community as he worked with UNESCO and the World Federation for Mental Health. (p. 278)

Sullivan in fact died "while laboring on interdisciplinary conferences concerned with world problems" (Crowley, 1981, p. 211), and he was a social critic of the first order.

CONCLUDING THOUGHTS

Much more could be written about Sullivan, especially about his contributions to social science and sociology, which were summarized by Gardner Murphy, Elizabeth Cattell, Leonard Cottrell, Nelson N. Foote, and Charles S. Johnson in the original memorial symposium (Mullahy, 1952) and by Blitsten (1953); his role as a social critic (Crowley, 1981); the transpersonal and existential elements in his work (Frie, 2000, 2002;

Williams, 1994); his ethical views (Riepe, 1966); and his extensive but still unsystematized theory of sleep and dreaming.

Sullivan was, apparently, a complex man who was remarkably sensitive to his interpersonal context, in which he might appear as warm and loving or as cold, sarcastic, and withdrawn. On the whole, I suspect that those who wound up disliking him were those who committed interpersonal crimes against him or against their patients. I trust my own empathic understanding of him as a man who wanted only to be loved and accepted as he was.

Regarding Sullivan's work, I am inclined to agree with Fiscalini (1995), who said: "I have always found Sullivan's writing filled with human insight and truth, a telling of human experience the way it is, in fact, lived. Sullivan's psychoanalytic concepts always seemed closer to what humans were about than Freudian ideas did" (p. 2)–a statement which hints at Sullivan's empathy as well as the existential-phenomenological essence of his work. And I agree with Cottrell and Foote (1952), who said of his clinical style that it involved

> just a matter-of-fact getting down to business in helping to solve the patient's difficulties in living, yet a solution fundamental in every sense, philosophical, medical or otherwise. Such level-headed piercing to the heart of the problem–the interpersonal problems of the people involved–is perhaps one explanation for the brevity of Sullivan's writing. (pp. 204-205)

These authors also summarized Sullivan's social role:

> Harry Sullivan was not simply an intermediary who brought two disciplines, or the members of two disciplines, together. His magnificent talents as a matchmaker produced many more marriages of minds than that. He was responsible for hundreds of introductions across the boundaries of craft and clique–anthropologists, physiologists, government officials, academicians, hospital administrators, students, patients, publishers, writers. Had he never written a word, founded a journal, delivered a lecture, or helped to organize an institution or association, the abundance of his cosmopolitan friendliness would nonetheless have been an important force in knitting alliances between psychiatrists and all those who cope professionally with problems of living in present-day society. (pp. 181-182)

Otto Klineberg (1952), writing in a similar vein, described the meeting that led to the publication of Cantril's (1950) *Tensions That Cause Wars*. A Hungarian sociologist asked Cantril,

> "How did you get these people together; in particular, how did you have the genius to invite Harry Stack Sullivan to this meeting?" What he meant was that Sullivan had a kind of stimulating, disturbing, and finally soothing and coordinating effect on the group. This came out clearly in Sullivan's actual part in the proceedings, and it was related to his very real understanding of the way in which the psychiatrist and the social scientist could be mutually helpful. (Cottrell & Foote, 1952, p. 216)

I think it is appropriate to apply to Sullivan words that R. D. Laing applied to Gregory Bateson:

> The second to the last time that Bateson visited with me, I asked him what he would call a saint. He replied without a pause, obviously having thought about that question before and told me, "A saint is someone who sees things as they are and doesn't get angry about it." Bateson certainly got angry about things. He didn't think he was a saint. Neither do I. (Simon, 1993, p. 33)

Nor would Sullivan have thought himself a saint. He cared far too much about evil, "the unwarranted interference with life" (Sullivan, 1972, p. 4) to refuse to be angry. Instead he fought it, at the cost of his life itself.

NOTES

1. For a history of this controversial decision, see Bayer and Spitzer (1982).
2. Allen (1995) names Benjamin Weininger as a two-time sexual partner (p. 3).
3. For more on the Sullivan-Hadley relationship, see Bever, 1993.
4. Similarly, Swick Perry (1982) did not in print label the relationship between Margaret Stack, Sullivan's aunt, and her "woman companion" (p. 211) as the lesbian relationship she later acknowledged to Allen (1995) that it was.
5. Spurlock (2002) discusses Sullivan's views on homosexuality as representative of a developmental tradition which was gradually submerged as the psychiatric viewpoint became dominant. Harned notes that Sullivan "blurs the line between the heterosexual and homosexual, in part by insisting that the experience of homosexuality in preadolescence is necessary to overcome 'the stress of heterosexual adaptation' (1962b, p. 109)" (Harned, 1998, p. 306). Drawing on extensive clinical material, Sullivan "anticipates Kinsey's finding of a sexual continuum" (p. 306).

6. Allen's work is popularized in Hansen (2002).

7. The Second Colloquium on Personality Investigation was held under the joint auspices of the American Psychiatric Association Committee on Relations of Psychiatry and the Social Science Research Council, November 29-30, 1929, in New York City.

8. The book had an introduction by the psychologist of religion, Robert H. Thouless. Swick Perry (1982) noted that this book was reissued by Williams and Wilkins in 1929, probably at Sullivan's suggestion (p. 444, note 9). It was also published in Canada by Macmillan in 1929. The American and British publishers issued a second edition in 1948. That edition was reprinted in 1969 by Christian Classics in Westminster, Maryland. The Knights of Columbus Website currently describes the book as making "A sound case for abstinence" (www.kofc.org visited 28 May 2003).

9. Since 1992, John Fisher has been an acting teacher at the University of California at Berkeley, where he earned his PhD in 2001 with a dissertation on "De-camping: Towards a Gay-Political-Camp Theatre." The playwright founded his own Berkeley student theatre group, Sassymouth, to perform his productions (Cockrell, 1996/2003). He is currently co-artistic director of the Theatre Rhinoceros, which is billed on their Website as "The Nation's Longest-Running Lesbian, Gay, Bi-sexual & Transgender Theatre Company" (see http://www.therhino.org). It was founded in August 1977 by the late Allan B. Estes. Fisher's background sources for *Combat!* included Chapman (1976), Swick Perry (1982), and Bérubé (1990). Fisher depicts a sometimes drunk Sullivan who ultimately commits suicide, thus choosing to ignore, for the sake of a more interesting plot, the fact that the French police surgeon ruled Sullivan's death to be natural (Swick Perry, 1982, p. 417).

10. Sullivan also cited this story in his 1927 book review, focusing on the motto "We generally learn to leave well enough alone" (in Swick Perry, 1982, p. 339). Swick Perry in various places judges Sullivan's version of *The Mysterious Stranger* to be a confabulation. In her introduction to *Schizophrenia as a Human Process* (Sullivan, 1962b), she discusses this as an amusing example of the way that in the process of creation "each of many thinkers supplied ideas and concepts, words and phrases which went through a transformation in the sea of Sullivan's clinical observation and knowledge" (p. xxiv). In a footnote to *The Interpersonal Theory of Psychiatry* (Sullivan, 1953), she writes that the stories Sullivan used "are not in precise agreement with the legends and stories that we know: for instance, the published version of Mark Twain's *The Mysterious Stranger* has a different setting, characters, and events" (p. 329n). The story actually exists in several versions. The 1916 published version, now thought to be primarily a fabrication of its editor, and Twain's various manuscript versions of *The Mysterious Stranger* are compiled in Gibson (1969).

11. I am grateful to John Fisher for providing me with an electronic copy of his script, which has no page numbers or numbered scenes.

12. For example, Sullivan (1953) states that "the tension called anxiety primarily appertains to the infant's, as also to the mother's, communal existence with a *personal* environment, in utter contradistinction to the physicochemical environment . . . the relaxation of the tension of anxiety . . . is the experience, not of satisfaction, but of interpersonal security" (p. 42). Sullivan (1964) stresses the "*interpersonal induction* of anxiety, and the exclusively interpersonal origin of every instance of its manifestation" (p. 238).

13. Sullivan (1953) discussed his childhood fear of spiders and his rejection of the psychoanalytic interpretation in his preface to the dream of the web and the spider,

whose meaning has been probed by several later writers (Cushman, 1994; Gill, 1984; Levenson, 1984; Mendelson, 1984).

14. The dream apparently "cures" another problem as well: Sullivan reported a thorough dislike for the color blue, which he attributed to "his mother's use of the color on his baby clothes, which she preserved and exhibited proudly from time to time" (Swick Perry, 1982, p. 33).

15. Swick Perry (1982) gives the number of lectures as 246 (p. 393).

16. This anachronism does not occur in the 1981 version of the Broderick and Schrader history.

17. In a footnote Jackson and Lederer (1969) define compages as a whole formed by the compaction or juncture of parts, a framework or system of conjoined parts, a complex structure–O.E.D. (p. 55n).

18. Where individuals approach it, they are labeled 'schizoid' or 'autistic.'

19. I am grateful to Burston (1996) for steering me to this review.

20. Sullivan's description of this process is remarkably similar to the independently constructed theory of Cameron and Magaret (1951) in their descriptions of "the muting of communicative speech" (pp. 107-109) and "behavioral duplicity" (pp. 109-112). Sullivan would wholeheartedly have affirmed the description by these authors of the autistic community and the pseudocommunity–concepts acknowledging the interpersonal nature of the inner world.

21. A complete list of Mowrer's publications may be found in Mowrer (1983).

22. It is interesting, given Johnson's four-dimensional model, that Os Guinness (1973) regarded alienation as similarly four-dimensional: "The alienation of evil is theological, between God and man [thou]; sociological, between man and other men [we]; psychological, between man and himself [me]; and ecological, between man and nature [it]" (pp. 35-36).

REFERENCES

Ackerman, N. W. (1958). *The psychodynamics of family life: Diagnosis and treatment of family relationships*. New York: Basic/Harper.

Ackerman, N. W. (1966). *Treating the troubled family*. New York: Harper Torchbooks.

Ackerman, N. W. (1971). The growing edge of family therapy. *Family Process, 10*, 143-156.

Aden, L. (Ed.). (1988). Special issue: Boisen and pastoral care. *Journal of Psychology and Christianity*, 7(2), 3-89.

Allen, M. S. (1995). Sullivan's closet: A reappraisal of Harry Stack Sullivan's life and his pioneering role in American psychiatry. *Journal of Homosexuality, 29*, 1-18.

Anchin, J. C., & Kiesler, D. J. (Eds.) (1982). *Handbook of interpersonal psychotherapy*. New York: Pergamon Press.

Anomaly. (1927). *The invert and his social adjustment*. London: Abilliere, Tindall & Cox.

Bateson, G., Jackson, D. D., Haley, J., & Weakland, J. H. (1956). Toward a theory of schizophrenia. *Behavioral Science, 1*, 251-264.

Bayer, R., & Spitzer, R. L. (1982). Edited correspondence on the status of homosexuality in DSM-III. *Journal of the History of the Behavioral Sciences, 18*, 32-52.
Beavers, W. R. (1977). *Psychotherapy and growth: A family systems perspective*. New York: Brunner/Mazel.
Beels, C. C. (1976). Family and social management of schizophrenia. In P. Guerin (Ed.), *Family therapy: Theory and practice* (pp. 249-283). New York: Gardner Press.
Benjamin, L. S. (1996). *Interpersonal diagnosis and treatment of personality disorders* (2nd ed.). New York: Guilford Press.
Benjamin, L. S. (2003). *Interpersonal reconstructive therapy: Promoting change in nonresponders*. New York: Guilford Press.
Bérubé, A. (1990). *Coming out under fire: The history of gay men and women in World War Two*. New York: Plume/Penguin Books.
Bever, C. T. (1993). Collaboration and conflict: Ernest E. Hadley and Harry Stack Sullivan, 1930-1945. *Journal of the American Academy of Psychoanalysis, 21*, 387-404.
Blitsten. (1953). *The social theories of Harry Stack Sullivan: The significance of his concepts of socialization and acculturation*. New York: William-Frederick Press.
Bloch, D., & Simon, R. (Eds.). (1982). *The strength of family therapy: Selected papers of Nathan W. Ackerman*. New York: Brunner/Mazel.
Bodin, A. M. (1981). The interactional view: Family therapy approaches of the Mental Research Institute. In A. Gurman & D. Kniskern (Eds.), *Handbook of family therapy* (pp. 267-309). New York: Brunner/Mazel.
Boisen, A. T. (1926). Personality changes and upheavals arising out of the sense of personal failure. *American Journal of Psychiatry, 5*, 331-351.
Boisen, A. T. (1936). *Exploration of the inner world*. New York: Harper & Brothers.
Boisen, A. T. (1938). Types of dementia praecox. A study of psychiatric classification. *Psychiatry, 1*, 233-236.
Boisen, A. T. (1939a). Economic distress and religious experience. *Psychiatry, 2*, 185-194.
Boisen, A. T. (1939b). Review of James S. Plant's *Personality and the culture pattern*. *Psychiatry, 2*, 294-296.
Boisen, A. T. (1942a). Book review of Erich Fromm's *Escape from Freedom*. *Psychiatry, 5*, 113-117.
Boisen, A. T. (1942b). Form and content of schizophrenic thinking. *Psychiatry, 5*, 23-33.
Boisen, A. T. (1942c). Religion and personality adjustments. *Psychiatry, 5*, 209-218.
Boisen, A. T. (1955). *Religion in crisis and custom: A sociological and psychological study*. New York: Harper & Brothers.
Boisen, A. T. (1958). Religious experience and psychological conflict. *American Psychologist, 13*, 568-570.
Boisen, A. T. (1960). *Out of the depths: An autobiographical study of mental disorder and religious experience*. New York: Harper & Brothers.
Boszormenyi-Nagy, I., Grunebaum, J., & Ulrich, D. (1991). Contextual therapy. In A. Gurman & D. Kniskern (Eds.), *Handbook of family therapy* (2nd ed., pp. 200-238). New York: Brunner/Mazel.

Bregman, L. (1979). Anton Boisen revisited. *Journal of Religion & Health, 18*, 213-229.

Broderick, C. B., & Schrader, S. S. (1981). The history of professional marriage and family therapy. In A. Gurman & D. Kniskern (Eds.), *Handbook of family therapy* (pp. 5-35). New York: Brunner/Mazel.

Broderick, C. B., & Schrader, S. S. (1991). The history of professional marriage and family therapy. In A. Gurman & D. Kniskern (Eds.), *Handbook of family therapy* (2nd ed., pp. 3-40). New York: Brunner/Mazel.

Burston, D. (1996). *The wing of madness: The life and work of R. D. Laing*. Cambridge, MA: Harvard University Press.

Burton, A. (1971). *Interpersonal psychotherapy*. Englewood Cliffs, NJ: Prentice-Hall.

Cameron, N., & Magaret, A. (1951). *Behavior pathology*. Boston: Houghton Mifflin.

Cantril, H. (Ed.). (1950) *Tensions that cause wars*. Urbana, IL: University of Illinois Press.

Carson, R. C. (1969). *Interaction concepts of personality*. Chicago: Aldine.

Chapman, A. H. (1976). *Harry Stack Sullivan: The man and his work*. New York: G. P. Putnam's Sons.

Chapman, A. H. (1990). Sullivan, Harry Stack. In K. A. Garraty & M. C. Carnes (Eds.), *American National Biography. Vol. 21* (pp. 109-110). New York: Oxford University Press.

Chapman, A. H., & Chapman-Santana, M. (1980). *Harry Stack Sullivan's concepts of personality development and psychiatric illness*. New York: Brunner/Mazel.

Chatelaine, K. L. (1978). *Harry Stack Sullivan–The formative years (1892-1930). Dissertation Abstracts International*, 40(03A). (UMI No. 7820760).

Chatelaine, K. L. (1981). *Harry Stack Sullivan, the formative years*. Washington, DC: University Press of America.

Cockrell, C. (1996, December 4). To John Fisher, all the UC world's a stage. *Berkeleyan*. Retrieved June 1, 2003, from http://www.berkeley.edu/news/berkeleyan/1996/1204/stage.html

Cottrell, L. S., & Foote, N. (1952). Sullivan's contributions to social psychology. In P. Mullahy (Ed.), *The contributions of Harry Stack Sullivan: A symposium on interpersonal theory in psychiatry and social science* (pp. 181-205). New York: Hermitage House.

Crowley, R. M. (1981). Harry Stack Sullivan as social critic. *Journal of the American Academy of Psychoanalysis, 9*, 211-226.

Cushman, P. (1994). Confronting Sullivan's spider: Hermeneutics and the politics of therapy. *Contemporary Psychoanalysis, 30*, 800 844.

Evans, F. B. (1996). *Harry Stack Sullivan: Interpersonal theory and psychotherapy*. New York: Routledge.

Examiner staff. (1999, January 20). "Combat" best new local play. *San Francisco Examiner*. Retrieved June 1, 2003, from http://www.sfgate.com/cgi-bin/article.cgi?file=/examiner/archive/1999/01/20/STYLE10210.dtl

Fiscalini, J. (1995). Harry Stack Sullivan [1938]. Introduction. In D. B. Stern, C. H. Mann, S. Kantor, & G. Schlesinger (Eds.), *Pioneers of interpersonal analysis* (pp. 1-7). Hillsdale, NJ: Analytic Press.

Fisher, J. (1996). *Combat! An American Melodrama.* Unpublished play script, San Francisco, CA.

Foa, U. G. (1961). Convergences in the analysis of the structure of interpersonal behavior. *Psychological Review, 68*, 341-353.

Frie, R. (2000). The existential and the interpersonal: Ludwig Binswanger and Harry Stack Sullivan. *Journal of Humanistic Psychology, 40*, 108-129.

Frie, R. (2002). Binswanger, Sullivan and the problem of agency in contemporary psychoanalysis. *Contemporary Psychoanalysis, 38*, 635-673.

Fromm, E. (1941). *Escape from freedom.* New York: Holt, Rinehart & Winston.

Gibson, W. M. (Ed.). (1969). *Mark Twain's Mysterious stranger manuscripts.* Berkeley: University of California Press.

Gill, M. M. (1984). "Harry Stack Sullivan: The web and the spider": Discussion. *Contemporary Psychoanalysis, 20*, 189-196.

Goldwert, M. (1995). A forgotten pioneer: Anton T. Boisen and religious psychosis. *Psychological Reports, 76*, 1033-1034.

Green, J. (1996, March 5). Gay musicals prepared him for "Combat." *San Francisco Examiner.* Retrieved June 2, 2003, from http://www.sfgate.com/cgi-bin/article.cgi?file=/examiner/archive/1996/03/05/STYLE5057.dtl

Guerin, P. (1976). Family therapy: The first twenty-five years. In P. Guerin (Ed.), *Family therapy: Theory and practice* (pp. 2-22). New York: Gardner Press.

Guinness, O. (1973). *The dust of death. A critique of the establishment and the counter culture–and a proposal for a third way.* Downer's Grove, IL: InterVarsity Press.

Haley, J., & Hoffman, L. (1967). The growing edge. An interview with Carl Whitaker. In *Techniques of family therapy* (pp. 265-360). New York: Basic Books.

Hall, C. E., Jr. (1967). Some contributions of Anton T. Boisen (1876-1965) to understanding psychiatry and religion. *Bulletin of the Menninger Clinic, 31*, 42-53.

Hansen, B. (2002). Queer health professionals of historic note. *American Journal of Public Health, 92*(1), 36-44.

Harned, J. (1998). Harry Stack Sullivan and the gay psychoanalysis. *American Imago, 55*, 299-317.

Havens, L. L. (1977). Harry Stack Sullivan's contribution to clinical method. *Contemporary Psychoanalysis, 13*, 360-364.

Hiltner, S. (1972). *Theological dynamics.* Nashville, TN: Abingdon Press.

Holifield, E. B. (1983). *A history of pastoral care in America: From salvation to self-realization.* Nashville: Abingdon Press.

Holifield, E. B. (1990). Johnson, Paul E. (1898-1974). In R. J. Hunter, H. N. Malony, L. O. Mills, & J. Patton (Eds.), *Dictionary of pastoral care and counseling* (p. 613). New York: Abingdon Press.

Hunt, J. M. (1984). Orval Hobart Mowrer (1907-1982). *American Psychologist, 39*, 912-914.

Jackson, D. D. (1961). The monad, the dyad, and the family therapy of schizophrenics. In A. Burton (Ed.), *Psychotherapy of the psychoses* (pp. 318-238). New York: Basic Books.

Jackson, D. D., & Lederer, W. J. (1969). *Mirages of marriage.* New York: Norton.

Johnson, P. E. (1957). *Personality and religion.* New York: Abingdon Press.

Johnson, P. E. (1967). *Person and counselor.* Nashville: Abingdon Press.

Johnson, R. C., Dokecki, P. R., & Mowrer, O. H. (1972). *Conscience, contract, and social reality; theory and research in behavioral science*. New York: Holt, Rinehart and Winston.

Jourard, S. (1964). *The transparent self*. New York: Van Nostrand Reinhold.

Kiesler, D. J. (1983). The 1982 interpersonal circle: A taxonomy for complementarity in human transactions. *Psychological Review, 90*, 185-214.

Kiesler, D. J. (1996). *Contemporary interpersonal theory and research: Personality, psychopathology, and psychotherapy*. New York: Wiley.

Klerman, G., & Weissman, M. M. (Eds.). (1993). *New applications in interpersonal psychotherapy*. Washington, DC: American Psychiatric Press.

Klerman, G., Weissman, M. M., Rounsaville, B., & Chevron, E. (1984). *Interpersonal psychotherapy of depression*. New York: Basic Books.

Kvarnes, R. G., & Parloff, G. H. (Eds.). (1976). *A Harry Stack Sullivan case seminar: Treatment of a young schizophrenic*. New York: W. W. Norton.

Laing, R. D. (1963). Review of *Schizophrenia as a human process* by H. S. Sullivan. *International Journal of Psychoanalysis, 44*, 3.

Laing, R. D. (1965a). *The divided self: An existential study in sanity and madness*. New York: Penguin Books. (Original work published 1959)

Laing, R. D. (1965b). Mystification, confusion, and conflict. In I. Boszormenyi-Nagy & J. L. Framo (Eds.), *Intensive family therapy: Theoretical and practical aspects* (pp. 343-363). New York: Harper & Row/Hoeber Medical Division.

Laing, R. D. (1969). *Self and others*. New York: Pantheon Books. (Original work published 1960)

Leary, T. F. (1957). *Interpersonal diagnosis of personality*. New York: Ronald Company.

Levenson, E. A. (1984). Harry Stack Sullivan: The web and the spider. *Contemporary Psychoanalysis, 20*, 174-189.

Levenson, E. A. (1992). Harry Stack Sullivan: From interpersonal psychiatry to interpersonal psychoanalysis. *Contemporary Psychoanalysis, 28*, 450-466.

Macmurray, J. (1979). *Persons in relation*. Atlantic Highlands, NJ: Humanities Press. (Original work published 1961)

Markowitz, J. C. (1997). Interpersonal psychotherapy for dysthymic disorder. Washington, DC: American Psychiatric Press.

Marziali, E., & Monroe-Blum, H. (1994). *Interpersonal group psychotherapy for borderline personality disorder*. New York: Basic Books.

McGoldrick, M., Gerson, R., & Shellenberger, S. (1999). *Genograms: Assessment and interventions* (2nd ed.). New York: W. W. Norton.

Mead, G. H. (1934). *Mind, self, and society* (C. W. Morris, Ed.). Chicago: University of Chicago Press.

Mendelson, M. D. (1984). "Harry Stack Sullivan: The web and the spider": Discussion. *Contemporary Psychoanalysis, 20*, 196-204.

Miller, D. R., & Sobelman, G. (1985). Models of the family: A critical review of alternatives. In L. L'Abate (Ed.), *The handbook of family psychology and therapy. Volume I* (pp. 3-37). Homewood, IL: Dorsey Press.

Minuchin, S. (1974). *Families and family therapy*. Cambridge, MA: Harvard University Press.

Minuchin, S. (1984). *Family kaleidoscope: Images of violence and healing*. Cambridge: Harvard University Press.
Minuchin, S., & Fishman, H. C. (1981). *Family therapy techniques*. Cambridge, MA: Harvard University Press.
Minuchin, S., & Nichols, M. P. (1998). *Family healing: Tales of hope & renewal from family therapy*. New York: The Free Press.
Mowrer, O. H. (1950). *Learning theory and personality dynamics: Selected papers*. New York: Ronald Press.
Mowrer, O. H. (1961). *The crisis in psychiatry and religion*. Princeton, NJ: Van Nostrand Insight.
Mowrer, O. H. (1964). *The new group therapy*. Princeton, NJ: Van Nostrand.
Mowrer, O. H. (1966). *Abnormal reactions or actions? (An autobiographical answer)*. Dubuque, IA: Wm. C. Brown.
Mowrer, O. H. (Comp.). (1967). *Morality and mental health*. Chicago: Rand McNally.
Mowrer, O. H. (1974). O. Hobart Mowrer. In G. Lindsay (Ed.), *The history of psychology in autobiography. Vol. VI* (pp. 327-364). Englewood Cliffs, NJ: Prentice-Hall.
Mowrer, O. H. (1976). Changing conceptions of neurosis and the small-groups movement. *Education, 97*, 24-62.
Mowrer, O. H. (1983). Autobiography. In *Leaves from many seasons: Selected papers* (pp. 317-328). New York: Praeger.
Mowrer, O. H., & Vattano, A. J. (1974). *Integrity groups: The loss and recovery of community*. Urbana, IL: Integrity Groups.
Mufson, L., Moreau, D., Weissman, M. M. et al. (1993). *Interpersonal psychotherapy for depressed adolescents*. New York: Guilford Press.
Mullahy, P. (Ed.). (1952). *The contributions of Harry Stack Sullivan: A symposium on interpersonal theory in psychiatry and social science*. New York: Hermitage House.
Mullahy, P. (1970). *Psychoanalysis and interpersonal psychiatry: The contributions of Harry Stack Sullivan*. New York: Science House.
Mullahy, P., & Melinek, M. (1983). *Interpersonal psychiatry*. New York: SP Medical & Scientific Books.
Neill, J. R. (1982). Biographical introduction to the work of Carl Whitaker. In J. R. Neill & D. P. Kniskern (Eds.), *From psyche to system: The evolving therapy of Carl Whitaker* (pp. 1-20). New York: Guilford Press.
Neill, J. R., & Kniskern, D. P. (Eds.). (1982). *From psyche to system: The evolving therapy of Carl Whitaker*. New York: Guilford Press.
Nichols, M., & Schwartz, R. (1998). *Family therapy: Concepts and methods* (4th ed.). Boston: Allyn and Bacon.
Patton, J. (1988). Physicians of the soul: Boisen on pastoral care and counseling. *Journal of Psychology and Christianity, 7*(2), 44-53.
Paul, N. L. (1966). Effects of playback on family members of their own previously recorded conjoint therapy material. *Psychiatric Research Reports, 20*, 175-187.
Paul, N. L. (1967a). The use of empathy in the resolution of grief. *Perspectives in Biology and Medicine, 11*, 153-169.
Paul, N. L. (1967b). The role of mourning and empathy in conjoint marital therapy. In G. Zuk & I. Boszormenyi-Nagy (Eds.), *Family therapy and disturbed families*. Palo Alto, CA: Science and Behavior Books.

Paul, N., & Grosser, G. (1965). Operational mourning and its role in conjoint family therapy. *Community Mental Health Journal, 1*, 339-345.

Pearce, J. (1985). Harry Stack Sullivan: Theory and practice. *American Journal of Social Psychiatry, 5*, 5-13.

Powell, R. C. (1977). Anton T. Boisen's "Psychiatric examination: Content of thought" (c. 1925-31): An attempt to grasp the meaning of mental disorder. *Psychiatry: Journal for the Study of Interpersonal Processes, 40*, 369-375.

Pruyser, P. W. (1967). Anton T. Boisen and the psychology of religion. *Journal of Pastoral Care, 21*, 209-219.

Riepe, D. (1966). Ethical views of Harry Stack Sullivan. *International Journal of Social Psychiatry, 12*, 255-260.

Ruesch, J., & Bateson, G. (1949). Structure and process in social relations. *Psychiatry: Journal for the Study of Interpersonal Processes, 12*, 105-124.

Ruesch, J., & Bateson, G. (1951). *Communication: The social matrix of psychiatry*. New York: W. W. Norton.

Schlapobersky, J. (2000, September 28). Obituary: Robin Skynner. *The Guardian*. Retrieved May 20, 2003, from http://books.guardian.co.uk/Print/ 0,3858,4069149,00.html

Segal, H. (1973). *Introduction to the work of Melanie Klein* (new, enlarged ed.). New York: Basic Books.

Shainess, N. (1978). Reflections on the contributions of Harry Stack Sullivan. *American Journal of Psychoanalysis, 38*, 301-315.

Silverman, H. L. (1955). The psychology and psychiatry of Harry Stack Sullivan. *Psychiatric Quarterly Supplement, 29*, 7-22.

Simon, R. (1984, November/December). Stranger in a strange land: An interview with Salvador Minuchin. *Family Therapy Networker, 8*(6), 21-25.

Simon, R. (1993). Still R. D. Laing after all these years. In *One-on-one: Conversations with the shapers of family therapy* (pp. 21-33). Washington, DC: The Family Therapy Network/Guilford Press. (Original work published 1983)

Skynner, A. C. R. (1976). *Systems of family and marital psychotherapy*. New York: Brunner/Mazel.

Spurlock, J. C. (2002). From reassurance to irrelevance: Adolescent psychology and homosexuality in America. *History of Psychology, 5*, 38-51.

Stuart, S., & Robertson, M. (2002). *Interpersonal psychotherapy: A clinician's guide*. London: Edward Arnold.

Sullivan, H. S. (1924). Schizophrenia: Its conservative and malignant features. *American Journal of Psychiatry, 81*, 77-91.

Sullivan, H. S. (1927a). Affective experience in early schizophrenia. *American Journal of Psychiatry, 6*, 468-483.

Sullivan, H. S. (1927b). The common field of research and clinical psychiatry. *Psychiatric Quarterly, 1*, 276-291.

Sullivan, H. S. (1927c). The onset of schizophrenia. *American Journal of Psychiatry, 1*, 105-134.

Sullivan, H. S. (1927d). Review of *The invert and his social adjustment*. *American Journal of Psychiatry, 7*, 532-537.

Sullivan, H. S. (1929). Research in schizophrenia. *American Journal of Psychiatry, 9*, 553-567.

Sullivan, H. S. (1931-1932). The modified psychoanalytic treatment of schizophrenia. *American Journal of Psychiatry*, *88*, 519-540.

Sullivan, H. S. (1938). The data of psychiatry. *Psychiatry*, *1*, 121-134.

Sullivan, H. S. (1942). Sullivan, Harry Stack. In M. Block & E. M. Trow (Eds.), *Current biography: Who's news and why 1942* (pp. 812-813). New York: H. W. Wilson.

Sullivan, H. S. (1945). *Conceptions of modern psychiatry*. Washington, DC: William Alanson White Psychiatric Foundation. (Original work published 1940)

Sullivan, H. S. (1953). *The interpersonal theory of psychiatry* (Ed. H. Swick Perry & M. Ladd Gawell). New York: Norton.

Sullivan, H. S. (1954). *The psychiatric interview* (Ed. H. Swick Perry & M. Ladd Gawell). New York: Norton.

Sullivan, H. S. (1956). *Clinical studies in psychiatry* (Ed. H. Swick Perry, M. Ladd Gawell, & M. Gibbon). New York: Norton.

Sullivan, H. S. (1962). *Schizophrenia as a human process* (Ed. H. Swick Perry). New York: W. W. Norton.

Sullivan, H. S. (1964). *The fusion of psychiatry and social science* (Ed. H. Swick Perry). New York: Norton.

Sullivan, H. S. (1972). *Personal psychopathology: Early formulations* (Ed. H. Swick Perry). New York: Norton.

Swick Perry, H. S. (1982). *Psychiatrist of America: The life of Harry Stack Sullivan*. Cambridge, MA: Belknap Press/Harvard University Press.

Teyber, E. (1997). *Interpersonal process in psychotherapy: A relational approach (3rd ed.)*. Pacific Grove, CA: Brooks/Cole.

Thompson, C. (1962). Harry Stack Sullivan, the man. In H. S. Sullivan, *Schizophrenia as a human process* (Ed. H. Swick Perry; pp. xxxii-xxxv). New York: W. W. Norton. (Original work published 1949)

Vande Kemp, H. (1981). The dream in periodical literature: 1860-1910. *The Journal of the History of the Behavioral Sciences*, *17*, 88-113.

Vande Kemp, H. (1992). G. Stanley Hall and the Clark school of religious psychology. *American Psychologist*, *47*, 290-298.

Vande Kemp, H. (1996). Psychology and Christian spirituality: Explorations of the inner world. *Journal of Psychology and Christianity*, *15*, 161-174.

Vande Kemp, H. (1999). Diana Baumrind: Researcher and critical humanist. In D. Moss (Ed.), *Humanistic and transpersonal psychology: Historical and biographical sourcebook* (pp. 249-259). New York: Greenwood Press.

Vande Kemp, H. (2000). Gordon Allport's pre-1950 writings on religion: The archival record. In J. Belzen (Ed.), *Aspects and contexts: Studies in the history of psychology of religion* (pp. 129-172). Atlanta: Rodopi.

Vande Kemp, H. (2001). The patient-philosopher evaluates the scientist-practitioner: A case study. In B. D. Slife, R. N. Williams, & S. H. Barlow (Eds.), *Critical issues in psychotherapy: Translating new ideas into practice* (pp. 171-185). Thousand Oaks, CA: Sage.

Weissman, M. K. (2000, October 10). *History of IPT*. Retrieved June 2, 2003, from http://www.interpersonalpsychotherapy.org/

Weissman, M. M., Markowitz, J. C., & Klerman, G. L. (2000). *Comprehensive guide to interpersonal psychotherapy*. New York: Basic Books.
Wilfley, D. E., Mackenzie, K. R., Welch, R. R, Ayres, V. E., & Weissman, M. M. (Eds.). (2000). *Interpersonal psychotherapy for groups*. New York: Basic Books.
Williams, P. S. (1994). Harry Stack Sullivan: Opening the door for a transpersonal vision? *Humanistic Psychologist*, *22*, 62-73.
Winn, S. (1998, February 14). Fisher's 'Combat!' carries the day. History, sexuality merge in ambitious, passionate epic. *San Francisco Chronicle*. Retrieved June 1, 2003, from http://www.sfgate.com/cgi-bin/article.cgi?file=/chronicle/archive/1998/02/14/DD94185.DTL
Witenberg, E. G. (Ed.). (1973). *Interpersonal explorations in psychoanalysis. New directions in theory and practice*. New York: Basic Books.
Wynne, L. (1984). Review of *The strength of family therapy: Selected papers of Nathan W. Ackerman*. *Family Process*, *23*, 279-295.

Empathy, the Easily Aroused Child and Antidotes for Bullying

Elizabeth A. Rock

SUMMARY. This article presents the results of a qualitative interview study of the experience of empathy in the easily aroused child. Participants were asked about their perception and vicarious experience of emotions in others and the cognitive process used to choose responses. These children were able to identify and differentiate emotions of both themselves and the victims. They used a complex cognitive process that considered the action, the context, strategies, and possible consequences. Reactions of peers, the need to assist the victims, and providing intervention for the aggressor were major themes they discussed. The violation of the sense of fairness was critical in their choice of responses. This article also discusses temperamental characteristics of the easily aroused child, emotional expression, and self-regulation. The findings of this study led to the development of a bully prevention program which incorporates the elements of the experience of empathy identified by the children. The program can be used at the K-5 level. Components include (a) identifying types and characteristics of bullies, (b) recognizing feel-

---

Elizabeth A. Rock, PhD, is a school psychologist currently working in Powell, WY, with children in the public school setting. Her special interests include children with social cognitive skills deficits, poorly developed self-regulation and emotional expression, and difficulty with attention and focus to their environment. The program discussed in the article is currently in use in the Park County School District #1, Powell, WY. Address correspondence via e-mail at <earock@park1.k12.wy.us>.

[Haworth co-indexing entry note]: "Empathy, the Easily Aroused Child and Antidotes for Bullying." Rock, Elizabeth A. Co-published simultaneously in *The Psychotherapy Patient* (The Haworth Press, Inc.) Vol. 13, No. 1/2, 2004, pp. 63-86; and: *Saints and Rogues: Conflicts and Convergence in Psychotherapy* (ed: Robert B. Marchesani, and E. Mark Stern) The Haworth Press, Inc., 2004, pp. 63-86. Single or multiple copies of this article are available for a fee from The Haworth Document Delivery Service [1-800-HAWORTH, 9:00 a.m. - 5:00 p.m. (EST). E-mail address: docdelivery@haworthpress.com].

http://www.haworthpress.com/web/TPP

Digital Object Identifier: 10.1300/J358v13n01_03

ings of victims, (c) perspective taking, (d) problem solving applied to frequently encountered school bully situations, and (e) strategies for victims and witnesses. A variety of activities and materials are included in the program. Results of surveys done with classes are presented, and the impact of the program on the school community is discussed. An important aspect of the program has been the participation of the classroom teacher and site administrator. Students need to know they can report bully behavior and obtain assistance with intervention. This works towards creating a change in the school climate that is more supportive to students becoming part of a sharing community.

KEYWORDS. Empathy, bullying, elementary schools, temperament, arousal, emotional regulation

INTRODUCTION

To be emotionally competent means to have the skills necessary to decide on behavior that is efficacious in a variety of situations (Saarni, 1999). These skills include the ability to know one's own feelings, to be able to label them, and to rely on them to guide behavior (Park & Park, 1997). It is also critical to be able to recognize feelings in others and to use that information to accurately interpret actions and predict behaviors (Park & Park; Saarni).

Many children enter school with an understanding of what is expected of them in social situations involving emotional expression. These children have a strong sense of self-efficacy that allows them to try out new strategies in interpersonal situations. These children are not concerned about evaluation of their behavior by others. They are confident in their ability to evaluate a situation and respond with an appropriate display of emotions and behaviors. Other children enter school with less emotional competence and lack the ability to make good decisions about their behavior.

One indicator of deficits in emotional competence is the display of antisocial behaviors. This includes a range of aggressive actions that can be either direct or indirect (Berkowitz, 1993). These violations of social rules are as diverse as (a) physical aggression such as hitting, pushing, or tripping; (b) verbal abuse such as name-calling or excessive teasing; and (c) defiance of authority or violation of rules. The strongest aggressive actions are directed toward what is perceived to be the source of unpleasant feelings (Loeber & Hay, 1997). Bullying includes most of these antisocial behaviors. Any aggressive action, whether direct or indirect, that is repeatedly directed at another is considered bullying (Olweus, 1991).

Lack of ability to self-regulate emotional responses is also seen as lack of emotional competence. Adults see children who have limited self-regulation of their emotions as unable to experience the empathy for others needed to engage in prosocial behaviors (Eisenberg et al., 1998; Zahn-Waxler, Radke-Yarrow, Wagner, & Chapman, 1992). This leads to the assumption that antisocial behaviors manifested by a child represent pathology and results in efforts to force the child to conform to a predetermined manner of response (Chess & Thomas, 1999). This undermines the child's own ability to interact with and gain mastery over the environment.

Behaviors seen as pathological may be the result of the child's inability to understand what behavior is required for acceptable interaction with the environment (Chess & Thomas, 1999). According to Chess and Thomas, behavior patterns some adults perceive as psychological disorders are a manifestation of a poor fit between a child's temperament and the environment. The fit of the child's temperament with the environment has an impact on how emotional competence develops (Park & Park, 1997). As the child matures the interaction among temperament, experience, social context, and caregivers shapes emotional response and self-regulation (Rothbart & Ahadi, 1994). The response a child receives from others evokes a specific reaction from the child, which leads to established patterns of behavior (Caspi, 1998). Unfortunately, these patterns of responses may result in negative interactions with both peers and adults.

Temperament-based behaviors may cause adults to have certain expectations about children (Graziano, Jensen-Campbell, & Sullivan-Logan, 1998). Children respond by engaging in the expected behaviors. Easily aroused children are often perceived by adults as lacking in the ability to experience empathy and engage in appropriate prosocial behaviors. Their emotional sensitivity, impulsive response style, and lack of self-regulation can result in adults assuming that negative interactions with peers represent pathology. These behaviors may be a misguided attempt on the part of these children to demonstrate empathy towards peers.

Easily aroused children are highly emotional and quick to become angry. Therefore, they often engage in reactive aggressive behaviors. Instead of planned and calculated acts of aggression towards their peers, the easily aroused child may be expressing their frustration and anger after being provoked and losing control (Schwartz, Dodge, Petit, & Bates, 1997).

TEMPERAMENT

Temperament has been characterized as a form of reactivity to stimulation in the environment and self-regulation of the response and is considered biologically rooted (Rothbart & Bates, 1998; Rothbart, Ahadi, & Evans, 2000). Temperament is a behavioral style and not the content of the behavior itself (Chess & Thomas, 1999). There are nine categories of temperament. Chess and Thomas explain the application of these categories to children:

Intensity refers to the amount of energy involved in the response to an event. Emotions are felt and possibly expressed with greater intensity.

Sensory threshold refers to the level of stimulation in sensory input, environmental objects, and social contacts required to evoke a response from the child. A child with a low sensory threshold will react more quickly to social situations. The reactions may include inappropriate perceptions of the stimulus and exaggerated emotional responses.

Activity describes the amount of physical activity in the child's response. This could include striking out, pushing, shoving, running after another child, or other types of physical aggression.

Negative mood would include a large amount of unpleasant or possibly unfriendly behavior.

Distractibility is how easily children are distracted from a task or behavior. Children may have difficulty remembering appropriate responses they have been taught and revert to previously established inappropriate behaviors.

Predictability refers to the consistency with which the child responds to certain demands for behavior. The child may consistently become defiant when asked to perform routine behaviors.

Approach is the ease with which a child enters into new situations or meets new people. The easily aroused child may react negatively and attempt to avoid new places or people.

Adaptability refers to the flexibility in the child when changes are made in routine or plans are disrupted. The easily aroused child has difficulty accepting unexpected changes.

Persistence means the ability of the child to stay with a task until completed. The child may become frustrated easily and even express intense anger at a task that does not bring success quickly and easily.

With high ratings in these nine categories, children may be more likely to react quickly, physically, and with anger to situations they perceive as hurtful to others or to self. The perception that they are unable to feel empathy for peers is reinforced by these behaviors because adults do not consider them prosocial. The perception of lack of empathy is also supported by an inability on the part of the easily aroused child to appropriately apply problem-solving skills or to control their impulses. The easily aroused child, with a high level of emotionality combined with lack of self-regulation, often engages in aggressive actions leading to rejection by peers (Pelligrini, Bartini, & Brooks, 1999). This pushes them to further affiliate themselves with other aggressive peers, or to increased levels of anger and frustration.

Dimensions of temperament seen will fluctuate depending on the situation in which the individual is observed (Rothbart et al., 2000). However, arousability is a physiological response of the central nervous system that is more or less consistent throughout life (Strelau, 1994). It determines the amount and intensity of reaction and thinking in response to stimuli. Easily aroused individuals will have lower perceptual thresholds and rapid and reactive cognitive processing. Easy arousability is characterized by more intense reactions. The level of arousal in the individual mediates emotionality such as distress, fear, and anger. Those individuals high in emotionality are more highly aroused (Strelau).

Fluctuation of the levels of arousal is related to adaptation and regulation of responses such as fear, frustration, and motivation. Easy arousability to fear will be shown in situations the individual is not familiar with (Rothbart et al., 2000). As the events become familiar the arousal of fear diminishes.

Temperamental differences in children appear early in life and initially are relatively independent of socialization (Kochanska, 1993). Temperamental differences are not a product of cognitive development, but their expression is modified by cognitive factors. Socializing agents such as teachers and parents observe temperamental differences and expect certain behaviors and developmental consequences (Graziano et al., 1998). Expectations about behaviors may encourage those behaviors to occur (Caspi, 1998).

Temperamental traits usually associated with both internalizing and externalizing behavior problems include (a) irritability-difficultness, (b) inhibition-fearfulness, and (c) impulsivity-unmanageability (Guerin, Gottfried, & Thomas, 1997). These traits affect the development of behavior both directly as a continuous trait and indirectly through the child's impact on parents and others (Rothbart & Bates, 1998).

The trait most associated with externalizing behavior problems and lack of prosocial behavior is impulsivity-unmanageability (Caspi, Moffitt, Newman, & Silva, 1996; Rothbart & Bates, 1998). The typical behavior seen in this type of child is failure to comply with attempts by parents or other adults to stop or redirect action (Bates, Pettit, Dodge, & Ridge, 1998). The high impulsivity-unmanageability child may also have a strong attraction to external rewards and lack the ability to inhibit responses.

EMPATHY

Empathy has been defined as an affective response that is the result of a state or condition in another person (Hoffman, 1990). Empathy elicits vicariously induced reactions with the clear idea that the other person is distinctly separate. Empathy as a response becomes associated with cognition through operant and social learning processes (Saarni, 1999).

Hoffman (1990) discusses four developmental stages of empathy. The first stage is global empathy, which occurs during infancy. Infants experience empathetic distress when hearing another child cry. This type of empathy is not the result of the infant's awareness of being distinct from others but is merely a general feeling of unpleasantness. At about the age of 1 year children begin to develop mental images that represent themselves and others as separate. Children at this point have the sense that the distress felt is actually coming from the other person's pain. It is the beginning of awareness that another person may be crying and that the cry they hear is separate from their own.

The third stage of empathy begins during the second and third year of life. Children start to learn adherence to standards and feel anxiety in response to disapproval (Hoffman, 1990). Children display the emotions of guilt and shame that indicate the beginning of role-taking ability. Interventions to comfort others begin during the third stage. Children are now aware that other people have distinct feelings of their own. As children's cognitive skills develop they expand the array of emotions integral to the experience of empathy. Children at this level engage in cognitive activity that allows empathy when presented with information about another without having to observe the person.

The most advanced level of empathy occurs in late childhood (Hoffman, 1990). The child has the ability to see self and others as having separate identities. By the age of 8 or 9 years the child begins to focus on inner processes and can reflect on the other person's inner experience of emotion. The other's inner states are vicariously experienced as the child's own.

Complex cognitive activity shapes the empathetic response (Bengtsson & Johnson, 1992). The behavior that results from an empathetic response to social situations is based on a series of steps in cognitive processing. Children interpret cues, determine what their options are for behavior, and then make a choice about the action to be taken.

EMOTIONAL EXPRESSION

Emotions have both intrapersonal and interpersonal consequences when they are expressed (Zeman & Shipman, 1996). Social relationships can be established, preserved, or destroyed based on the appropriateness of the manner in which emotions are expressed (Cole, Zahn-Waxler, & Smith, 1994; Zeman & Garber, 1996). Children learn to regulate their display of emotions for others based on what has been taught through the socialization process (Saarni, 1999). Children perceive that expression of emotions in a socially acceptable manner is important. Children learn to expect certain responses from others depending on not only the emotion but also the expression of it.

Children learn at a young age that the expression of negative emotion may not be acceptable and may have detrimental consequences for interpersonal relations (Zeman & Garber, 1996). They are more likely to control their expressions of negative emotions when peers are present. Children are also less likely to show true feelings when an authority figure is present, such as a teacher (Cole, 1986). Children may decide whether or not to express negative emotions if the person present is the target of those emotions (Zeman & Garber).

A child who is socially rejected by peers tends to attribute hostile intent to the actions of others (Dodge & Somberg, 1987). The bias towards attribution of negative intent is most pronounced in situations that provoke anxiety in the child. This child's choice of actions may be aggressive rather than productive (Saarni, 1999). Failure of an action to resolve a situation increases the tendency of the child to attribute negative intent to the actions of others (Dorsch & Keane, 1994). Thus, inappropriate behaviors that the child has learned continue to place him or her in situations that elicit negative or hostile actions from peers.

REGULATION

Self-regulation is the ability to manage and control emotions, thinking, and subsequent actions in a variety of situations (Saarni, 1999). Emotional regulation refers to (a) the subjective experience of a particular feeling, (b) the intensity and duration of the feeling, and (c) the expression of the feeling (Gross, 1998). Emotional regulation has also been defined as the management of responses within a framework of both cognition and personal experience (Brenner & Salovey, 1997). It is a process that occurs during the course of interactions with others. Individuals who have had success regulating their emotional responses learn to express socially appropriate emotions and engage in prosocial behaviors. Children who are excessively controlled may have difficulty expressing feelings and reacting spontaneously (Cole, Michel, & Teti, 1994). This may result in general avoidance of situations or interactions with others. Lack of control that results in extreme inhibition of behavior can also reduce contact with others (Kagan, 1998).

Regulation of emotional response is linked to level of arousal and learned behaviors (Bates et al., 1998; Eisenberg et al., 1998). The highly aroused child may be more attentive or vigilant towards the emotional responses of others than would a less aroused child and be more sensitive to others (Park & Park, 1997). This greater sensitivity combined with inadequate cognitive techniques for analyzing emotions may result in poor judgment and inappropriate decisions about reactions. These children are often excluded by peers, punished by adults for inappropriate behaviors, and lose the opportunity to learn more appropriate ways of responding as they are isolated from interaction with their environment.

Arousability and regulation are interrelated. The child's temperament influences how the child regulates emotional responses (Eisenberg, Fabes, & Losoya, 1997). Overarousal may result in both inhibition of a behavioral response as well as uncontrolled behavior. With lack of regulation the predominant emotion expressed may be hostility (Rubin, Chen, & Hymel, 1993). Overcontrol often results in anxious behavior.

Prosocial behavior and empathy are related to the control element of negative affect (Rothbart et al., 2000). Children who are prone to fear may also be more responsive to cues that indicate punishment or other undesirable results for their behavior. Internalized components of negative affect also result in discomfort that result in prosocial characteristics such as guilt or shame (Rothbart, Ahadi, & Hershey, 1994). These children may be more easily conditioned to resist antisocial behaviors such as physical aggression.

Children who effectively attend to others and focus on results of their behavior are more capable of engaging in prosocial actions (Kochanska, 1997). These children have an overall greater level of emotional regulation. Adequate regulation of self and emotions contributes to (a) a feeling of mastery of the social environment, (b) connectedness to others, and (c) overall sense of well-being (Thompson, 1994; Walden & Smith, 1997).

THE STUDY

A group of ten children were interviewed to examine the experience of empathy in the easily aroused child. These children were selected from referrals made by classroom teachers based on their perception of easily arousability and a history of antisocial behaviors. There were six boys and four girls ranging in age from 9.5 to 11.3 years.

The major concern with all of the students was their behavior. Specifically, the behaviors described by the teachers included (a) fighting, (b) bullying other students, (c) defiance of adult direction, (d) destruction of school property or possessions of other students, (e) disruptive classroom behavior, (f) failure to turn in or complete assigned work, (g) social isolation and withdrawal, and (h) inappropriate emotional responses to events. Teachers also described many of these students as inattentive in class or large group activities and very demanding of individual attention.

The objective of the study was to discover elements of the phenomenon of empathy in easily aroused children who are perceived as aggressive by peers and adults in the environment. Components of the cognitive and affective framework used by the easily aroused child to interpret actions of others were identified. The interview allowed exploration of the unique inner experience of empathy in the easily aroused child. Interviewing provided information that would not otherwise be available to the researcher.

The children were questioned in three areas. The first area was how the child identifies feelings in others. It was important to know if the child was experiencing personal distress and acting to relieve that or if there was another rationale used to explain behavior. The ability to recognize affect in self and others is a critical aspect of empathy. It was also essential that the child be able to make a distinction between self and others. The actions of the child needed to reflect that the choice of behavior was a way to relieve the suffering or distress of others and not his or her own discomfort.

A second area of questioning was the cognitive process used by the child. The child should be able to correctly attribute intent to the actions of others and know who the victim is. Determining whether or not the child had adequate cognitive skills to correctly evaluate the situation of others and make appropriate choices for action was an important area of this investigation. The easily aroused child can be impulsive and act before thinking carefully about consequences. The easily aroused child can also display inappropriate learned behaviors in response to distress in others. These behaviors are learned because adults or peers have reinforced them.

The third area of questioning explored what the child identified as appropriate behavior in response to the distress of others. How the child has learned a particular set of behaviors and possibly how those behaviors continue to be reinforced would be useful information in recommendations for interventions. To fully understand the children's experiences, it was important to have them explain how specific responses were chosen. This question area provided insight into the complexity of their thinking.

INTERVIEW RESULTS

Categories of Responses

The interview responses were grouped into four categories:

a. causative events,
b. context,
c. strategies, and
d. consequences.

Causative events are those things identified in the conversations of the children that produced their responses. The actions of peers were described as a form of retaliation. Some children expected this would occur if they intervened.

The actions of adults described by the children were seen as directed at them. These actions included the possibility of punishment for intervention that might not be considered acceptable in some way. Some children expressed confusion or worry about their choice of action because of this concern. The children also saw adults as available to provide the intervention for them. If they wanted the victim rescued in some way that they could not accomplish, an adult could do it for them.

The context for the responses of the children included the location of the event and the people who were present. All of the children described events that occurred either on the playground or in the classroom. All the children mentioned the presence of peers. This included (a) the aggressors, (b) other participants, (c) observers, and (d) peers identified as friends by the children. Those peers labeled as friends by the children were described as possible sources of support. The children also recognized the possibility that these friends might find their action unacceptable in some way and exclude them from their group.

If adults were present in the situations described by the children, they became a consideration in decisions about their actions. Adults could provide intervention and relieve them of taking action that might prejudice them with their peers. Adults could also be the source of punishment if the action the children chose was deemed inappropriate.

The children described several strategies for intervention in the situations, which included talking to the victim, the aggressor, or both. They would tell the victim to ignore the aggressor or walked away. Half of the children said they told victims that comments made by the aggressors were not true or not fair to make them feel better. They tried to help victims recognize one or more strong points they had to help them feel less sad.

Comments to the aggressors all addressed the issue of fairness. The children attempted to explain to the aggressors that their behavior was not right because they were bigger or stronger and the victim had not done anything directly to them.

Asking friends for help was also discussed by some of the children. They said that it was important that all the friends agree on the course of action to be taken. Being friends and helping each other required honesty in this type of discussion. Walking away from the situation was an option for only two children. Both stated that they walked away because they did not want the same thing to happen to them.

Getting an adult to help was one of the last choices mentioned by the children. They all used other options before going to an adult. They were concerned that they might get in trouble along with the aggressor if they told an adult because the aggressor would lie about what happened.

Physical intervention such as hitting, pushing, or chasing the aggressor was mentioned. Some of the children said that they think about doing that but do not because they know they will be punished. Two said they hit or push if they are very angry with the aggressor. These two children also stated that the aggressor in their situations had caused problems for them in the past and they knew just how the current victim felt.

The consequences of intervention in the situations the children described were important to the children as they decided on a plan of action. They expressed fear of losing a friend or being isolated from others because they took action that might not be considered acceptable by peers. Several of the children were concerned that the aggressor might victimize them as retaliation for intervention.

Rescue of the victim was mentioned as a consequence. They wanted to rescue the victims to relieve their sadness, show friendship as support, and because they identified with how the victim felt. The feelings expressed were anger at the aggressor and sadness or loneliness for the victim.

Rectifying wrongdoing was another reason children chose to intervene. The children discussed the fairness of the actions of the aggressors. It was not fair if the aggressor was bigger, more popular, a bully, or had favor with an adult. They also commented on lack of fairness if the victim was innocent of any action that directly affected the aggressor. They seemed to recognize that the aggressor was using the victim as a scapegoat.

Themes of Responses

Two major themes emerged: the empathetic response to the victim and the cognition leading to a decision about the action to take. The empathetic response to the victim had four components: (a) recognition of the victim's situation, (b) violation of their sense of fairness, (c) memory of a personal experience, and (d) an emotional response. Cognition leading to the decision regarding behavior had three components: (a) concern about the feelings of the victim, (b) awareness of possible peer responses that might occur such as retaliation or support for their actions, and (c) consideration of either help or punishment by adults as a consequence for actions.

The responses of the children to the interview questions produced an eloquent story of their experience of empathy. The emotional aspect of their response was evident as they described their experiences. The process they used to determine their actions was explained.

The children clearly identified that a peer was hurting another child in some manner. They described the behavior of the aggressor in detail.

> One time there was a new kid in our class and his name was the same as another kid. We already had a kid by this name in our class and so we called them 1 and 2. Well, 1 and his buddies went over to him and acted nice but then started telling him he was ruining his life because he was the only one with his name allowed in our class. That wasn't right because 2 can't help what his name is. (Child 4)

> One time this kid was chasing a little kid around and then the little kid tripped. This kid and some others were laughing at him. They knew he would probably trip because he can't run very well and they can scare him easy and make him run. (Child 2)

> The other day this kid kept teasing another kid and telling him he was fat. This kid is so teeny, how could he ever be fat? He was just wearing this puffy coat and it was sort of too big and everything, but he likes to wear it cause that just how he is. But I could tell his feelings were hurt and he was kind of mad about being called fat even if he knows he isn't. It's like the other kid was making fun of how he dressed. (Child 9)

Some children included elements of their own memories of having been in the victim's situation.

> I feel lonely when I get hurt, like if someone won't play with me or makes faces at me. I can take care of myself and all that but I still feel lonely and sad. I know what it feels like to want someone to play with you or talk to you and nobody does it. (Child 6)

> I sometimes do really dumb stuff like without thinking you know. And kids will tell me how stupid I act and won't play with me or

> throw me the ball cause they think I'll just act goofy. I don't mean to and I feel really sad and lonely when they talk to me like that. I get mad at myself, too. (Child 5)

They expressed emotional responses towards both the victim and the aggressor.

> I feel real sad if I see some kid who doesn't get to play soccer with us. It's just because he can't play good or something. Then they just have to stand around and wish they could play with us, but the other kids ignore him or some even call him names. (Child 1)

> I'm glad if a teacher sees a kid making fun of someone because they deserve it. I don't tell on them because that would be tattling but it makes me mad to see them get away with stuff. I want to see somebody hurt them. (Child 7)

> I felt angry when I saw him laughing at that girl. And I also felt like he should get in big trouble for doing it. It's not fair that kids like that can get away with stuff just because other kids are afraid of them. They are just ugly bullies. (Child 5)

The violation of their sense of fairness and what was right or wrong in terms of behavior towards others was evident in their responses.

> When kids tell someone they can play with them but then another friend comes over and they tell the first one they can't play anymore. It's not fair because everyone has a right to play with someone and you can't tell them to go away after you already start playing like they aren't good enough anymore. (Child 10)

> I always see this one kid being teased and I don't like him because he calls other kids names, even me. But it still isn't right. He gets hurt and fights back because he is mad and his feelings are hurt and he doesn't know what else to do. (Child 4)

The children demonstrated an understanding of why the victims were experiencing hurtful feelings. The victim's feelings that concerned them were usually identified as sadness or fear. This understanding was part of their consideration of what action to take.

> I knew my brother was really scared, like oh no he's probably going to hit me or something. The other kids were scared too because this guy is really mean and he has lots of friends that might gang up after school and hurt you if he doesn't like what you do. Everybody was scared, even the boys, and we didn't know what to do at first. (Child 10)

> I wonder about how that kid feels if they are all making fun of him because he can't help the way he talks and stuff like that. You can tell by their face that they want to cry because they are sad and think no one likes them, but they won't cry because then they would really get laughed at and be called baby and stuff. It would not be a good thing. (Child 3)

> I wanted to do something to help her but she had her friends with her. I figured they would all get on me later. So I waited for them to leave and then I tried to cheer her up and tell him not to listen to those girls because they were just snobby. They really aren't any better just for having better stuff. (Child 8)

> One kid couldn't swim in the river with all the rest of us because of some medical problem and he was hassling everyone else because he was by himself. I figured he would be more mad if I just yelled at him so I went over and tried to talk to him and ask him to fish in the creek on the other side with me. He's pretty good at fishing and has a new telescoping pole. It's pretty awesome. Maybe he would stop being mad if I did that, you know, made him feel like he was more expert or something. (Child 7)

They thought about the reaction of peers and what they should do within the context of their expectation of how they would behave.

> The guy doing the hurting needs to be helped too but you can't just say anything to them because they will get embarrassed and be more mad. So maybe I can talk to them later or something like that. But I don't want to get them mad at me because then they'll try to hassle me too. You got to be real careful with some of these guys. They just want to look tough to the other guys. (Child 5)

> I talk to my friends first. If more of my friends are around we can do something because there is more of us. It's like making them

> think our group is better and we know more. If you can't do that you have to stay out of that and just try to be friendly to the girl they are teasing. You might want to play with them later or like get invited to their birthday next week. You got to be real careful about that. (Child 10)

Adult responses were also a factor but not the major determinant of their choice of action unless they were fearful of physical harm or felt they could not stop the abuse of the victim.

> I was really afraid of that kid and just figured he would punch me or something. So that's when I went to tell the aide what was going on. He was really out of control and somebody could have gotten hurt bad if no one stopped him. (Child 3)

> Telling a teacher is like tattling and we have a rule in our class about that. And you have to have witnesses and everything. It's easier to just settle it yourself. I'm pretty good at talking to kids and I just tell the little kids to go away and play somewhere else. Teachers would just do that. They won't do anything except maybe make then stand against the wall for the rest of recess. (Child 2)

EMPATHETIC RESPONSE

The empathetic experience for the children in this study began with their recognition of the pain and emotional state of the victims. They reflected on their own prior experience and used this to identify and describe the feelings of the victim. The children experienced an emotional response related to their own history of being hurt by someone else.

Seeing another child being hurt in some way caused distress for the children in this study. The actions of peers that caused the victim's distress were familiar to these children. They had all been in the victim's position. They attributed negative intent to the actions of the aggressors based on their previous experience. This was a learned social response that occurs when children experience aggression and rejection from peers. Their sense of fairness was violated as they experienced a connection to the victim. They knew what it felt like and what they wanted to see done about it.

These children were able to reflect on their own experience to take the perspective of the victim. The victims were seen as separate and distinct from themselves. Taking the perspective of another person allowed the children to respond in a manner that addressed the needs of the victim and not just their own needs.

Although it has been proposed that easily aroused children lack the ability to regulate emotional responses, these children showed they had the ability to self-regulate in a thoughtful manner. The level of arousal of affect in the children was intense. The ability of the children to experience the emotions of the victim helped motivate them to take an action that would relieve the discomfort of the other child.

The children were able to keep their emotional responses under control and responded with behaviors that show empathy and are prosocial. Their feelings were intense, but they were not so aroused that they felt they could not control the feelings. The children felt competent to make a decision regarding their behavior and act on it because they perceived themselves to be in control of their own emotions.

Expressing their feelings to the victim as a choice of behavioral response was seen as an appropriate way to bring comfort to the victim and to themselves. Perhaps the children saw the potential for developing new relationships as they intervened on behalf of the victims. The expression of affect was not seen as a detriment to their interpersonal relationships with their peers when it was expressed to the victim.

Some of the children in this study chose to express feelings to the aggressor. Perhaps they saw that as the only alternative available to stop the aggressor from continuing to harass the victim. It may also reflect a sense of confidence on the part of these children in their ability to keep their emotional reactions under control.

The cognitive skills the children used to respond were developed as part of their experiential process. This experience allowed the children to evaluate and modify the intensity of their emotional responses. The children were familiar with the feelings of anger, fear, and sadness that they vicariously experienced watching the aggressors and victims. They were able to maintain their arousal level low enough to give them a sense of being in control of the feeling. These children had made an adaptation to the affect associated with the negative events they described. The events were very familiar to them.

Impulsivity and inability to inhibit responses is also a trait of the easily aroused child with externalizing behaviors. The children in this study showed they had the ability to inhibit portions of their emotional responses. A lack of emotional regulation would be seen in responses that were hostile and possibly directed towards the aggressors.

The children addressed the rightness or wrongness of the actions of the aggressors. They expressed this to themselves, the victims and aggressors, and as an important component of their responses in the interview. They looked at the context of each event. They were particularly conscious of the presence of peers and possible ramifications of their choice of actions with their peer group. They wanted to take action to rectify the wrong they saw done but did not want to place themselves in the position of being victims. The previous experience of these children as victims of aggressors led them to recognize the hostile intent. They also considered the effect their actions would have on the situation. They chose not to respond with aggression that would not have been a productive solution.

The children thought through their actions. If they felt too threatened by peer presence, their intervention was with the victim to comfort and encourage them. If they felt more confident with their peers and their ability to regulate their emotional response, they directed their intervention to the aggressor. Approaching the aggressor could cause an argument escalating to physical aggression. Choosing this action shows greater ability to monitor and control an emotional response. These children knew the aggressors and had experience with the behaviors they observed. The children had an expectation of certain emotional and behavioral responses from their peers based on their own choice of behaviors.

Watching another child being hurt by a peer caused strong emotional responses in these children. Their actions, however, were not intended just as a relief of their own distress. They also wanted to seek justice in some manner and to convey to others the right way they should behave toward each other. Instead of engaging in antisocial behavior when experiencing strong emotional arousal, these children showed constraint and thoughtfulness in their actions.

Some of the children expressed concern about being punished for their actions. Some indicated they would only seek adult attention as a last resort because of this. Past experience of punishment for antisocial behaviors was a factor. Adults would expect anger, aggression, and other inappropriate expressions of emotion. The children in this study did not see adults as fair and unbiased in their interventions.

IMPLICATIONS

The easily aroused child has been viewed as possibly lacking in the ability to experience empathy for others, and engage in prosocial behaviors. The responses of the children interviewed suggest that in fact this type of child may be able to (a) recognize the feelings of others, (b) relate them to their personal experiences yet keep them separate, and (c) make reasoned decisions about their actions.

What may be lacking for the easily aroused type of child is knowledge of specific intervention strategies. These children are expressing a violation of their sense of fairness with associated anger. If they do not have specific strategies available to use, then they may engage in what adults consider being antisocial behaviors. This would include physical or verbal aggression. Providing skills training for the easily aroused child could eliminate undesirable behaviors for some children.

An important implication of the interview results is the need for adults to become more sensitive to the keen sense of fairness that these children have. Disciplinary interventions should consider this aspect of their behavioral choices. What has been perceived as strictly antisocial behavior may be merely a distortion of prosocial behavior to aid victims because of lack of skills to choose alternative behaviors.

Counseling programs should also consider this sense of fairness these children have and address it as a critical component of problem solving and other cognitive skills training. It would be appropriate to help them learn to take the perspective of the aggressor and not just the victim. The children in this study have not only been victims but have also been in the role of aggressor. These children recognize the problem. They know what they want for a solution. What they need is assistance with learning to recognize resources and practicing more alternatives for their behavior depending on specific situations they find themselves in.

THE BULLY PREVENTION PROJECT

The school site where this interview study was conducted has begun to identify a need to make adjustments in the school discipline program to address the issue of bullying. A new classroom instruction program has been started. This program incorporates the elements of the experience of empathy identified by the children: actions, context, strategies, consequences, and intervention with both the aggressor and the victim.

It is a program that can be used at grades 3-5. Classroom teacher participation in the instruction and follow-up actions as well as support from the school site administrator is critical.

The instructional component for students includes (a) perspective taking, (b) communication skills to assist in better expressing their feelings, (c) problem solving, and (d) conflict resolution. These skills are taught through a variety of activities which vary with the grade level. Older students participate in role-playing, cooperative learning groups, and group discussions addressing actual events from their school day experience. Other activities include making posters to "advertise" the no bullying ideas, group games using problem-solving skills, and discussion groups. All students work together to develop class rules regarding bullying. These rules help the students identify the need to include everyone in their activities as a major tool to preventing bullying, as well as general statements that bullying will not be tolerated.

Also included in this program is an emphasis on working together as a community to help each other. Students are encouraged to listen to their peers and aid those they see being victimized. Teachers will be encouraged to listen to students with a new perspective that recognizes that apparent antisocial behavior may be learned responses on the part of a child with good intentions. They may also consider that some children need changes in the environment and expectations for their behavior in order function at their best and learn new patterns of behavior.

Parents are provided with support materials for use at home as needed. They are kept informed of the progress of the program through the school newsletter. Parents are encouraged to talk with their children about bullying issues and to report incidents to the school administration. They can also ask for assistance for themselves or their child in dealing with specific issues that arise.

At the beginning of instruction in bully prevention at each class level, the students were asked to complete a survey. Various questions were asked regarding the frequency and type of bully behavior they experienced or engaged in with peers. Verbal aggression was reported occurring at least twice each week by 41% of both boys and girls in the 3rd grade and by 38% of those in the 4th grade. Physical aggression was reported occurring at least twice a week by 29% of the boys and 24% of the girls in the 3rd grade. Physical aggression was reported by 44% of 4th grade students. The students were also asked who at school they turned to for help in dealing with bullying. The majority who had indicated they were bullied stated they told no one and received help from no one. Those who sought help did so from parents or siblings.

Since completion of the initial series of lessons, six students in grades 3 and 4 were informally interviewed to elicit their view of the impact of the bully prevention lessons. Although these students were not included in the original study of empathy, they did fit the profile of the easily aroused child. They were also students who had been identified as engaging in some bully behavior with other students.

All of these six students stated that bullying had decreased in their classes. They related the decrease to two main factors. They said that the bullies were now being watched by teachers more carefully so they didn't get away with the behavior as often. They also said that other kids were inviting them to play more often or letting them play if they asked to be included in a game. These are both specific skills taught as part of the bully prevention classes.

Two of the students who had previously been involved in bully behaviors with peers have not been referred for aggressive behaviors since the lessons started. They both talked about playing with other peers. One of them stated that he had "found some other guys to play with who liked me because I don't get into so much trouble any more."

One of the girls interviewed tearfully talked about not having any friends to play with anymore since the lessons had begun. Two girls who had been her playmates stated that they just "didn't want to be with her if she was going to act mean." This girl is now beginning to reflect on her own behaviors and possibly look for alternatives to improve her peer relations.

The bully prevention program was in the early stage of implementation when the students were interviewed. Those lessons now are moving into the second phase. As the program progresses, further information will be gathered from the students about their experiences with peers as it relates to bullying and their emotional reactions to it. This preliminary feedback from the children involved as victims and aggressors provides an echo of the comments made by the easily aroused children in the original study. They kids are sensitive to the reactions or adults, are relieved to see them becoming more alert to the problem, and also seem to be learning how to relate in a different manner to some of their peers.

It is important to recognize that easily aroused children are capable of great empathy. They are also capable of engaging in appropriate behaviors in response. These abilities need to be expanded and reinforced so that these children will be better able to develop their interpersonal skills. A bully prevention program is one example of a potentially powerful tool to use with these children.

REFERENCES

Bates, J. E., Pettit, G. S., Dodge, K. A., & Ridge, B. (1998). Interaction of temperamental resistance to control and restrictive parenting in the development of externalizing behavior. *Developmental Psychology, 34*, 982-995.

Bengtsson, H., & Johnson, L. (1992). Perspective taking, empathy, and prosocial behavior in late childhood. *Child Study Journal, 22*, 11-22.

Berkowitz, L. (1993). *Aggression: Its causes, consequences and control*. Philadelphia: Temple University Press.

Brenner, E. M., & Salovey, P. (1997). Emotion regulation during childhood: Developmental, interpersonal, and individual considerations. In P. Salovey & D. J. Sluyter (Eds.), *Emotional development and emotional intelligence* (pp. 168-192). New York: Basic Books.

Caspi, A. (1998). Personality development across the life course. In W. Damon (Series Ed.) & N. Eisenberg (Vol. Ed.), *Handbook of child psychology: Vol. 3. Social, emotional, and personality development* (5th ed., pp. 311-387). New York: Wiley.

Caspi, A., Moffitt, T. E., Newman, D. L., & Silva, P. A. (1996). Behavioral observations at age 3 predict adult psychiatric disorders: Longitudinal evidence from a birth cohort. *Archives of General Psychiatry, 53*, 1033-1039.

Chess, S., & Thomas, A. (1999). *Goodness of fit: Clinical applications from infancy through adult life*. Philadelphia: Brunner/Mazel.

Cole, P. M. (1986). Children's spontaneous control of facial expression. *Child Development, 57*, 1309-1321.

Cole, P. M., Michel, M. K., & Teti, L. O. (1994). The development of emotion regulation and dysregulation: A clinical perspective. *Monographs of the Society for Research in Child Development, 59*, 73-100.

Cole, P. M., Zahn-Waxler, C., & Smith, K. D. (1994). Expressive control during a disappointment: Variation related to preschoolers' behavior problems. *Developmental Psychology, 30*, 835-846.

Dodge, K. A., & Somberg, D. R. (1987). Hostile attributional biases among aggressive boys are exacerbated under conditions of threat to the self. *Child Development, 58*, 213-224.

Dorsch, A., & Keane, S. P. (1994). Contextual factors in children's social information processing. *Developmental Psychology, 30*, 611-616.

Eisenberg, N., Fabes, R. A., & Losoya, S. (1997). Emotional responding: Regulation, social correlates, and socialization. In P. Salovey & D. J. Sluyter (Eds.), *Emotional development and emotional intelligence* (pp. 129-163). New York: Basic Books.

Eisenberg, N., Fabes, R. A., Shepard, S. A., Murphy, B. C., Jones, S., & Guthrie, I. K. (1998). Contemporaneous and longitudinal prediction of children's sympathy from dispositional regulation and emotionality. *Developmental Psychology, 34*, 910-924.

Graziano, W. G., Jensen-Campbell, L. A., & Sullivan-Logan, G. M. (1998). Temperament, activity, and expectations for later personality development. *Journal of Personality and Social Psychology, 74*, 1266-1277.

Gross, J. J. (1998). The emerging field of emotion regulation. *Review of General Psychology, 2*, 271-299.

Guerin, D. W., Gottfried, A. W., & Thomas, C. W. (1997). Difficult temperament and behavior problems: A longitudinal study from 1.5 to 12 years. *International Journal of Behavioral Development, 21*, 71-90.

Hoffman, M. L. (1990). Empathy and justice motivation. *Motivation and Emotion, 14*, 151-172.

Kagan, J. (1998). Biology and the child. In W. Damon (Series Ed.) & N. Eisenberg (Vol. Ed.), *Handbook of child psychology: Vol. 3. Social, emotional, and personality development* (pp. 177-235). New York: Wiley.

Kochanska, G. (1993). Toward a synthesis of parental socialization and child temperament in early development of conscience. *Child Development, 64*, 325-347.

Kochanska, G. (1997). Multiple pathways to conscience for children with different temperament: From toddlerhood to age 5. *Developmental Psychology, 3*, 228-240.

Loeber, R., & Hay, D. (1997). Key issues in the development of aggression and violence from childhood to early adulthood. *Annual Review of Psychology, 48*, 371-410.

Olweus, D. (1991). Bully/victim problems among schoolchildren: Basic facts and effects of a school-based intervention program. In D. J. Pepler & K. H. Rubin (Eds.), *The development and treatment of childhood aggression* (pp. 411-448). Hillsdale, NJ: Erlbaum Associates.

Park, L. C., & Park, T. J. (1997). Personal intelligence. In M. McCallum & W. E. Piper (Eds.), *Psychological mindedness: A contemporary understanding* (pp. 133-168). Mahwah, NJ: Lawrence Erlbaum Associates.

Pellegrini, A. D., Bartini, M., & Brooks, F. (1999). School bullies, victims, and aggressive victims: Factors relating to group affiliation and victimization in early adolescence. *Journal of Educational Psychology, 91*, 216-224.

Rothbart, M. K., & Ahadi, S. A. (1994). Temperament and the development of personality. *Journal of Abnormal Psychology, 103*, 55-66.

Rothbart, M. K., Ahadi, S. A., & Evans, D. E. (2000). Temperament and personality origins and outcomes. *Journal of Personality and Social Psychology, 78*, 122-135.

Rothbart, M. K., Ahadi, S. A., & Hershey, K. L. (1994). Temperament and social behavior in childhood. *Merrill Palmer Quarterly, 40*, 21-39.

Rothbart, M. K., & Bates, J. E. (1998). Temperament. In W. Damon (Series Ed.) & N. Eisenberg (Vol. Ed.), *Handbook of child psychology: Vol. 3. Social, emotional, and personality development* (5th ed., pp. 105-176). New York: Wiley.

Rubin, K. H., Chen, X., & Hymel, S. (1993). Socioemotional characteristics of withdrawn and aggressive children. *Merrill-Palmer Quarterly, 39*, 518-534.

Saarni, C. (1999). *The development of emotional competence*. New York: The Guilford Press.

Schwartz, D., Dodge, K. A., Petit, G. S., & Bates, J. E. (1997). The early socialization and adjustment of aggressive victims of bullying. *Child Development, 68*, 665-675.

Strelau, J. (1994). The concepts of arousal and arousability as used in temperament studies. In J. E. Bates & T. D. Wachs (Eds.), *Temperament: Individual differences at the interface of biology and behavior* (pp. 117-142). Washington, DC: American Psychological Association.

Thompson, R. A. (1994). Emotional regulation: A theme in search of definition. In N. Fox (Ed.), The development of emotion regulation: Behavioral and biological considerations. *Monographs of the Society for Research in Child Development, 59* (Serial No. 240), 25-52.

Walden, T., & Smith, M. C. (1997). Emotion regulation. *Motivation and Emotion, 21,* 7-25.

Zahn-Waxler, C., Radke-Yarrow, M., Wagner, E., & Chapman, M. (1992). Development of concern for others. *Developmental Psychology, 28,* 126-136.

Zeman, J., & Garber, J. (1996). Display rules for anger, sadness, and pain: It depends on who is watching. *Child Development, 67,* 957-973.

Zeman, J., & Shipman, K. (1996). Children's expression of negative affect: Reasons and methods. *Developmental Psychology, 32,* 842-849.

Psychological Perspectives on the Stigmatization of Italian Americans in the American Media

Elizabeth G. Messina

SUMMARY. A central sociopolitical and psychological problem confronting Italian Americans in the United States today is the media's relentless stereotyping of Italian Americans as criminals who are in some way connected to Mafiosi. These negative representations are controlling images because they are created and perpetuated by dominant social institutions to make the ethnic treatment of Italian Americans seem *natural* and *normative.*

Stereotypes of Italian Americans have strong negative connotations that reflect the history of this identity group in the United States and in Italy. These historically based negative stereotypes underlie representa-

---

Elizabeth G. Messina, PhD, is Adjunct Assistant Professor of Psychology at Fordham University and a faculty member in the Department of Psychiatry at Lenox Hill Hospital, New York. She maintains an active psychotherapy practice in Manhattan. As a researcher she has conducted cross-cultural research in Italy and the United States focusing on gender egalitarianism and cancer pain. Her current research interests focus on culture and gender, and intergenerational migration trauma. She is the author of numerous articles focusing on Italian Americans and is the editor of *In Our Own Voices: Multidisciplinary Perspectives on Italian and Italian American Women* (2003, Lafayette, Indiana: Bordighera Press). She is past Vice-President of the American Italian Historical Association.

[Haworth co-indexing entry note]: "Psychological Perspectives on the Stigmatization of Italian Americans in the American Media." Messina, Elizabeth G. Co-published simultaneously in *The Psychotherapy Patient* (The Haworth Press, Inc.) Vol. 13, No.1/2, 2004, pp. 87-121; and: *Saints and Rogues: Conflicts and Convergence in Psychotherapy* (ed: Robert B. Marchesani, and E. Mark Stern) The Haworth Press, Inc., 2004, pp. 87-121. Single or multiple copies of this article are available for a fee from The Haworth Document Delivery Service [1-800-HAWORTH, 9:00 a.m. - 5:00 p.m. (EST). E-mail address: docdelivery@haworthpress.com].

http://www.haworthpress.com/web/TPP

Digital Object Identifier: 10.1300/J358v13n01_04

tions of Italian Americans in the print and entertainment media today. Such negative representations continue to disfigure and misrepresent Italian Americans in American society.

There is now significant cross-disciplinary evidence that Italian Americans have occupied an ambiguous identity in American society as *stigmatized marginalized* whites.[1] Unfortunately, research examining the psychological and social effects of ethnic racism, prejudice and stereotyping related to Italian Americans is virtually nonexistent. Italian Americans still remain conceptually invisible in psychological and psychoanalytic research literature.

This essay represents an attempt to synthesize historical, sociological, and psychoanalytic perspectives of Italian Americans with social psychological research that has examined the nature of stereotyping and prejudice. The purpose of this paper is threefold: (a) to provide a brief overview of the concepts of prejudice, stereotyping and racism in the scientific literature as they pertain to Italian Americans, (b) to review the historical roots of prejudice and stereotyping about Italian Americans during the twentieth century that have impacted media portrayals of Italian Americans today, (c) and lastly to demonstrate the ways in which Italian Americans have been made to carry America's every sociological and psychological *shadow*[2] from the early days of industrial capitalism to the postmodern era.

KEYWORDS. Italian Americans, stereotyping, media, ethnic racism, prejudice, skin privileges, Mafiosi, Italian American directors, artists

THEORY OF PREJUDICE, STEREOTYPING, AND SCAPEGOATING

As Gordon Allport (1954) noted in his groundbreaking psychological treatise on prejudice, stereotypes may not be inherently dangerous or inherently demeaning.[3] In early experimental laboratory studies of prejudice, social psychologists encountered a powerful phenomenon: Researchers found that after the flip of a coin, participants assigned to one of two random groups displayed significant bias in favor of their group (*us*) and against the other group (*them*).[4] This classification, in turn, initiates *bias*: Once categorized, people tend to automatically value others in their own group. Moreover, research repeatedly shows that individuals tend to evaluate members of the *in-group* (us–we are better than they are) more positively and members of the *out-group* (them–they are inferior to us) more negatively.[5] Prejudice outside the laboratory, however, is a more complex phenomenon. While racism reflects, in part, the universal tendency to favor the *in-group,* societal variables, as will be discussed shortly, transform this basic process into a more systemic insidious phenomenon.[6]

Prejudice refers to "negative attitudes against certain out-groups and their members that are *irrationally* [emphasis is mine] based . . . accompanied by a faulty generalization or *stereotypes*."[7] For example, when we say an individual is prejudiced against Italian Americans, we mean that he or she is primed to feel or behave negatively toward Italian Americans, and that he or she feels justified in thinking that Italian Americans are pretty much the same.

According to Dovido and Gaertner (1998), people's first thoughts and impressions of others occur, spontaneously and automatically, from categorization.[8] The mere classification of people into social groups allows people to understand others with regard to a few main characteristics, such as their age, gender, social role, or physical appearance. However, stereotyping goes one step beyond categorization: a *stereotype* is a simplistic generalization (albeit of questionable validity) about a group of people in which identical characteristics, consistent with one's prejudices, are assigned to all members of that group (Aronson et al., 2002; Fiske, 1998). For example, media representation of Italian Americans as gangsters and criminals obscures their variability because these portrayals are not counterbalanced by positive images reflecting the diversity of the Italian American community. The media rarely, if ever, portrays Italian Americans as they truly are: a diverse subgroup of American society with its share of political leaders, scientists, writers, filmmakers, business leaders, physicians, attorneys, psychologists and psychiatrists.

A study conducted in 1999 by the Italic Studies Institute of New York analyzed 1,078 Hollywood films that featured Italian Americans from 1931 to 1998 and found that only twenty-seven percent or 152 films portrayed Italian Americans positively, while seventy-three percent or 781 films portrayed Italian Americans negatively. Social psychologist Susan Fiske (1998) observes that to the extent that a stereotype obscures individual differences and variation in a group of people it is *potentially abusive*. The results of this and other surveys affirming Americans' perceptions of Italian Americans' criminality demonstrate the effect of negative or *potentially abusive* stereotyping in action. As the Italic Studies survey demonstrates, to the millions of Americans whose principal views of Italian Americans are shaped by what they see on the television screen, negative stereotypes of Italian Americans exist as repetitive variations played upon inaccurate yet widely endorsed negative stereotypes.

These mixed and mostly negative portrayals of Italian Americans are exacerbated by the fact that such representations are rarely counterbalanced by Italian Americans characters that are cast in more positive portrayals such as expert authorities, professionals, executives, or newsmakers. Thus, rather than helping to overcome the negative image of Italian Americans fostered by entertainment programming, the media reinforces negative images by failing to *counterbalanc*e these images with more positive portrayals.

Journalism scholars Wilson and Gutierrez (1995) have pointed out two particularly pernicious features of stereotyping: (1) the *vicious cycle* aspect–once stereotypes are expressed and learned, they are reinforced, validated and perpetuated; (2) once validation occurs, it solidifies stereotypes into *norms* that suggest how certain individuals and groups should be treated.

Research also indicates that once formed, stereotypes are resistant to change.[9] Because stereotypic information is reinforced throughout one's life, it provides "an *unconscious* belief system for perceiving the world."[10] Socially ingrained, yet often unconscious, ethnic/racial stereotyping is so strongly socialized within United States culture that most people are not conscious of the control they exert over their thoughts, feelings, and behaviors. Once activated they unconsciously bias people's perception, judgments, and intentions.[11]

Unfortunately, stereotyping of Italian Americans as an identity group prone to criminality, violence and murder has become normative in American society. For example, surveys have shown that many citizens in the United States endorse stigmatizing attitudes about Italian Americans and their alleged connections to the Mafia today. In a recent study (2000) commissioned by Commission of Social Justice,[12] a division of the Order of the Sons of Italy, over seventy-four percent of the respondents endorsed the belief that most Italian Americans have a connection to the Mafia. Such generalizations about Italian Americans' criminality and violence are not based in fact: Italian Americans are involved in only two percent of all homicides, just slightly higher than the English and Irish.[13] Moreover, the FBI reports that less than two percent of every ten thousand Italian Americans are involved in organized crime.[14]

Psychoanalytic and Jungian thought has much to contribute to our knowledge and understanding of group and collective life as it relates to stereotyping and prejudice. One of Jung's greatest contributions to psychoanalytic thought is the discovery of the reality of the *collective unconscious* and the "presence of the unconscious in the collective and the collective in the unconscious."[15] In Jungian psychological terms, a *scapegoat* is an ancient archetype and activity (dating back to human sacrifice) that is created by *projecting* the darker side of life (elements of the group psyche that are unacceptable to collective consciousness) to an *out-group* perceived to be separate and apart from the *in-group*.[16]

In the context of collective life, scapegoating activity represents the group's push toward its own wholeness. Scapegoating "represents the transfer of negative attributions from one part of the system to another in order to fulfill what is perceived to be necessary for the system to survive as a whole."[17] In his book *Up from Scapegoating* (1995), Jungian psychiatrist Arthur D. Colman argues that groups, like individuals, will create scapegoats rather than "accommodate diversity with its corpus."[18] Groups may need to find a scapegoat to deal with the threat and tension of fragmentation and disintegration.

Italian peasants in Italy and Italian immigrants in America served as convenient scapegoats for the problems that plagued the new republic of Italy and the anxieties that plagued Americans in a rapidly changing industrial capitalist economy. Moreover, although Italian Americans in the twenty-first century have acquired power and resources unavailable to their immigrant ancestors, they continue to be receptacles of attributes unwanted in the ideal postmodern American.

As I will discuss shortly, attributes such as violence and criminality continue to be "disowned" and "split off" from the collective American psyche and projected onto Italian Americans. In turn, debasing Italian Americans alters and inflates the self-image of Americans. The "badness" of Italian Americans appears to be an ongoing and unifying organizing principle in the psychic lives of Americans evinced by the media's stereotyping of Italian Americans as criminals and Mafiosi.

Inequities of power and history make some stereotypes worse than others. Operario and Fiske (1998) observe that stereotypes "based on power differential between groups have the most potential to harm."[19] *Power,* which is defined as the "ability to control the outcomes of others," entails the power to "classify and categorize outgroups via changing scientific standards, the power to enact race-based laws via political dominance, and the power to subordinate via social and economic control."[20] For several decades following the unification of Italy in 1860, in order to maintain power, privilege, and dominance, members of the elite classes (landowners, the borghesi, and the Catholic Church of the south) colluded with the northern-dominated government to promote stereotypes of peasant southerners as "Africans" and "cannibals," disparaging both their moral character and intelligence[21] (Verdicchio, 1994). The elite and politically powerful of Italy used their power to define southern peasants in dehumanizing terms to justify their domination and colonization of the southern peninsula. Scientific support for these stereotypes were found in the research of Italian anthropologist Cesare Lombroso and his followers, Enrico Ferri, and Alfredo Niceforo, who established the "racial inferiority" and "criminality" of southern Italians through "cranial measurements and other pseudoscientific criteria."[22]

Ethnicism[23]/racism is an intractable problem that is dependent on the maintenance of a power differential that enables dominant groups to define the 'self' in opposition to an 'other.' In Italy racial positivist arguments were used to explain the

> congenital inability of Southerners to accept the discipline of an organization . . . their anarchic individualism, made them disorderly, liable to rebellion, and unsuited to long term political preparation.[24]

Viewed through the lens of psychoanalytic theory, it is reasonable to theorize that the collective ego of the post-unification Italian elite embodied the ethic of discipline, restraint and control. In order to sustain this "ideal" image, the powerfully elite unconsciously rejected "primitive" parts of themselves that were incompatible with their "civilized" self-image. The elite, in turn, projected these disowned "primitive" parts onto Italian peasants. Thus, members of the elite political hegemony of the newly formed Italian republic did not accurately perceive Italian peasants. Instead they projected onto peasants unconscious aspects of themselves that have been rejected as incompatible with their civilized self-image. As a result, the northern Italian vision of peasant Italians' reality is mediated, obscured and obstructed by a variety of prejudicial and discriminatory projections.

Power underlies the psychological discrepancy between those who control and those who are controlled. Social psychologists theorize that racism renders members of lower-power groups vulnerable to subordination and exploitation by those who control resources. The northern Italian government used military power to repress southern Italian rebellion against the economic injustices of the newly formed republic. Southern resistance fighters were characterized as "criminals," and at least ten thousand southerners died and twenty thousand were imprisoned or banished by the government for their acts of rebellion (Verdicchio, 1994). Historian Donna Gabaccia (2000) observes that the *criminalization* of Italy's migrants originated in Italy's post-unification civil war between the state and peasantry.[25] Italian peasants who fought their oppressors were stigmatized by the Italian government as violent criminals. This explanation of the etiology of the stereotyping of southern Italians as criminals contradicts popular mythology that perpetuates the false belief that southern Italians' transplantation of the Mafia of Italy to the United States was the origin of this defaming stereotype.[26] In fact, the Mafia that grew to power subsequent to the era of prohibition in the United States was not linked to the Mafia in Italy. Up until the 1920s the Irish controlled the Mafia in the United States.

OVERVIEW OF CULTURAL CATEGORIZING OF ITALIAN AMERICANS

The tendency to treat white European Americans as a monolithic group who have uniformly enjoyed the power and privilege of their "whiteness" has been a problem in understanding American culture. Psychologists Landrine, Klonoff and Brown-Collins suggest that there are significant differences between Americans of European ancestry. Therefore, in their view, European ethnic and cultural groups should not continue to be viewed monolithically within contemporary multicultural research paradigms.[27] As Hope Landrine puts it:

> As long as "cultural diversity" means "how those minorities are different" (from whom?), diversity discourse eloquently eludes addressing, yet quietly maintains, existing social arrangements. Until the focus on culture regards European American cultures as being as salient and in need of analysis as the cultures of others, cultural diversity belittles culture while exploiting it. Culture will be regarded with dignity and the sociology of knowledge altered only when European American cultures are treated like all others.[28]

While many Italian Americans may have benefited from the economic advantages equated with the "skin privileges" of whiteness since

World War II, the emerging body of scholarly research suggests Italian Americans as a whole have not possessed the same social or political power and status of other white European ethnic groups in the United States. The editors *In the Making and Unmaking of Whiteness*[29] note the complexities of "whiteness" and explain:

> how whites themselves are internally differentiated, how the same white skin that has facilitated the integration, assimilation, and enrichment of some does not guarantee that others . . . might not also experience . . . stigmatization and subjugation.

At the turn of the century when the social sciences were developing, researchers adopted biased macrolevel approaches to classify people into races. Social scientific racists argued that there were several European "races" and generally accepted the idea that there was a hierarchy of races with northern and western Europeans at the top, and southern and eastern Europeans at the bottom. In this tradition race-defining variables included ethnicity (e.g., German "race"), religion and language (e.g., the Jewish "race"), and geography (e.g., Mediterranean race).[30] The Anglo-Saxon, Germanic, Teutonic and other Aryan or Nordic races were thought to be biologically and racially superior to the "new immigrants." According to Guetrl,[31] "old immigrants" were folded into a pan-whiteness identity which included those of "English, Dutch, and French" ancestry. Nativists[32] asserted that "new immigrants" including Italians were *racially distinct* from Americans of northern European descent.

There was a perception among Americans nativists that the "new immigrants" were reproducing at higher rates than native-born Americans and that their greater numbers were vitiating the quality of America's intellectual gene pool. This perception was amplified by the realities of the changing demographics in America's urban centers. For example, by 1910 half or more of America's largest cities, including New York, appeared to be "more foreign" in 1900 than in 1850: almost fifteen percent of the America's urban population was of foreign birth.[33] Moreover, at the turn of the century Italians constituted the numerically largest group of "new immigrants."

Beginning in the 1860s, Charles Darwin's treatise on the origin of the species and his ideas about natural selection or "survival of the fittest" provided America's Social Darwinists with an explanation for the biological superiority of white Americans whose civilization was rooted in northern Europe. Reflecting the Darwinian thinking prevalent during the late nineteenth century, the idea was that just as different species of animals struggled for survival and competed for superiority, so too did human races.[34] Implicitly analogizing racial group membership to the groupings of animals, racial difference was thought to represent a "natural difference which must always exist."[35]

In the early part of the twentieth century, Americans cast Italian immigrants into racial idioms similar to those of their homeland. The asymmetrical social power between immigrant Italians and native-born Americans in the United States functioned to perpetuate racial prejudice and stereotypes about southern Italians similar to those made by higher power groups in Italy. As early as 1867 the *New York Times* commented about the Italian immigrant's "natural inclination toward criminality."[36] By 1885 Italian immigrants were cast by the American press into stereotypical icons of the subhuman racially inferior "other." Italian immigrants were portrayed as intellectually and physiologically inferior and were characterized as "ignorant, dirty, lazy, servile, superstitious, dishonest and bloodthirsty."[37] One journalist remarked in 1885 that

> by all odds the most vicious, ignorant and degraded of all the immigrants who come to our shores are the Italian inhabitants . . . a seething mass of humanity, so ignorant, so vicious, so depraved that they hardly seem to belong to our species, Men and women; yet living, not like animals, but like vermin![38]

Such virulent racism reveals the presence and the extent of intense anti-Italian prejudice that existed prior to the mass migration of Italians to the United States during the first decade of the twentieth century.

From the standpoint of American nativists and racist "reformers," inferior biology and "stilletto-weilding dagoes" from Italy were thought to have brought with them to the United States the "bad" blood of their race (Hooton, 1939). Ironically, racist arguments similar to those of the Italian Positivists were made by nativist Americans about "phylogenetically" inferior Italian immigrants who were perceived to be unworthy of and unprepared for American citizenship.

Italians were almost always described by the American press as "swarthy" and "kinky-haired." According to historian Robert Orsi, the perceived physical features of the Italian "brown" "olive-skinned" newcomers did not easily adhere to racial categories of "white or black," the only two possibilities in the domestic racial taxonomy.[39] The genetic ambiguity of the racial status of Italian immigrants constituted, in the words of historian John Higham, the Italian's racial "inbetweeness."[40]

Social psychologist Gordon Allport (1954) observed that "*dark skin implies more than pigmentation, it implies social inferiority.*"[41] Far from merely contributing to appearance, surface features pointing toward the unseen moral, intellectual, or psychological properties of race were thought to represent one's racial essence.[42] The Immigration Restriction League founded in 1896 by Ivy League educators and intellectuals, such as Prescott F. Hall and Henry Cabot Lodge, highlighted the notion of the "non-whiteness" of southern Europeans and Italians by suggesting there was the

> possibility of African blood [flowing through the veins of] . . . the dark peoples living in the Mediterranean shores . . .[43]

Pasquale Verdicchio (1994) posits that the "whiteness" of Italian Americans was erased in American society by a socially constructed ideology that excluded Italian Americans from this racial category and considered them to have been socially "black."[44] Culturally Italian Americans still bear the invisible psychological stigmata of social "blackness."[45]

VIOLENCE AGAINST ITALIAN IMMIGRANTS IN THE AMERICAN SOUTH

In the late 1880s American white southerners referred to the "uncivilized" newly arrived Sicilian immigrants as "black dagoes."[46] One Italian diplomat remarked that Sicilian immigrants were regarded as "white negroes."[47] In 1891, southern racial hatred of Sicilian Italian immigrants culminated in the largest mass lynching (as measured by the number of people illegally killed in one place at one time) in United States history.[48]

Between 1886 and 1910, Italians suffered the largest number of lynchings in the American South than any other *non-black* minority. Historian Clive Webb documents that although Sicilians comprised less than four percent of the white male population between 1890 and 1910, about forty percent of the white men murdered by lynch mobs were Sicilians.[49] Yet Italian Americans are the ones who have been stereotyped as violent murderers.

EUGENICISM, ETHNIC RACISM, AND PSYCHOLOGY'S INTELLIGENCE TESTING MOVEMENT

Charles Darwin's theories of evolution provided nativists with a powerful and allegedly scientific basis for supporting the restriction of the influx of "new immigrants" who were seen as "less fit" for the duties and responsibilities of American citizenship. Eugenicists argued that studies had "proven" those members of the lower classes and non-white peoples had "inferior genes."[50]

Immigrant Italians were a natural target for racial purists. According to professor of Puerto Rican studies, Richie Perez, in the early 1900s American expansionists, eugenicists, scientists, and policymakers embarked on the pursuit of "racial purity" goals similar to those embraced by the Nazis.[51] As eugenicists rose to power in America, writes Perez, politicians used "scientific claims" to justify the "sterilization of the unfit" and restriction on the "further immigration of inferior people."[52]

The ideas of Social Darwinism gave new impetus for restrictions on migration itself. To reduce the entry of newcomers to the United States, several legislative acts were aimed at reducing the number of Italian immigrants and other "newcomers" entering the United States.

Eugenicists and scientific racists who believed in the supremacy of the "white" race made use of invalid "scientific studies" to prove that Italians, among other "new immigrants" (Jews, Portuguese, and Eastern Europeans), had innately "inferior" intelligence and represented "races" still close to the "barbarians." Psychologists who led the intelligence testing movement were mostly hereditarians (who believed that observed differences among individuals for a particular trait are due to genetics), eugenicists (who believed that improvement in the human race should be encouraged through selective breeding) and social reformers. Lewis Terman, Stanford University scholar, researcher, test developer (of the Stanford-Binet Intelligence Test),[53] ideologue and social reformer, molded the intelligence testing movement. Terman's value-laden idea that the *intellectual level* of an individual predicted their *educability* had significant implications for the stratification of white, minority and immigrant children in the educational system.[54] Terman believed in the power of intelligence tests to assess and predict a child's educability and course of study. For example, in his *Measurement of Intelligence* (1916) Terman discussed the cases of two Portuguese brothers with borderline intelligence (with measured IQs of 77 and 78) and predicted that each brother would "doubtless become a fairly reliable laborer at unskilled work . . . and will probably never develop beyond the 11- or 12-year level [of intelligence] or be able to do satisfactory school work beyond the fifth or sixth grade."[55] Terman's sentiments about the intelligence levels and educability of immigrants and their children were unequivocally racist.

The first mass group-administered intelligence tests[56] (tests that could be administered to groups in one sitting) were administered to over two million army recruits during World War I. Psychologists accrued intelligence test data on 12,407 foreign-born army draftees during this time and found that draftees from Italy, Russia and Poland (who were not bilingual) scored lowest on intelligence tests while draftees from England, Scotland, Denmark, Germany, Sweden and Canada scored highest.[57] Psychologists viewed the lower IQ scores of southern and eastern Europeans as an indication of innately inferior intellectual capacities rather than as a reflection of their socioeconomic, cultural-biological conditions and limited English proficiency.

This body of research unjustly stigmatized Italian Americans as genetically and intellectually inferior and uneducable. The army intelligence test data was later used to justify discriminatory immigration and educational policies against Italian Americans (Kamin, 1974). The initial publication of the army intelligence data in 1921 occurred during the same year in which Congress passed a temporary emergency measure placing a numerical limitation on immigration (Kamin, 1974).

In his book, *A Study of American Intelligence* (1923),[58] Princeton University psychologist Carl Brigham[59] argued that American intelligence was declining in direct proportion to the number of new immigrants entering the United States who possessed "inferior blood." Brigham based his conclusions on an invalid analysis and interpretation of army intelligence test data.

Eugenicists like Carl Brigham advocated such policies as preserving "racial purity" by restricting immigration of "less developed" ethnic and racial groups (southern and eastern Europeans) and controlling the reproductive behavior of "inferior stock" individuals. In the concluding chapter of his book Brigham (1923) wrote:

> The deterioration of American intelligence is not inevitable, however, immigration should not only be restrictive but highly selective. . . . The *really important steps are those looking toward the prevention of the continued propagation of defective strain* [emphasis added] in the present population. . . . [60]

Thus, Brigham argued not only for immigration restriction but implicitly recommended controlling the reproductive behavior of immigrants possessing "inferior genes."

On February 20th, 1923, Francis Kinnicut of the Immigration Restriction League cited Brigham's "scientific" findings in his testimony before the United States Senate Committee on Immigration. Kinicutt strongly urged Congress to:

> . . . further restrict immigration from southern and eastern Europe . . . *the intelligence of the Italian immigration* . . . is of a very low grade . . . all rank far below the average intelligence for the whole country.[61]

A month earlier, in January 1923, psychologist Dr. Arthur Sweeney's book, *Mental Tests for Immigrants*, was made part of the appendix to the hearings of the House Committee on Immigration and Naturalization (Kamin, 1974). Testifying before the House Committee on Immigration and Naturalization, Sweeney characterized "Latin" [Italian] immigrants as "imbeciles" who possessed primitive brain structures "scarcely superior the ox . . . who think with their spinal cord rather than the brain."[62] He, too, urged Congress to "apply the new weapons of science [intelligence tests] to protect ourselves against the degenerate horde."[63]

During the 1920s "race psychologists" (a term then used for cross-cultural psychologists) also administered thousands of intelligence tests to native-born American and American-born children of Italian immigrants residing in New York, New Jersey and California (Young, 1922; Pinter, 1923; Maud, 1926; Graham, 1926; Mead, 1926; Hirsch, 1927; Kimball, 1930). Racist conclusions about the intellectual inferiority of American-born Italian children of Italian immigrants were drawn by several researchers affiliated with Ivy League academic institutions. In 1920, Katharine Murdoch, an instructor in psychology at Columbia University School of Social Work, wrote confidently in an academic journal, *School and Society*, that *Italian children* were *more retarded* [being overage for one's grade level] in their intellectual development than were "Negroes or Jews." Murdoch (1920) wrote:

> On the whole the colored boys seem to be about halfway between the Hebrews and the Italians. The *Italians* still maintain their position at the foot of the four races . . . this fact shows *that more retardation of the less gifted races does take place. . . .* [64]

For Italian American children, ability-stigmatizing stereotypes[65] drawn by "race psychologists" virtually locked them out of the upward flow of educational and social mobility. Formal intellectual achievement was made more difficult for our ancestors in our nation's intellectual institutions because most were regarded as not highly educable. This made it easier for the dominant white majority society to block our Italian ancestors' access to opportunities that required institutional credentials.

Psychology's intelligence testing's extrascientific agenda helped Congress to pass racist immigration laws that transformed American society and the lives of Italian American immigrants and their descendants. Intelligence testing data supported the passage of racist legislation in 1921 and again in 1924 that imposed a quota on Italian emigration to the United States. The first Emergency Quota Act was passed in 1921 and permitted the admission of only three percent of the numbers of each national group reported for the census of 1910.[66] This law favored countries of northern and western Europe, excluding those from southern and eastern countries. The second law, the 1924 Johnson-Reed Act, cut the previous quota to two percent by assigning each country an annual allowable quota based on the census of 1890, prior to the massive influx of southeastern Europeans after 1900. This law once again gave comparative advantage to the peoples of northern Europe. The Johnson Reed Act of 1924 dramatically reduced the volume of Italian immigrants entering the United States to below 29,000 per year after a peak of 349,042 in 1920 coming from southern and eastern Europe This quota was enforced for over forty years until it was repealed in 1965.[67]

INTELLECTUAL ABILITY STIGMATIZATION OF ITALIAN AMERICANS IN THE MEDIA

Today network, cable television and feature films are replete with stereotypical images of Italian Americans who are intellectual ability-stigmatized. Italian American protagonists are featured as either lacking in intelligence or as intellectually unsophisticated. Examples of feature films are: *Rocky I* (1976), *Saturday Night Fever* (1977), *Married to the Mob* (1988), and *My Cousin Vinny* (1992). Each of these films features protagonists who are uneducated but "street smart." Throughout the latter film, *My Cousin Vinny* (1992), attorney Vincent La Guardia Gambini (Joe Pesci) and girlfriend Mona Lisa Vito (Marisa Tomei) are ridiculed as vulgar, naïve, street-smart fools. Only at the penultimate moment in the film are both characters shown to be highly intelligent and extremely competent.

On prime-time television, Vinnie Barbarino, in *Welcome Back, Kotter*, is cast as an academic failure, more concerned about his sexual appeal to woman than his performance in school. On *Taxi* the role of villain Louie DePalma's and Carla Tortelli's role in *Cheers* confirms the media's tendency to portray Italians as uneducated individuals, occupying low status jobs and behaving in a vindictive manner.[68] In *Who's the Boss*? Tony Micelli (Tony Danza) is portrayed as an uneducated boxer turned domestic worker who is employed by a college-educated WASP female executive. More recently, in a prime-time television series, *That's Life* (2000), a New Jersey working-class, Italian American female protagonist was featured struggling to overcome her college professor's perception of her as an intellectual ability-stigmatized student who does not belong in college. This anecdotal account of intellectual ability-stigmatized Italian American characters portrayed in the media is validated by the empirical research of Lichter and Lichter, 1982, and Lichter, Lichter and Rothman, 1991.

The Center for Media and Public Affairs study found that in television prime-time programs during the period 1980-81, negative portrayals of Italian Americans outnumbered positive ones by a margin of nearly two to one. Moreover, the portrayal of Italian American criminals exceeded the portrayal of the total number of educated Italian American professional and business executives.[69] Specifically they found that one in six Italian Americans were portrayed as professional criminals, and only one in seven were portrayed as professionals or business executives. Most characters held low status jobs, and the majority of Italian-American protagonists did not speak proper English, frequently making them the butt of jokes. Historian's Iorizzo and Mondello (1980) traced the history of the portrayal of Italian Americans between the period of 1900-1979 in television, film, comic strips and comic books. They found that Italian American characters were depicted as comical, menacing and terrorizing.

In sum, Italian Americans are "ghettoized" in mostly negative portrayals and few, if any, Italian American characters are portrayed as prosperous, authoritative and well educated. It is indeed difficult to find examples of Italian American characters in mainstream Hollywood cinema or network television that are complex and self-determining.

SCAPEGOATING, ARCHETYPAL IMAGES OF ITALIANS AS ROGUES AND OUTLAWS

In the early part of the twentieth century Italian immigrants were valued in American society solely for their willingness to perform backbreaking physical labor that Americans were unwilling to undertake. They were seen as a cheap source of human labor to fuel the expanding industrial and economic growth of the American economy. As the largest of all immigrant groups, Italian immigrants encountered some of the most oppressive working conditions in the American labor market of industrial capitalism.

The heroic efforts of Italian laborers to survive and find meaning in a "heartless"[70] capitalist society that was rejecting of them have, rarely, if ever, been portrayed in feature films or network television. The courage, stoicism, perseverance, resilience, and toughness of Italian laborers who rose to the challenge of transforming and even sacrificing their lives in order to ensure the survival of their families and future generations of Italian Americans still remains invisible in the entertainment media and, therefore, to the general public. Unlike the archetypal outlaw, the archetypal hero, like the protagonist featured in Pietro Di Donato's *Christ in Concrete* (1939/1966), is principled, feels outraged by injustice and fights to protect society as well as for the values that are sacred to them. Rarely, if ever, are Italian Americans portrayed in the media as the upstanding and, at times, courageous citizens most Italian Americans are.

Despite the great artistic contributions of many Italian Americans to the Hollywood film industry, Italian Americans and their ancestors are continuously featured in the entertainment media as *rogue outlaws* who are driven by profit, greed, and competition to obtain power. These *outlaws* range free on the fringe of society, killing without conscience. Their drive for power outweighs any kind of moral value or sense of responsibility to the individual or to society.

For fully a century in feature films and network television, the Italian *mobster/outlaw* has psychologically carried America's *shadow*. America's collective disapproval of feelings, wishes and behaviors related to violence, greed, murderous rage, criminality and disregard for human life have been split off from the collective American psyche and displaced and projected onto the Italian American *rogue/mobster*. These are feelings, the expression of which all people are ambivalent about and deny in themselves. The most recent example of this phenomenon is America's ambivalent love affair with the hit HBO series *The Sopranos*.

The Sopranos, written and directed by third-generation Italian American David Chase (born David De Cesare), has stimulated many scholarly debates[71] among Italian American intellectuals and other non-Italian academics. However, the debate has yet to include a psychoanalytic and social psychological perspective that might illuminate the dynamics of power and social status that perpetuate *modern* ethnic racism.[72]

Late twentieth and early twenty-first century American corporate culture has bred individuals who commit "white-collar crime" with impunity, causing financial ruin for many innocent citizens by defrauding and betraying stockholders, employees and the public's trust. The naked financial greed of these white-collar criminals, like the greed of mobster/outlaw, is unmediated by any sense of moral or social responsibility to the community. As corporate culture unravels and America's family life is severely challenged by the voracious demands of postmodern corporate life, the nation's attention is riveted on Sunday evenings by the Home Box Office series, *The Sopranos*. This award-winning television series has metaphorically put its finger on the psychological and social ills that currently threaten the integrity of our social fabric as a nation and a society.

The Sopranos, in the words of cultural critic Elaine Showalter, is a "cultural Rorschach test." It is, observes professor of cultural journalism Ellen Willis,

> a parable of corruption and hypocrisy in the postmodern middle class, . . . But at the primal level, the inkblot is the unconscious. The murderous mobster is the predatory lust and aggression in all of us; his lies and cover-ups are ours; the therapist's fear is our own collective terror of peeling away those lies. The problem is we can't live with the lies, either.[73]

As Ellen Willis suggests, Tony Soprano *is* our mythical, lovable, murderous, psychopathic scapegoat. To maintain an inner sense of "goodness" and to defend against vulnerability, the viewing public develops the fantasy that "badness" is out there (in the Mafia) and can be controlled. This psychological process involves the defense mechanism of *projective identification*. If the viewer's identification with the dark side of Tony Soprano remains unconscious then the viewer does not have to experience their own aggression, greed, dissimulation or emotional emptiness. As a result, these unwanted parts of themselves can continue to be split off and projected onto the protagonists of *The Sopranos.* In turn, Italian Americans as a group can continue to be devalued. Devaluing Italian Americans as a group unconsciously permits dominant groups in American society to maintain their own sense of "goodness."

Rather than consciously confront the political and moral crises in our society brought about by the extant corruption in our institutions, and the betrayal of the public's trust by many of our corporate and political leaders, we prefer, as social psychological and psychoanalytic theory predict, to *unconsciously* locate our cultural demons in the 'other.' Television's critically acclaimed, *other*, Tony Soprano, of *The Sopranos*, is our cultural *other.* According to Colman, the scapegoat [like Tony Soprano] is a collective creation, a symbolic compromise for many individuals' negative projections which allows society's denials of its own negative tendencies. Colman says:

> A scapegoat is humanity's societal vessel, for the [group's] *shadow* . . . this has required sophisticated rationalizations based on what Erik Erikson (1972) has called pseudo speciation [speculation] to describe how a ruling or dominant group can justify locating the scapegoating function in its slave or any other group cast as different and lower than itself. We have many modern examples, the "greedy" Jew, the "stupid" black, the *"corrupt" Italian* . . . [74] [emphasis added]

Italian Americans have served as repositories of American society's unwanted or unacceptable feelings or impulses. Our national obsession for violence, and blood and our out-of-control appetite for wealth and power is siphoned off and projected onto Italian organized crime. Rather than consciously confront the corruption in our dominant society, we scapegoat organized crime. Arthur Colman (1995) writes:

> We use victims to siphon off our darkest, guiltiest thoughts and feelings . . . we use scapegoats to carry our guilt, to assure ourselves that we are innocent victims.[75]

By definition unconscious material is painful because it is too painful to acknowledge: We want to be entertained and diverted from our national pain at any cost.

Stereotypical images of Italian Americans as mobsters also serve to support the maintenance of hierarchical social power arrangements in which Italian Americans retain a subordinate position to other European American whites. In a society where today's robber barons may become tomorrow's philanthropists, Tony Soprano, during a psychotherapy session with Dr. Melfi, concisely sums up the hypocrisy (from his perspective) of America's capitalist system. Tony alludes to the historical experiences of Italian Americans that led him to choose an "alternate route to success." Tony explains to Dr. Melfi:

> Men like the Carnegies and the Rockefellers needed "worker bees" to build their cities and dig their subways to make them richer. But some of us refused these terms. Some of us wanted a piece of the action. We weren't educated like Americans, but we had the balls to take what we wanted.[76]

Fierce, defiant, and arrogant, Tony the *outlaw*, like white-collar criminals (who often but not always stop short of murder), does not bow down to convention or the law. Tony's observations also emphasize the differences between Americans and Italian Americans who did not acquire formal education (reinforcing the stereotype of intellectual ability stigmatization) in American institutions and, hence, are forced to value alternative forums of success such as lawful (and unlawful) entrepreneurship.

Carby (1987) writes that the purpose of stereotypes is not to reflect reality accurately but to serve as a disguise for societal reality. The disguise serves many purposes. It soothes the conscience of a society whose espoused ideals were blatantly contradicted by the behavior of its members. Many viewers who may be feeling trapped in their everyday conventional lives may vicariously identify with Tony's freedom to operate successfully outside of many of today's institutions in which power concentrated in the hands of a few increasingly trumps the values of our nation's "meritocracy." Tony's success gives viewers a sense of how things could be if we were outlaws and took matters into our own hands.

The mythic Italian American "mobster kinship groups" like the "Sopranos and Corleones," observes cultural critic Sandra Gilbert, "strike a special chord in the hearts of the heart of our country."[77] Might it be that in the spiritual wasteland of our twenty-first century, the deep and pervading sense of loss of the value of human connection could only be confronted in the web of violence of the mythic mobster family?

On-screen portrayals of Italian American families where loyalty, honor, responsibility to the family, and preservation of kinship ties are placed above individual self-interest have always received acclaim from American audiences. However, most portrayals of the mythic Italian American family occur in the context of Mafia kinship groups or in dumbed-down network television series, such as the current Emmy award-winning series *Everybody Loves Raymond* (2003) (although Raymond is a professional sports writer, his career is peripheral to the central dynamics of the show which focuses on emotionally intense family relationships). In this context, Italian Americans are still regarded as an *outgroup* who are disrespected by the dominant majority group but are thought to possess socially redeeming qualities.[78]

The Sopranos perpetuate pernicious stereotypes of Italian Americans. The national and international distribution of the syndicated series has a devastating impact on Italian America: Negative stereotypes of Italian Americans are given "eternal life" by the recycling of *The Sopranos* and *The Godfather* films. This takes on added significance when we consider that social psychological studies demonstrate that when people do not have direct contact with an ethnic group, their attitudes about an ethnic group is formed by portrayals of that ethnic group in the mass media.[79]

Many scholars concur that *The Godfather* perhaps more than anything else written about Italian Americans (except perhaps for *The Sopranos*) has done the greatest harm to the image of Italian Americans. The 1969 publication of Mario Puzo's novel *The Godfather*–which was on the *New York Times* bestseller list for sixty-seven weeks–and its commercially successful screen adaptations helped popularize the image of Italian Americans as gangsters. While twenty-one films featuring an Italian American main character as a mobster were produced between the end of the Second World War and the release of *The Godfather* in March 1972, at *least 300 crime stories* modeled on the saga of the Corleone family were produced between 1969 and 1975.[80] Unfortunately, Mafia stereotypes of Italian Americans have been popularized by some of the most celebrated Italian American directors, Francis Ford Coppola, Martin Scorsese, and writer Mario Puzo.[81] These talented and creative artists may be perceived by some Italian Americans as having entered a Mephistophlean bargain of selling their souls to dominant American establishments in order to be successful. The Italian American community's ambivalent perception of these great artists may oscillate between recognizing them as heroes and cultural role models to be emulated and or as "Uncle Toms" who also betrayed Italian America by perpetuating negative stereotypes.

For many Italian Americans artists, like Coppola, Scorsese, and Puzo, to sustain the political sensitivity of an ethnic minority identity in the film industry may not be conducive to becoming successful players in the game of professional advancement. In the film industry (particularly during the 1970s), being a symbol or representative of all persons of Italian American ancestry could be conflictual: One can be torn between their symbolic image to their community and their own professional tasks and goals.

Italian American writers and filmmakers have employed varying methods in confronting and responding to their institutionally disadvantaged position as Italian Americans. For example, the great *American* filmmaker and director Frank Capra (e.g., *It Happened One Night* [1934]; *Mr. Deeds Goes to Town* [1936]; *Mr. Smith Goes to Washington* [1939]; *It's a Wonderful Life* [1946]) was born in Sicily in 1903 and emigrated with his family to America when he was six years of age. Not surprisingly, most of America, including Italian America, is still unaware that Capra was a first-generation Italian American!

Several years after graduating from the California Institute of Technology with a degree in engineering, he began his career as a filmmaker. While Capra's film images and actors were as "American as apple pie," his films were emotionally infused with humanistic Italian moral and social values including the values of compassion, patience, hard work, individualism, humility, courage in the face of adversity and self-sacrifice. Capra the immigrant, writes film critic Lee Lourdeaux, "championed Italian virtues for a greedy, profit-driven America"[82] Lourdeaux observes that Capra was an idealist and a pragmatist who succeeded in Hollywood by (1) distancing himself from his ethnicity, (2) featuring "mainstream couples with Italian ideals"[83] and (3) using "blonde, non-ethnic women and all-American men to put across his intensely Italian vision of the country."[84]

Distancing from the Italian American community is understandable as an attempt at accommodation and survival. Despite Capra's silence about his Italian American identity, he appeared to possess sufficiently healthy self-esteem to creatively construct a successful film career at a time in American history when anti-Italian prejudice was blatant. In order to gain credibility and support in the film industry, Capra portrayed *nonvisibly Italian American* characters in white skin. Although one might view Capra's approach to success in the Hollywood film industry as akin to "passing as a white non-Italian European," the ethos of his films is intensely Italian.

However, one must also consider the psychological cost of "passing," invisibility, and compartmentalizing one's ethnic identity. The act of self-silencing represents another form of social oppression. The psychic energy a person is forced to expend to conceal important aspects of one's life is considerable. In fact the psychological and cultural literature on people of color document the negative psychological effects of passing as a long-term mechanism for managing discrimination (Gomez, 1999; West, 1999).

MODERN ETHNIC RACISM

Social psychological research has demonstrated that since the 1970s a more subtle form of racism has developed in the United States and Europe. While discrimination and prejudice has not been eradicated, the normative principles governing the expression of blatant racist or prejudiced attitudes have changed. Specifically, people have learned to act or to appear unprejudiced while inwardly maintaining their stereotypical views–this phenomenon is called *modern racism*.[85] In sum, people have learned to hide prejudice in order to avoid being labeled racist. Thus, blatant forms of racism are replaced with a modern form of objectivity that leaves the door open for *subtle bias*. Indeed there are many white Americans who intellectually reject racial bias and who strive to behave in fair and unbiased ways yet are unaware of their racial bias.

Social psychologists have demonstrated that *subtle racism* is much more insidious than overt racism because the perpetrator is unaware of his or her racial bias.[86] For example, social psychologists Thomas Pettigrew and Roel Meertens (1995) demonstrated the existence of *blatant* as well as *modern subtle racism* in three major western European countries: France, the Netherlands and Great Britain. In all three countries, those who scored high on the blatant prejudice scale were in favor of sending immigrants back to their home countries and expressed interest in restricting the civil rights of immigrants. In contrast, those who scored high on the subtle racism scale but low on the blatant racism scale rejected immigrants in more covert and subtle ways. Specifically, while they were not in favor of sending immigrants back to their home countries, they were *unwilling* to do anything to improve their relations with the immigrant population nor would they go along with efforts to increase the civil rights of that population. Moreover, participants who scored low on both blatant and subtle prejudice scales were prepared to take action to help immigrants remain in the country and were willing to proactively improve relations between immigrants and natives.

The subtlety prejudiced try not to be openly unfair but avoid meaningfully confronting targets of prejudice and their issues. The acting out of subtle prejudice toward Italian Americans is prevalent in "innocent jokes" and other cues indicating that Italian Americans are still perceived by dominant American society as an *outgroup*. For example, in her memoir *Were You Always an Italian?* (2000), journalist and essayist Maria Laurino writes about experiences in which her last name is frequently a target of Mafia-related "innocent jokes." Laurino writes:

> For second and third generations and beyond being an Italian American is a deceptively difficult legacy . . . [although] organized crime represents a minuscule fraction of Italian Americans (as everyone says they know, but people actually seem not to have registered, judging from the number of Mafia comments about my Italian name). . . . [87]

The remarks described by Laurino make the subtlety of these forms of individual level prejudice hard to document: Italian Americans who call attention to such harassment often appear to other whites as "too sensitive." Blatant discrimination is more easily documented.

The acting out of subtle prejudice toward Italian Americans in the public domain is also prevalent. In an interview with a journalist, former Governor Mario Cuomo related an experience regarding ethnic prejudice that he encountered with then Mayor John Lindsay. Mario Cuomo describes the encounter as follows:

> John Lindsay never understood it, he never understood it. He invited me to the [mayor's] mansion to see *The Godfather* with Matilda. He was trying to get me to join his administration. I said, "How can you invite me to see *The Godfather*? . . . This guy who kills people, murders them, plucks their eyes out, drugs them, and he's treated as a great guy, the whole community loves him. What are you saying with this movie?" He recalled that Lindsay replied, "Oh, it's only a movie, you're too sensitive."[88]

Like most of the subtlety prejudiced, former Mayor John Lindsay's subtle racism is insidious because he is blithely unaware of his ethnic bias.

Thirty years later, in October 2002, New York's Mayor Bloomberg boycotted the Annual New York Columbus Day Parade when the parade's organizers, the Columbus Foundation, objected to Bloomberg's having invited Italian American actors Lorraine Bracco (Dr. Melfi) and Dominic Chianese (Carrado, Uncle Junior) to march in the parade as his guests of honor. Both actors are cast members of *The Sopranos*. The Columbus Foundation objected to the mayor's having extended an invitation to these actors because they were cast members of a television program that openly defames Italian Americans. Mayor Bloomberg did not back down, he could not understand what the "fuss" was all about; he reasoned that he was honoring two accomplished Italian American actors; if they didn't march, he wasn't marching. The Columbus Foundation sought legal resolution to the conflict; the mayor withdrew from the Columbus Day parade in Manhattan and instead marched alongside both actors in the Bronx, Arthur Avenue, Columbus Day Parade. At no point in the public conflict did the mayor recognize or substantively address the issue of the defamation of Italian Americans. The mayor's response and the media's coverage of the conflict suggested that the parade's sponsor's were being "overly sensitive" about a *fictive* television series. The mayor and the media's defensive rcsponse were to act as if the Columbus Foundation's accurate perception of defamation was unwarranted. In so doing both the media and the mayor (as a representative of a government institution) failed to acknowledge their roles in perpetuating the defamation of Italian Americans. Until there is a willingness to understand that the defamation of Italian Americans is *real,* no resolution or reconciliation can take place.

As these anecdotes suggest, subtle ethnic racism exists not only at the level of the individual, but at the higher levels of institutions and culture. Cultural racism operates from the top-down and race prejudice operates from the bottom-up; their joint effect is institutional racism (Jones, 1998).[89]

CONCLUSION

In this essay I have argued that images of Italian Americans in the media have been determined for centuries by political, economic and historical contexts, and that these images are at variance with current and past southern Italian and Italian American realities. Negative stereotyping exerts an invisible yet psychologically powerful effect on Italian American's psyches, our aspirations, life chances, self-image, ethnic identity and self-esteem. Negative stereotyping of Italian Americans may also result in subtle forms of discrimination socially, professionally, and politically. Moreover, prejudice related to Italian Americans' perceived connection to the Mafia has placed a stigma on individuals of Italian descent.

While Italian Americans may have not had to deal with everyday racism as experienced by visible persons of color, the persistence of negative stereotyping of Italian Americans is a form of *subtle* racism. It is essential that derogatory stereotypes of Italian Americans be understood for what they are: a reflection of *subtle* racism that powerful and racially dominant majority groups use to rationalize their power privilege (Banks & Eberhard, 1998). As an identity group we have yet to acquire sufficient power and influence in the social hierarchy to alter the institutional arrangements that perpetuate stereotyping of Italian Americans in the media. Professor of law David Richards (a third-generation Italian American) writes that the Italian American story has been

> obscured and deformed by the demands of Americanization under circumstances of injustice. In fact, Italian Americans were themselves victimized by racism, both in Italy and the United States, and have good reasons in contemporary circumstances to refuse a continuing cultural acquiescence in an American cultural racism that is as unjustly stigmatizing of them as it is of Americans of color.[90]

If we are to relate as equals–along with other groups in the United States then Italian Americans need to be represented fairly, honestly, and accurately in public and academic cultures. In order for this to occur, Italian Americans need to conduct a power analysis of our place in the social hierarchy. Such a power analysis can point to new arenas for action on legal, legislative, and political as well as on personal levels.

NOTES

1. See David R. Roediger. (1994). *Towards the Abolition of Whiteness: Essays on Race, Politics, and Working Class History*. London: Verso; Vecoli, Rudolph J. (1994). Are Italian Americans just white folks? In Mary Jo Bona & Anthony Tamburri (Eds.), *Through the looking glass: Italian & Italian/American images in the media, Vol. 27*, 29-50. Staten Island, New York: American Italian Historical Association; and Jennifer

Gugliemo & Salvatore Salerno (Eds.) (2002). *Are Italians white? How race is made in America.* New York: Routledge Press.

2. C. G. Jung described ways in which individuals and cultures have *shadows*–qualities that are judged unacceptable and hence are hidden and denied. Cultures and individuals do not wish to acknowledge their own shadow, so they project them on to others, seeing those others as the problem.

3. Stereotypes are oversimplifications that we employ to make sense of the complex social environment that we live in. The process of stereotyping is thought to have evolutionary value in that, given our limited capacity to process constant complex stimuli in our environment, it allows us to take shortcuts and adopt certain rules of them to understand people. See Aronson et al. 2002.

4. Hogg, M. A., & Abrams, D. A. (1988). *Social identifications: A social psychology of intergroup relations and group processes.* London: Routledge.

5. See Wilder, D. A. (1986). Social categorization: Implications for creation and reduction of intergroup bias. In L. Berkowitz (Ed.), *Advances in experimental social psychology* (Vol. 19), San Diego, CA: Academic; Reichl, A. J. (1997). Ingroup favouritism and outgroup favouritism in low status minimal groups: Differential responses to status-related and status-unrelated measures. *European Journal of Social Psychology, 27*, 617-633.

6. Operario & Fiske, 46.

7. Susan Fiske. (1998). *Handbook of social psychology*, 264.

8. Research indicates that people can categorize others within microseconds after first seeing them. See Don Operario & Susan T. Fiske. (1998). Racism equals power plus prejudice: A social psychological equation for racial oppression, 33-53; and John F. Dovidio & Samuel L. Gaertner. (1998). On the nature of contemporary prejudice: The causes, consequences, and challenges of aversive racism, 6. In Jennifer L. Eberhardt & Susan T. Fiske (Eds.), *Confronting racism: The problem and response.* Thousand Oaks, CA: Sage Publications, Inc.

9. Aronson, 461; Susan T. Fiske. (1998). Stereotyping, prejudice, and discrimination. In D. T. Gilbert, S. T. Fiske, & G. Lindzey (Eds.), *Handbook of social psychology, Vol. 2*, 357-411. New York: McGraw Hill.

10. Don Operario & Susan Fiske. (1998). A social psychological equation of racial oppression. In Eberhardt, Jennifer & Fiske, Susan (Eds.), *Confronting racism: the problem and the response.* Thousand Oaks, CA: Sage, 42.

11. Operario & Fiske, 42.

12. See National Italian American New Bureau, February 26, 2001. *Italian Americans challenge stereotypes in The Sopranos.* Washington, D.C., 2.

13. See Robert S. Lichter, Linda S. Lichter, & Stanley Rothman. (1991). *Watching America.* New York: Prentice Hall, 198.

14. Richard Gambino. (1985). Italian Americans and the media: An agenda for a more positive image. In Lydio F. Tomasi (Ed.), *Italian American new perspectives in Italian immigration and ethnicity.* Staten Island, New York: Center for Immigration Studies, 67-77.

15. Arthur Colman. (1995). *Up from scapegoating: Awakening consciousness in groups.* Wilmette, Illinois: Chiron Publications, xv.

16. Colman, 7.

17. Colman, 7.

18. Colman, 5.

19. Don Operario & Susan Fiske. (1998). Racism equals power plus prejudice: A social psychological equation for racial oppression, 41.

20. Operario & Fiske, 34, 38.

21. Paolo Verdicchio. (1994). "If I was six feet tall, I would have been Italian American," Spike Lee's Guineas. In Peter Carravetta (Ed.), *Differentia: Review of Italian thought*. Flushing, NY: Queens College Press, 178.

22. Paolo Verdicchio, 179.

23. Psychoanalyst Michael Adams Vannoy suggests that "race" or "color" will gradually become less relevant and "ethnicity" more significant as a "category" given the sheer number, diversity, and differences between cultures in the United States. Thus, problems related to becoming conscious of the "diversity of diversity" of ethnic groups is, in Vannoy's view, best conceptualized as *ethnicism*. See Vannoy, Michael Adams. (1996). *The multicultural imagination: Race, color, and the unconscious*. New York: Routledge, 245.

24. Gabriella Garibaudi. (1996). Images of the South. In David Forgas & Robert Lumley (Eds.), *Italian cultual studies*, 17.

25. See Donna R. Gabaccia. (2000). *Italy's many diasporas*. Seattle, WA: University of Washington Press. Gabaccia states that ". . . charges of criminality, along with anarchy and violence, followed Italians everywhere, generating long lasting stereotypes" (189).

26. Historian Humbert Nelli dates the origin of the Mafia in Italy to the historical period of post-unification Italy in 1860. Nelli observes that subsequent to unification the economic conditions of the masses worsened; impoverished and helpless, peasants and farmers sought a protector to look out for their interests in a time of need. A locally important person, a *capo mafioso*, became a patron of a large number of people. Government authorities and members of the ruling classes also exploited the Mafia as a means of controlling the peasants. For example, landowners hired mafioso to collect rents and intimidate workers. Gradually, the Mafia assumed control of large estates by paying absentee landowners and replaced many feudal owners as members of the new ruling class. While the Mafiosa engaged in noncriminal and nonviolent activities, their power inhered from the fact that they would "engage in violence and crime of any time to reach their goals" (11). Under these conditions, observes Nelli, the Mafia in Sicily "functioned and flourished as an extralegal (and parallel) form of government" (8). Moreover, in the United States, up until the 1920s, most of organized crime in America was controlled by the Irish. Italian immigrants who joined youth gangs in ethnic "colonies" in America were not, as many thought, former members of Mafia groups in Italy. According to Nelli (1976), the *Black Hand* [Mano Nera] gang members were common criminals, many of whom had criminal records in Italy not connected to Mafia activities. They preyed upon Italian immigrants through extortion and blackmail and were unsuccessful in extending their power outside of the Italian community (70). In the earlier part of the twentieth century, the *Black Hand* [Mano Nera] was neither as powerful or effective as post-prohibition Mafia groups. Italian domination of organized crime did not occur until the emergence of post-prohibition Mafia groups who formed powerful criminal syndicates, often in combination with Jewish associates. See Humbert Nelli. (1976). *The business of crime*. New York: Oxford University Press.

27. Landrine, Klonoff, & Brown-Collins. (1995). Cultural diversity and methodology in feminist psychology: Critique, proposal, empirical evidence. In Hope Landrine (Ed.) *Bringing cultural diversity to feminist psychology: Theory, research and practice*. Washington, D.C.: American Psychological Association, 55-76.

28. Hope Landrine. (1995). Introduction: Cultural diversity, contextualism, and feminist psychology. In Hope Landrine (Ed.), *Bringing cultural diversity to feminist psychology: Theory, research, and practice.* Washington, D.C.: American Psychological Association, 16.

29. Bridget Brander Rasmussen, Eric Klineberg, Irene J. Nexica, & Matt Wray. (Eds.). (2001). *The making and unmaking of Whiteness.* Durham, NC: Duke UP, 8.

30. Operario & Fiske, 36.

31. Guterl, Matthew Pratt. (2001). The color of race in America. Washington: Washington State University Press, 18.

32. Native-born Americans hostile to newcomers or "new immigrants" were called "nativists."

33. Gabaccia. (2000), 153, 239.

34. R. Richard Banks & Jennifer L. Eberhardt. (1998). Social psychological processes and the legal bases of racial categorization. In Jennifer L. Eberhardt & Susan Fiske (Eds.), *Confronting racism: The problem and the response.* Thousand Oaks, London: Sage Publications, 65.

35. Banks & Eberhardt, 67.

36. Clive Webb. (2002). The lynching of Sicilian immigrants in the American South, 1886-1910. *American Nineteenth Century History.* Spring, *3* (1) Webb, 54.

37. Rudolph Vecoli. (1985). The search for an Italian American identity: Continuity and change. In Lydio Tomasi (Ed.), *Italian Americans new perspectives in Italian immigration and ethnicity.* Staten Island, New York: Center for Migration Studies of New York, Inc., 100.

38. George E. Pozzeta. (1979). The mulberry district of New York City: The years before World War One. In Robert F. Hanney and Jean Vincenza Scarpaci (Eds.), *Little Italies in North America.* Toronto: Multicultural History Society of Ontario, 23.

39. Robert Orsi. (1992). The religious boundaries of an in-between people: Street *feste* and the problem of the dark-skinned other in Italian Harlem, 1920-1990. *American Quarterly, 44* (3), 314.

40. Robert Orsi, 314, 315.

41. Gordon Allport. (1954). *The nature of prejudice.* Cambridge, MA: Addison Wesley, 136.

42. Pavalko, Ronald M. (1980, October). Racism and the new immigration: An interpretation of the assimilation of white ethnics in American society. *Sociology and Social Research, 65* (1), 60.

43. Donna R. Gabaccia. (2000), 125.

44. Pasquale Verdicchio, 178.

45. The long-term psychological effects of the ambiguities of our racial status in American society are surfacing in the cultural productions of contemporary Italian American writers. For example, in her book, *Taking Back My Name* (1991), Italian American writer Maria Mazzotti Gillan addresses the social and psychological realities of growing up Italian American in the 1950s. In her poem, "In the Still Photograph, circa 1950," she writes: "Even in the standard family picture,/we do not look American" and in "Memory We Are Walking," "We laugh and capture mulberries . . ./I am happy. I do not know./that in the houses neighboring the park/people have watched us. They hate/our dark skin, our immigrant clothes." In "Growing Up Italian" she remembers how "I hoped for a miracle that would turn my dark skin light,/that would make me pale and blonde and beautiful;/ . . . I woke up cursing/all those who taught me to hate

my dark, foreign self." See Maria Mazzotti Gillan. (1991). *Taking back my name*. San Francisco, CA: malafemmina press.

46. According to Professor Richard Gambino (1998), the British originated the idiom "dagoe" (a term similar in meaning to the American term "greenhorn") to cast Italian immigrants in negative racist terms. See Richard Gambino. (1977). *Vendetta: The true story of the largest lynching in U.S. history*. Garden City, NY: Doubleday.

47. Webb, 57.

48. Richard Gambino, 8.

49. Clive Webb, 54.

50. Richie Perez. (1997). From assimilation to annihilation: Puerto Rican images in U.S. films. In Clara Rodriguez (Ed.), *Latin looks*. Boulder, CO: Westview Press, 146.

51. Richie Perez, 146.

52. Richie Perez, 146.

53. French psychologists Alfred Binet and Theodore Simon developed the first cognitively based intelligence measure that was intended for use as a basic screening instrument to determine which children in then overcrowded public schools would benefit from a mainstream curriculum. The French Binet-Simon scale was translated and imported to America and significantly revised by Lewis Terman in 1911 and 1915. Terman standardized the revised test near Stanford, California, hence, the "Stanford-Binet" Intelligence Test. See Richard R. Valencia & Lisa A. Suzuki. (2000). In *Intelligence testing in minority students: Foundation, performance, factors, and assessment issues*. Thousand Oaks: Sage Publications, Inc.

54. Terman strongly supported the use of intelligence tests as educational tests for educational tracking via homogeneous tracking, and he also argued for tests to be used for determining one's vocational fitness in the workforce.

55. Quoted in Richard R. Valencia & Lisa A. Suzuki. (2001). Historical issues in intelligence testing and minority students. In *Intelligence testing in minority students: Foundation, performance, factors, and assessment issues*. Thousand Oaks, London: Sage Publications, Inc., 6.

56. Army Alpha and Beta tests adapted from the Binet-Simon intelligence scales assessed memory, comprehension, attention, judgment and reasoning.

57. Leon Kamin. (1974). *The science and politics of IQ*. Potomac, MD: Erlbaum Associates, 290.

58. Carl Brigham. (1923). *A study of American intelligence*. Princeton, NJ: Princeton University Press.

59. Dr. Carl Brigham who developed the infamous Scholastic Aptitude Test (SAT) recanted the validity of the Army test data for use as an accurate measure of racial differences between the foreign-born and native Americans. In his words: "For purposes of comparing individuals or groups, it is apparent that tests in the vernacular [English] must be used only with individuals having equal opportunities to acquire the vernacular of the test. . . . This review has summarized some of the more recent test findings which show that comparative studies of various national and racial groups may not be made with existing tests, and which show, in particular, that one of the most pretentious of these comparative racial studies–the writer's own–was without foundation." Carl Brigham. (1930). Intelligence tests of immigrant groups. *Psychological Review, 37*, 165.

60. Carl Brigham. (1923), 210.

61. Hearings before the Committee on Immigration, United States Senate, February 20, 1923. Washington, D.C.: Government Printing Office, 1923, 80-81.

62. Hearings before the Committee on Immigration and Naturalization, House of Representatives, December 26, 27, and 31, 1923, and January 2, 3, 4, 5, 7, 8, 9, 10 and 19, 1924. Washington, D.C.: Government Printing Office, 1924, 589-594. The most primitive part of the brain shared with all species is the brainstem surrounding the top of the spinal cord. This primitive structure regulates basic life functions such as breathing and metabolism. For Sweeney to allege that the "Latin" thinks with their spinal cord is to accord the "Latin" the same place on the evolutionary scale as that of a reptile. Sweeny's remarks imply that the "Latin" lacks the neurological structures (the neocortex) and capacities that make us uniquely human, i.e., the human ability to think, process information, make abstractions, or learn from experience.

63. Hearings before the Committee on Immigration, 589-94.

64. Katharine Murdoch. (1920). Educational research and statistics. *School and Society*, *XI* (266), 150.

65. Social psychologist Claude M. Steele's research has demonstrated how negative stereotypes about a group's intellectual abilities can impede an individual's academic achievement. See Claude M. Steele. (1998). A threat in the air: How stereotypes shape intellectual identity and performance. In Jennifer L. Eberhardt & Susan T. Fiske (Eds.), *Confronting racism: The problem and the response*. Thousand Oaks, London: Sage Publications, 202-232.

66. Stefano Luconi. (2001). *From paesani to White ethnics*. Albany, New York: State University of New York Press, 44.

67. Stefano Luconi, 49.

68. Robert S. Lichter, Linda S. Lichter, & Stanley Rothman. (1991). *Watching America*. New York: Prentice Hall Press, 244.

69. Robert S. Lichter & Linda S. Lichter. (1982). *Italian American characters in television entertainment*. West Hempstead, NY: Commission for Social Justice, i-ii.

70. See Pietro Di Donato's revolutionary and thinly disguised autobiographical novel, *Christ in Concrete* (1939) which immortalizes oppressed Italian immigrant laborers. Di Donato's novel critiques the systems of capitalism and Catholicism that exploit and oppress immigrant laborers; the novel's protagonists engage in an heroic struggle against the terrible injustices brought upon them by a "heartless" society. Di Donato was a bricklayer, novelist, playwright and short story writer. See Pietro Di Donato. (1966). Reprint. *Christ in Concrete*. Indianapolis, IN: Bobbs-Merrill.

71. See Glen O. Gabbard. (2002). *The psychology of the Sopranos: Love, death, desire and betrayal in America's favorite gangster family*. New York: Basic Books; Regina Barreca (Ed.). (2002). *A sitdown with The Sopranos: Watching Italian American culture on TV's most talked-about series*. New York: Palgrave Macmillan; David R. Simon with Tamar Love. (2002). *Tony Soprano's America: The criminal side of the American dream*. Boulder, CO: Westview Press; David Lavery. (Ed.). (2002). *This thing of ours*. New York: Columbia UP.

72. Social psychologists suggest that despite the apparent reduction of visible stereotyping of African Americans and other racial minorities, a new and more subtle kind of racism has taken its place: modern racism. In modern racism people on the surface appear not to harbor prejudice when in fact racist attitudes exist just beneath the surface. See Gaertner, S. L., & Dovidio J. F. (1986). The aversive form of racism. In J. F. Dovidio & S. L. Gaertner (Eds.), *Prejudice, discrimination, and racism: Theory and research*. Orlando, FL: Academic P, 61-89.

73. Ellen Willis. (2002). Our mobsters, ourselves. In David Lavery (Ed.), *This thing of ours: Investigating the Sopranos*. New York: Columbia University Press, 8.

74. Colman, 9.
75. Colman, 16.
76. Quoted in E. Anthony Rotundo. (2002). Wonderbread and stugots: Italian American manhood and *The Sopranos*. In Regina Barreca (Ed.), *A sitdown with The Sopranos: Watching Italian American culture on TV's most talked-about series*. New York: Palgrave Macmillan, 49.
77. Sandra Gilbert. (2002). Life with the (God) father. In Regina Barreca (Ed.), *A sitdown with The Sopranos: Watching Italian American culture on TV's most talked-about series*. New York: Palgrave Macmillan.
78. Research conducted by Princeton University social psychologist Susan Fiske has shown that there are two kinds of *outgroups* in American culture today. The first kind of *outgroup* is respected but disliked; this type of *outgroup* is seen as competent but not sociable, e.g., Jews, Germans, Asians, militant gay men, nontraditional women (lesbians, feminists and career women) and militant African Americans. They are seen as competent but not sociable. The second type of *outgroup* is disrespected but liked, e.g., traditionally subordinate African Americans, Hispanics, Native Americans, traditional women, feminine gay men and the physically disabled. They are seen as incompetent but have some socially redeeming traits. Perceptions of Italian America as portrayed in the media clearly indicate that Italian Americans belong to the second type of outgroup, i.e., Italian Americans, like many minorities, are disrespected and viewed as incompetent but are liked because they are warm, emotional, family-oriented, artistic and interested in food. Ambivalent racism posits that an outgroup can be respected but disliked, or disrespected but not liked but *not* both liked and respected. See Susan T. Fiske. (1998). Stereotyping, prejudice, and discrimination. In D. T. Gilbert, S. T. Fiske, & G. Lindzey (Eds.), *Handbook of social psychology, Vol. 2*. New York: McGraw Hill, 357-411.
79. Richie Perez. (1997). Puerto Rican images in U.S. films. In Clara Rodriguez (Ed.), *Latin looks*. Boulder, CO: Westview Press, 161.
80. Luconi, 49.
81. Second-generation Italian American writer Mario Puzo, born in New York City in 1920, was the son of illiterate Italian immigrants. As a critically acclaimed, but not well remunerated writer, Puzo wrote *The Godfather* while he was in his forties. Film director Francis Ford Coppola collaborated with Puzo on the scripts for the phenomenally successful and critically acclaimed films, *The Godfather Part I* (1972) and *The Godfather Part II* (1974). Third-generation Italian American film director Francis Ford Coppola grew up in a middle-class family and was the son of a successful symphony flutist (first flutist for Arturo Toscannini) who had always wanted recognition as a composer for films, "but his big break never came." The Coppola family's success ethic (to succeed in terms of money and public recognition), observes film critic Lourdeaux, would spur Coppola for years from one all-consuming project to the next.
82. Lee Lourdeaux. (1990). *Italian and Irish filmmakers in America*. Philadelphia, PA: Temple UP, 173.
83. Lee Lourdeaux, 132.
84. Lee Lourdeaux, 131.
85. Aronson, 492.
86. James Jones. (1998). The essential power of racism, 285. In Eberhardt & Fiske (Eds.).
87. Maria Laurino. (2000). *Were you always Italian*? New York: W. W. Norton.
88. Maria Laurino, 35.

89. James M. Jones. (1998). *The essential power of racism,* 282. In Eberhardt & Fiske (Eds.).

90. David Richards. (1998). *Italian American: The radicalizing of an ethnic identity.* NY: New York University Press, 236.

REFERENCES

Allport, Gordon W. (1954). *The nature of prejudice.* Cambridge, MA: Addison-Wesley.

Aronson, Elliot, Wilson, Timothy D., & Akert, Robin M. (2002). *Social psychology. 4th edition.* New Jersey: Pearson Education, Inc.

Barreca, Regina (Ed.). (2002). *A sitdown with The Sopranos: Watching Italian American culture on TV's most talked-about series.* New York: Palgrave Macmillan.

Brigham, Carl. (1923). *American intelligence.* Princeton, NJ: Princeton University Press.

Brigham, Carl. (1930). Intelligence tests of immigrant groups. *Psychological Review, 37,* 158-165.

Carby, H. (1987). *Reconstructing womanhood: The emergence of the African American woman novelist.* New York: Oxford University Press.

Colman, Arthur. (1995). *Up from scapegoating. Awakening consciousness in groups.* Wilmette: Chiron.

Di Donato, Pietro. (1939/1966). Reprint. *Christ in concrete.* Indianapolis, IN: Bobbs-Merrill.

Fiske, Susan T. (1998). Stereotyping, prejudice, and discrimination. In D. T. Gilbert, S. T. Fiske, & G. Lindzey (Eds.), *Handbook of social psychology, Vol. 2* (pp. 357-411). New York: McGraw Hill.

Forgas, David & Lumley, Robert. (Eds.). (1996). *Italian cultual studies.* New York: Oxford University Press.

Gabaccia, Donna R. (2000). *Italy's many diasporas.* Seattle, WA.: University of Washington Press.

Gabbard, Glen O. (2002). *The psychology of the Sopranos: Love, death, desire and betrayal in America's favorite gangster family.* New York: Basic Books.

Gambino, Richard. (1977). *Vendetta: The true story of the largest lynching in U.S. history.* Garden City, NY: Doubleday.

______. (1985). Italian Americans and the media: An agenda for a more positive image. In Lydio F. Tomasi (Ed.), *Italian American new perspectives in Italian immigration and ethnicity.* Staten Island, New York: Center for Immigration Studies, 67-77.

Gomez, J. (1999). Black lesbians: Passing, stereotypes, and transformation. In E. Brandt (Ed.), *Dangerous liaisons: Blacks, gays, and the struggle for equality* (pp. 161-177). New York: New Press.

Graham, Virginia Taylor. (1926). The intelligence of Italian and Jewish children in the habit clinics of the Massachusetts Division of Mental Hygiene. *Journal of Abnormal and Social Psychology, 20,* 371-376.

Guterl, Matthew Pratt. (2001). The color of race in America. Washington: Washington State University Press.

Harmon-Jones, E., Greenberg, J., Solomon, S., & Simon, L. (1996). The effects of mortality salience on intergroup biases between minimal groups. *European Journal of Social Psychology*, *26*, 677-681.

Hearings before the Committee on Immigration, United States Senate, February 20, 1923. (1923). Washington, D.C.: Government Printing Office, 80-81.

Hearings before the Committee on Immigration and Naturalization, House of Representatives, December 26, 27, and 31, 1923, and January 2, 3, 4, 5, 7, 8, 9, 10 and 19, 1924. (1924). (Washington, D.C.: Government Printing Office, 589-594.

Hogg, M. A. & Abrams, D. A. (1988). *Social identifications: A social psychology of intergroup relations and group processes*. London: Routledge.

Hooton, Earnest A. (1939/1972). *Crime and the man*. Westport: Greenwood Press.

Iorizzo, L. & Mondello, S. (1980). *The Italian Americans*. Boston: Twayne Publishers.

Kamin, Leon J. (1974). *The science and politics of IQ*. Potomac, MD: L. Erlbaum Associates.

Landrine, Hope, Klonoff, & Brown-Collins (Eds.): (1995). *Bringing cultural diversity to feminist psychology: Theory, research and practice*. Washington, D.C.: American Psychological Association.

Laurino, Maria. (2000). *Were you always Italian?* New York: W.W. Norton.

Lavery, David. (Ed.). *This thing of ours: Investigating the Sopranos*. New York: Columbia University Press.

Lichter, Robert, S. & Lichter, Linda S. (1982). *Italian American characters in television entertainment*. West Hempstead, NY: Commission for Social Justice.

Lichter, S. Robert, Lichter, Linda S., & Rothman, Stanley. (1991). *Watching America*. New York: Prentice Hall.

Lourdeaux, Lee. (1990). *Italian and Irish filmmakers in America*. Philadelphia, PA: Temple University Press.

Luconi, Stefano. (1999). Mafia-related prejudice and the rise of Italian Americans in the United States, *Patterns of Prejudice*, *33* (1), 43-51.

Luconi, Stefano. (2001). *From paesani to white ethnics*. Albany, New York: State University of New York Press.

Maud, Merrill, A. (1926). Mental differences in children referred to a psychological clinic. *Journal of Applied Psychology*, *10*, 470-486.

Mead, Margaret. (1927). Group intelligence tests and linguistic disability among Italian children. *School and Society*, *XXV* (642), 465-468.

Murdoch, Katharine. (1920). Educational research and statistics. *School and Society*, *XI* (266), 147-150.

National Italian American New Bureau. (February 26, 2001). *Italian Americans challenge stereotypes in The Sopranos*. Washington, D.C.

Nelli, Humbert S. (1976). *The business of crime*. New York: Oxford University Press.

Operario, Don & Fiske, Susan. (1999). A social psychological equation of racial oppression. In Eberhardt & Fiske (Eds.), *Confronting racism the problem and the response*. Thousand Oaks, CA, 33-53.

Orsi, Robert. (1992). The religious boundaries of an in-between people: Street *feste* and the problem of the dark-skinned other in Italian Harlem, 1920-1990. *American Quarterly*, *44* (3).

Pavalko, Ronald M. (1980, October). Racism and the new immigration: An interpretation of the assimilation of white ethnics in American society. *Sociology and Social Research, 65* (1), 56-77.

Perez, Richie. (1997). From assimilation to annihilation: Puerto Rican images in U.S. films. In Clara Rodriguez (Ed.), *Latin looks* (pp. 104-120). New York: Westview Press, a Division of Harper Collins.

Pettigrew, T.F. & Meertens, R.W. (1995). Subtle and blatant prejudice in Western Europe. *European Journal of Social Psychology, 25* (1), 56-76.

Pinter, Rudolf. (1923). Comparison of American and foreign children on intelligence tests. *Journal of Educational Psychology, 14*, 292-95.

Pozzeta, George E. (1979). The mulberry district of New York City: The years before World War One. In Robert F. Hanney & Jean Vincenza Scarpaci (Eds.), *Little Italies in North America.* Toronto: Multicultural History Society of Ontario.

Rasmussen, Bridget Brander, Klineberg, Eric, Nexica, Irene J., & Wray, Matt. (Eds.). (2001). *The making and unmaking of whiteness.* Durham, NC: Duke UP.

Reichl, A. J. (1997). Ingroup favoritism and out-group formation in low status minimal groups: Differential responses to status-related and status-unrelated measures. *European Journal of Social Psychology, 27*, 617-633.

Richards, David J. (1998). *Italian American: The radicalizing of an ethnic identity.* NY: New York University Press.

Rodriguez, Clara E. (1997). *Latin looks.* New York: Westview Press, a Division of Harper Collins.

Roediger, David R. (1994). *Towards the abolition of whiteness: Essays on race, politics, and working class history.* London: Verso.

Terman, Lewis. (1916). *The measurement of intelligence.* Boston, MA: Houghton Mifflin.

Wilder, D.A. (1986). Social categorization: Implications for creation and reduction of intergroup bias. In L. Berkowitz (Ed.), *Advances in experimental social psychology Vol. 19* (pp. 291-355). New York: Academic Press.

Wilson II, Clint C. & Gutierrez, Felix. (1995). *Race, multiculturalism and the media.* Second Edition. Thousand Oaks, CA: Sage.

Valencia, Richard R. & Suzuki, Lisa A. (Eds.). (2001). *Intelligence testing and minority students.* Thousand Oaks: Sage.

Vannoy, Michael Adams. (1996). *The multicultural imagination: race, color, and the unconscious.* New York: Routledge.

Vecoli, Rudolph J. (1985). The search for an Italian American identity: Continuity and change. In Lydio Tomasi (Ed.), *Italian Americans: New perspectives in Italian immigration and ethnicity* (pp. 88-112). Staten Island, New York: Center for Migration Studies of New York, Inc.

Vecoli, Rudolph J. (1994). Are Italian Americans just white folks? In Mary Jo Bona & Anthony Tamburri (Eds.), *Through the looking glass: Italian & Italian/American images in the media, Vol. 27* (pp. 29-50). Staten Island, New York: American Italian Historical Association.

Verdicchio, Paolo. (1994). "If I was six feet tall, I would have been Italian American," Spike Lee's Guineas. In Peter Carravetta (Ed.), *Differentia: Review of Italian thought* (p. 178). Flushing, NY: Queens College Press.

Webb, Clive. (2002). The lynching of Sicilian immigrants in the American South, 1886-1910. *American Nineteenth Century History*, Spring, *3* (1) 55.

West, C. (1999). Cornel West on heterosexism and transformation. In E. Brandt (Ed.), *Dangerous liaisons: Blacks, gays, and the struggle for equality* (pp. 290-305). New York: New Press.

Young, Kimball. (1922). Intelligence tests of certain immigrant groups. *Scientific Monthly*, *15*, 417-434.

With Him on the Trapeze

E. Mark Stern

SUMMARY. This is a collective telling of several psychotherapeutic relationships brought into a singular account. Be aware that each person in this article, living and dead, exists within the bounds of this account with the author's 50 years of the practice of psychotherapy remaining the sole constant. *[Article copies available for a fee from The Haworth Document Delivery Service: 1-800-HAWORTH. E-mail address: <docdelivery@haworthpress.com> Website: <http://www.HaworthPress.com> © 2004 by The Haworth Press, Inc. All rights reserved.]*

KEYWORDS. Therapeutic boundary, homelessness, roguishness, dual relationships, creativity, religiosity, disappointment, hospitalization

Unwashed hair, mottled and woven into a bun. Conjure somewhere in your mind a tall, quite thin, quixotic man, living on the social boundary.

E. Mark Stern, EdD, ABPP, is a Fellow of the American Psychological Association, the American Psychological Society, and the Acedemy of Clinical Psychology. Dr. Stern is Professor Emeritus, Graduate Faculty of Arts and Sciences at Iona College in New Rochelle, New York. He maintains a private practice in psychotherapy in New York City and in Dutchess County in upstate New York.

[Haworth co-indexing entry note]: "With Him on the Trapeze." Stern, E. Mark. Co-published simultaneously in *The Psychotherapy Patient* (The Haworth Press, Inc.) Vol. 13, No. 1/2, 2004, pp. 123-130; and: *Saints and Rogues: Conflicts and Convergence in Psychotherapy* (ed: Robert B. Marchesani, and E. Mark Stern) The Haworth Press, Inc., 2004, pp. 123-130. Single or multiple copies of this article are available for a fee from The Haworth Document Delivery Service [1-800-HAWORTH, 9:00 a.m. - 5:00 p.m. (EST). E-mail address: docdelivery@haworthpress.com].

http://www.haworthpress.com/web/TPP

Digital Object Identifier: 10.1300/J358v13n01_05

Jude's green eyes head on beyond my gaze into streams into madness. As they avoid human linkage, his vision is nonetheless poised.

Jude stood slumped in stature to a bit less than six feet. He wore an oversized Harlequin patterned shirt. On a seasonally hot, humid July New York day, Jude had invented for his comport a twirl of newspaper, leaving open spaces to provide cooling ventilation. Jude believed he kept company with the seasonal guardians. His entire wardrobe had been expropriated from the discard bin at a homeless shelter.

He walked the city streets barefoot through spring, summer and fall. Hibernal through most of winter, bundled rags crisscrossed his legs and feet reminiscent of a medieval wanderer.

His words were guarded, spoken almost in whispers supporting ours as a sacred match.

Jude was a pre-Christian son of the Catholic Church. Living in the midst of the 1960s, he would, during the "artists' mass" stately move himself into the procession of priest and alter-servers. During the rubrics of the consecration, he would once again move into the aisle glistening in rare liturgical dance. Languid arms raised, then dropped, as if, navigated into a mystical furrow.

There were times. The bishop's visit was one. Then trusted proctors, caring of Jude and just as loyal to clergy, would gently tweak him onto the outskirts. On the outskirts, Jude mumbled monotone malefic meditations. Through moments in the ritual, Jude bowed deeply. He never received the blessed sacrament, but, as the rubrics called for a final purifying of the chalices, Jude again slipped into a poetry of motion.

The priests at the university's Catholic chapel were then a tidy more tolerant. Themselves the desperadoes and adventurers of the 1960s, the two who come to mind left the official ministry of Church visible. In their way they each loved and feared Jude, seeing in him an incarnate gnosis.

Jude was, after all, messianic. More nymph than Christ. Sworn to the practice of *imitatio dei*, he was known, by some, for his unpredictable trippings with spasmodic demons. Yet those who heard these squalls with the devil's agents were often privy to the guardian spirits. Some liked being in Jude's company. Others despaired.

During the second of his two brief hospitalizations, Jude transformed his smearing practices to oozing poster paints and later acrylics onto newsprint. These were creased into balls and stuffed as insulation into his duffle. Sometime Jude was introduced by a master of traditional icons on the use of gold leaf. The crinkled and puckered papers, when finally unrolled, looked as if jewels had been set against backgrounds of mountainous masses of gray and black.

Jude was officially homeless, except for sharing movable quarters with Lucille, a former nun who had lately established a steady enough business of apartment and house sitting. It was in those many kitchens, on tables and countertops, that Jude set into new formats of his paper and gold leaf constructions. While sitting for an established abstract impressionist, Jude tore into several discarded drafts left in a recycling pile. These became a new medium for what even Lucille conceded to be a magical-mystical act. Even so, she was alarmed at the mania of his energy and bargained hard for him to contact me for psychotherapy.

I was, at the time, in addition to teaching and building my fee-for-service practice, an informal consultant to a pacifistic group of young volunteers of a faith-based bread-line and sometime overnight shelter. Living in the neighborhood of the shelter enabled me to be on call when emotional crises occurred. Lucille had become a mainstay of the community, so it was no surprise when she asked if I would agree to talk with Jude.

In fairness, Lucille had her doubts that he'd keep any kind of regular appointments. Yet, after ringing my doorbell, we set up a meeting time later that day. He brought his bundle of art, as he called it. Mendicancy, a few words commented on my office, and the tilt of his wispy curled beard filled the agenda. It was agreed that since he had no money, he would barter his art for my psychological help.

Our work invoked tenderness, remorse, a litany of regrets, but more importantly, an enthusiasm that, for once, he'd found someone who would unconditionally accept him. His expression began with a studied crudeness. Tenses shifted from present to the what might have been. There was a seafaring ancestry. His Newfoundlander mother hooked rugs which she sold from the side of their house. Tourists, when they appeared in summer, were foundations for apparitions. He looked first to their memories then to me and through me. Then he paced. His sights were set. I had a clear notion that he was attempting to see me in all dimensions. It would all count.

Some sort of cosmic sensibility. *Fortissimo*. Then a reverse pacing.

We scheduled the next five sessions. He introduced a sequence of seldom used words: "daft"; "recoil"; "exoneration"; "retract." Repetition of terms left me with an odd sense of duplicity. But the whispers grew stronger. The word groupings were tormenting. He grew paler.

Yet, sandwiched as in a cocoon, not so much eccentricity as an attempt at camaraderie.

He missed the sixth session. When we met later that week, he complained that too much time had elapsed. And besides, he wanted to give me a piece of art. It was due, he said. I could choose between five of his creations. I felt myself indulging in a bit of banditry. The larger trust could/might well be betrayed.

The painting I picked was night-veiled. A dock turned toward what appeared to be a sea in neverending expanse. Loneliness presided. It was twilight when I made my choice. And what I chose was revealing. Jude knew me for what I had taken of his. Cold cash never works that way. Propensity and partiality had been established. It was left to me to decipher whether there was something counterfeit in my choice. If so, then what of our work?

I asked the best of questions. He answered that he felt remorse, agony. "Can you enlarge on that?" He thought that there might be some vastness in his response. He felt sorry, he said, for the frustration teachers seemed to have; priests who, for a time, asked to hear his confession. He said he had to make up sins in order to make up for sins. When I asked him to explain, he said "Like what's happening right now." Like some anagram, the answer was there in all that was there.

Pierce into what, above all, what was he was expecting, or better, what was he needing from this process? Monologues, and there were many, made little sense.

How to proceed? "I want to retract?" he said, as he had said about other things? "No! Retract–retract." "Does God exist?" He insisted that that was a matter of how he could ask the question. "Do you exist?" he asked me, looking, as if seeing me now in a way. "Do you dance for Him? . . . Paint for Him?" It would have come to this: "I am Him." So I had finally asked him about his liturgical dances. Danced on the outskirts of the eleven o'clock artists' mass? The young volunteers attended that mass. They were welcome, even though chapel was for students and other members of the university community.

"Does Lucille know that god dances?" He said that he wouldn't want to count on anything, since being in and out of being god was puzzling. How did he decide the when of each feeling? "When 'when' boils over," he replied. There was no trace of a chuckle. "I circle around like an orbit circles and is a circle." I felt like a member of the trade as I asked when he first noticed. Then, in better words for me: "What epiphany? . . . How the awakening?" He made an attempt, stuttering as he spoke, telling me that that painful desire was his way of knowing desire. For him the tourists who purchased his mother's hooked scatter rugs desired. He had so little desire for his own mother. The tourists were the falcons who took what they wanted and brought it to their nests.

So to believe that Jude was/is a person? How come the switch to a god? Prowling around such questions became the provocation to ask about his father. "My father was a teacher and I was his incorrigible." "Was? Alive?" Jude left when he could and that was his kindness shown. He was not about to be his parents' "incorrigible." He thought it better to never see them again. "No, I have no reason to believe he's dead. But she died long ago." Again he looked at me for some sign. Again he entered into his litany of detached words: "recoil: I recoil; you recoil, they have recoiled?" Other words were conjugated: some were verbs, others nouns. "I and you; me and you; me alone; you alone." "And God?" I asked." "I am god; you are in the circumference of god."

"They were among life's lessons. Then there was the day my father opened the door to my room."

"And?"

"He called me pygmy. His best word for monstrosity. . . . He was right on in seeing me as descending from an irregular pattern. . . . I see myself that way. I am not of the obvious. Don't you see how my bushy eyelids grow sort of backwards. If you try to get a fix on who I am, if you stare too closely, you might never know that it is I who am peering at you."

True enough that his gaze registered some sort of extra comprehension. Like staring at a harpy; a level of presence that certainly demanded a sort of entangled attention.

His language was bunched tightly, as if the spoken words were coded–fleeting single phrases forming in whispers words that were charged with ambiguity.

"What makes you different from the others who claim special knowledge?"

"Early in the game, everyone was gone."

While attending junior high school, his mother began to speak with a hoarse voice. No one guessed that, by that time, she was in the midst of advanced throat cancer. Jude, confronting it now, indicated that he claimed to be little affected by her death. He continued to live as if he and his father were boarders in a house now run by a great aunt. He made no further pretensions of going to school. And it seemed as if no one cared. Still, I asked him if he were lamenting and not knowing how deep the feelings really were. How the loss of his mother was, in many ways, a reason for him to become heavily armored? His father divested himself of any involvement. Over and over again, he chided Jude for ever being born. Jude, the only child of a couple in misery. The ultimate of the unfortunate accident.

His father soon sold the house. They were never again in touch. Aside from his mother's aunt who moved back where she had been initially summoned, family became a closed issue. He was about to turn 16 when he became essentially homeless. Social services had provided him with a boarding arrangement, but Jude had already decided that he would be homeless. He spent hours at a branch library in an adjoining town. He read what he could, understood little, dozed when he wasn't being noticed.

The seasons of those first two years of homelessness were benign and warm enough. He took refuge on the outskirts of a town park. For a time, an elderly man gave him shelter. Jude hated the confinement. He took to street prostitution in a larger city. And he moved on as he felt dangers moving in. He haunted Catholic churches. Conferred the names of saints on himself.

"There's never been a conscience even after I started to go to confession." He invented sins: missing Sunday mass; minor thefts, blackmailing a businessman. Priests were usually displeased. Once he was screamed at and told never to return to the parish. He invented soft accents. Once an Irish brogue. He was told that his grandparents on both sides were Irish immigrants. For months on end, he spoke with a slight brogue. He knew little enough of his grandparents. They had no place in the architecture of his existence.

He eventually wandered into New York and took refuge in a lay Catholic shelter. There was a long waiting list, but he was assigned the bed of a man who was due to return after stomach surgery. The man never returned. He found clothes from the heap of garments donated to the shelter. It was summer and he was barefooted. The shelter had its dress code, but the young volunteer workers were in a constant state of flux. The shelter residents, too, had their pecking order. He was safest when he led the nightly rosary devotions.

"I was just 17, but I knew that I had a special place. Like it was Jesus had come in to live with the others."

"The Church decrees that Jesus was free of sin. And you keep knowing that without sin you could have never survived."

"That's where I go my way, and the church people go their way. . . . I'm on my magical trip, like Jesus was on his."

Our time was up for the day, and much remained to be kindled.

The next time we met, I had become his target and for over a year, the person he chose to stalk. He'd ring my office phone late into the night.

Attempted to break into my home shortly after I was married. It all made sense. But there seemed better ways. And, against better judgment, I continued to see Jude for his regular weekly sessions.

There was, of course, risk in continuing these sessions with Jude. But I never thought to look at a book of rules. He had threatened to wreak havoc in my office.

"And, if you destroy my furniture, I might decide that our contract no longer existed."

I wasn't pleased by my response. But quite serendipitously, someone showed me a reproduction of Max Ernst's painting *The Infant Jesus Being Spanked by the Virgin Mary in the Presence of Three Witnesses.* Ernst had been excommunicated for the painting. I described the painting to Jude.

He began to wonder if I wasn't suggesting that he return to the mental hospital. "It would be my beating." He was referring to the time he had been involuntarily admitted to a city hospital after being caught smearing feces on doorknobs in the homeless shelter. They administered high doses of Thorizine and Stelezine which, to cite Jude, "left me with no soul at all. They shamed me."

I asked him about the smearings and their possible relationship to the way he began to paint. "Painting and dancing and speaking in tongues have become my way of making the universe the way I think it ought to be. Jesus was punished for the same reason."

Soon after, he ceased stalking me. He phoned somewhere in the midst of several months of deciding that seeing me was no help at all. He called requesting that I return one of his paintings, but, in turn, he said he would replace it with two of his more recent productions. We met the following day and made the exchange.

The newer paintings were done in total blackness, except for some slight but obvious lines. I asked him about them. He was excited. Said that perched upon what seemed like a series of suspended trapezes were small figures. These were first inklings of any human presence in his art-work. "See," he pointed out with an abundance of excitement, "it's you with the Blessed Mother." I was able to follow the long narrow interspersing streaks.

I thanked him for the exchange. Our interchanges had been his hold onto his art. He, like Max Ernst, would for all time be an insurgent. Jude, who had been severely bullied throughout his school years, dismissed by his teachers, and verbally brutalized by his father, now knew that his "shit was golden"; that excrement was all he had to announce his presence.

Our work together had opened new pathways. Jude continued to reach out to the church's Sacrament of Penance. He needed to "get it all out, even if I have to invent most of it." He was describing his life, his right to his peculiarity, and his sense of wonderment about his own messianic mission.

I applauded him; his accomplishments and his way of being in the face of everything that had contributed to his survival. In this vein, I presented him with an article I had written on the deepest role of the Sacrament of Penance. I used the post-Vatican II Council's preferred term Sacrament of Reconciliation. I'd hope, I said, that he would value the article's pivotal point: Each time a penitent asks the priest to pray for forgiveness, the very act of such a request also asks God's mercy and forgiveness for the sins of all the church. Forgiveness, I suggested, had to be a reciprocal process to be authentic.

Jude identified with the negated Christ and underlined this identification with cosmic-ritualistic pantomime. Lucille he saw as the singular person who believed in his early career. She would always be the "voice crying out in the wilderness."

Jude died in his mid-40s. A young volunteer, who was then working at the shelter, wrote of his passing, noting a faint, but persistent overtone of something christologic having happened. In the end, Jude's credibility was no less than his cosmic dimensions spiraling into dance and painting.

As I reflect on my mission with Jude: He and I were, for that time, together, experiencing the all as on a trapeze. Always there was the dangle of risk; always the outstretched arms might possibly have missed the careening figure in space; always that certain reverence for that uncertain experience.

Third Gender: A Qualitative Study of the Experience of Individuals Who Identify as Being Neither Man nor Woman

Ingrid M. Sell

SUMMARY. The lives and experiences of 30 individuals (ages 29 to 77, from across the U.S.) who experience themselves as neither man nor woman, but "more like a third gender," were explored using in-depth interviews and qualitative content analysis based on Grounded Theory. This group exhibited a high degree of resilience, courage, compassion and creativity developed through lifelong struggles with identity and authenticity issues, and by facing ostracism, pressures to conform, and actual or threatened violence. Parallels suggested by third-gendered roles of non-Western cultures include a significant number (93%) reporting experiences of transcendent spiritual events or unusual abilities. Other

---

Ingrid M. Sell, PhD, is a clinician working with a rural adult population in southern Vermont and teaches in the distance-learning global program of the Institute of Transpersonal Psychology. This work, an earlier version of which was presented at the 109th convention of the American Psychological Association in San Francisco in 2001, received the Sidney Journal Award of APA Division 32 (Humanistic/ Transpersonal), and is drawn from her dissertation research at the Institute of Transpersonal Psychology.

[Haworth co-indexing entry note]: "Third Gender: A Qualitative Study of the Experience of Individuals Who Identify as Being Neither Man nor Woman." Sell, Ingrid M. Co-published simultaneously in *The Psychotherapy Patient* (The Haworth Press, Inc.) Vol. 13, No. 1/2, 2004, pp. 131-145; and: *Saints and Rogues: Conflicts and Convergence in Psychotherapy* (ed: Robert B. Marchesani, and E. Mark Stern) The Haworth Press, Inc., 2004, pp. 131-145. Single or multiple copies of this article are available for a fee from The Haworth Document Delivery Service [1-800-HAWORTH, 9:00 a.m. - 5:00 p.m. (EST). E-mail address: docdelivery@haworthpress.com].

http://www.haworthpress.com/web/TPP

Digital Object Identifier: 10.1300/J358v13n01_06

parallels include considerable numbers of artists, healers, and acting in mediating and leadership roles. *[Article copies available for a fee from The Haworth Document Delivery Service: 1-800-HAWORTH. E-mail address: <docdelivery@haworthpress.com> Website: <http://www.HaworthPress.com>*

KEYWORDS. Gender identity, gender variance, sex, gender, gender role, cross-cultural gender concept, transgender, third gender, authenticity, paranormal experience

If being born a biological male automatically makes one a man, and being born female automatically makes one a woman, why then is so much effort put into shaping ourselves into so-called "real men" or "real women"? If being a man or a woman is so natural, why does it require so much effort–and why does the nonconformance of others require so much policing, through means ranging from apparently benign joking to downright violence against those effeminate men and masculine women who violate cultural norms?

Why is it so disquieting when we are unable to tell whether someone is male or female? Why does it matter?

The power of the fear, fascination and repulsion that arises in response to gender-nonconforming people suggests that there may be forces beyond biology–or even social construction–at work. That power is recognized by many non-Western cultures where the ability to cross between the realms of male and female is seen as signifying a corresponding ability to mediate between the worlds of spirit and mundane (Bradford, 1983; Coleman, Colgan & Gooren, 1992; Eliade, 1964; Herdt, 1993; Jacobs & Cromwell, 1992; Kessler & McKenna, 1978; Murray & Roscoe, 1998; Nanda, 1986, 1993; Roscoe, 1988, 1991, 1993, 1998; Tafoya, 1992; Williams, 1992; Wilson, 1996).

In contrast, people who exist outside the norms of gender in Western culture are seen as sick or insufficiently developed. The DSM-IV definition of "gender dysphoria" lists as criteria of pathology "a strong and persistent cross-gender identification" and "persistent discomfort about one's assigned sex or a sense of the inappropriateness in the gender role of that sex" (p. 537). It also notes that "for clinically referred children, onset is usually between 2 and 4 and some parents report that their child has always had cross-gender interests" (p. 536). This parallels the early appearance of gender variance reported in some non-Western cultures

(Coleman, Colgan & Gooren, 1992; Gremaux, 1993; Herdt, 1993; Jacobs, Thomas & Lang, 1997; Kessler & McKenna, 1978; Nanda, 1986, 1993; Roscoe, 1988, 1991, 1998; Tafoya, 1992; Williams, 1992; Wilson, 1996), where the information is coded in a diametrically opposite way.

Nevertheless, despite this view of gender variance as pathology prevailing among many mainstream psychologists, it is counteracted by studies of transgendered individuals (e.g., Bolin, 1988; Cromwell, 1999; Devor, 1997) that show the transgendered to be in all other respects "normal," productive people. In light of the different treatment gender variance receives in non-Western cultures, it may be worth examining whether it is gender difference itself, or the definition of it as pathological, that is problematic.

The polarity of male-female is taken to be an absolute in modern Western cultures. It is used as the metaphorical basis of many other polarities, such as light/dark, active/passive, or strong/gentle, which in turn reinforce what we hold to be true about male and female, as well as the sense of things as being neatly divisible into polarized pairs.

The study presented in this paper explores the lives of a group of gender-variant North Americans who defy polarized thinking in the way in which they live and experience their genders, whose sense of themselves is best described as "*neither* man nor woman, but more like a *third* gender." After clarifying the distinctions between sex, gender, and sexual orientation, three key concepts which are very often confounded, several examples of third gender roles in non-Western cultures are presented in order to show some of the differing ways that gender is conceptualized. This is followed by some examples of the existing variety of Western gender variants. Finally, this sample and the findings on these North American "third gendered," which included a high degree of resilience, independence, leadership capabilities and authenticity as well as promising parallels to people in non-Western third-gendered roles, are discussed.

The question of what it is that makes one a man or a woman has been grappled with throughout Western history. Although in this materialistic era, biology is taken to be the starting point, historically, Western man was understood to be one gender, either metaphorically split in two, ever in search of the other missing half, as in Plato's conception (Rado, 1965), or with males seen as the complete being, with females seen as lesser, incomplete versions (Laqueur, 1990; Tannahill, 1980/1992).

Because contemporary Western culture takes physical manifestation to be the ultimate truth, biology is taken to be the determinant of both sex and gender. Thus, while *sex*–male or female–denotes biology, *gender*–man or woman–describes social roles (Money & Ehrhardt, 1972). Given the belief in an immutable, biologically based polarity, the terms are often used interchangeably, while the notion that beings follow bodies lies deeply entrenched and largely unexamined.

Of course, even biology is not so neat: A small but significant percentage of babies are born intersexed, with ambiguous physical sex markers. Yet rather than accepting these variations in nature, such births are treated as medical catastrophes requiring surgical and/or hormonal "corrections" with lasting devastating consequences for the individuals involved (Burke, 1996; Chase, 1998; Fausto-Sterling, 1993).

Cultural assumptions about the "natural" inevitability of gender following sex lead to further assumptions about what sorts of traits and behaviors are supposedly "natural" for each sex/gender (Collier & Yanagisako, 1987). Primary among these assumptions is the inevitability of the pairing of men and women. Thus, *sexual orientation* is the third key concept that is often confounded with notions about sex and gender.

This becomes clearer when we look at those who don't fit the mold in one way, and see how they are often confused with others who don't fit in another way. Thus, while sexual orientation is about desire, someone whose desire is for a person of the same sex may have their gender called into question, as in speculation whether gay men are "real men" or whether lesbians are in fact not quite female. On the other hand, gentle men and strong women are often presumed to be gay, regardless of whether they have any desire for someone of the same sex or not. And those whose gender identity is at odds with their birth sex–such as transsexuals and some transgendered people–are typically assumed to also be gay, although this is often not the case. One of the stereotypes of gay men and lesbians used to be that they "really" wanted to be the opposite sex.

VARIETIES OF GENDER DIFFERENCE

Non-Western Gender Variants

Gender is organized differently in non-Western cultures. Although of course males and females are recognized everywhere, gender, as opposed to sex, may be seen as a function of social, spiritual or occupational roles, rather than biology (Kessler & McKenna, 1978; Roscoe, 1993, 1998).

In contrast to the materially based Western categories, many non-Western cultures have socially established roles that recognize a third entity as neither male nor female. In numerous African tribes, women may become men through the institution of "*female husbands*," an economically based kinship arrangement in which they are recognized as men, with all the attendant privileges that men enjoy, but although the fact of their femaleness is not openly acknowledged, it is not forgotten (Carrier & Murray, 1998; O'Brien, 1977; Oboloer, 1980). In some instances, they may simultaneously still be married to men, in which case they are seen as wives (women) with their husbands and as husbands (men) with their wives. In the Balkan highlands of the former Yugoslavia and Albania, some women also step outside the strictures of a highly gender-polarized culture by becoming "*sworn virgins*," where they dress, work, and live as men, although they are understood to be "not-men" as well (Grémaux, 1993; Young, 2000).

In northern India, the *hijra* (Nanda, 1986, 1993) and in southern India, the *jogappas* (Bradford, 1983) are sacred "female men," biological males who wear women's clothing and are seen as female, although not entirely. In both instances, they are "called" to their position by mother Goddess figures, in whose service they perform at weddings, funerals and festivals, bestowing blessings upon the celebrants, and serve a recognized and mostly respected cultural function.

In Myanmar, the *acault* are men who showed cross-sex inclinations at a young age, where that is seen as evidence of being called to serve the goddess Manguedon. *Acault* take on feminine dress and behaviors, and act as shamans and seers. Their intermediate gender status is thought to bring with it considerable powers (Coleman, Colgan & Gooren, 1992).

In the South Pacific, variations on a third-gendered "half-man, half-woman" include the *mahu* of French Polynesia (Elliston, 1999), Tahiti and Hawaii as well as the Samoan *fa'afafine*, Tongan *fakaleiti* and *fakafafine* and Tuvaluuan *pinapinaaine* (Besnier, 1993), who typically are artists and carriers of cultural traditions, and who often act as mediators between island societies and outsiders. In particular, the *mahu* have been linked with shamanistic powers as well.

In Native North America, alternative gendered "*berdache*" roles have been documented in over 150 different tribes (Roscoe, 1998; Tafoya, 1992) in which either men or women, who had usually evidenced cross-sex tendencies early in life, assumed cross-gendered occupations and wore either opposite-sex clothing or a modified, third alternative. Known by a third- (or in some cases, a fourth [Roscoe,

1998]) gendered term, they were understood to be intermediate beings, between men and women, and appreciated as such as part of the fabric of the culture (Wilson, 1996).

A key distinction between these non-Western gender alternatives and the way in which gender difference is seen here is the acceptance that there is something other than just male or female–that these constitute a third, distinct gender category, *neither* male nor female. In contrast, believing that there are only two options here, many people find it difficult to see the variety in gender variance here. Virtually any movement away from conventional manhood or womanhood is seen as movement towards, and the desire to be, the "opposite" sex.

Western Gender Variants

Transsexuals are the most easily recognized gender alternative in our culture, as they most closely fit the paradigm of only two genders. Transsexuals experience themselves as the gender opposite to their birth sex and live as such, often undergoing surgical or hormonal alternations in order to achieve bodies that are congruent with their experience of themselves (Israel & Tarver, 1997).

Transvestites, on the other hand, are those who cross-dress for pleasure, but have no desire to give up their birth sex or sex-identified gender identities (Bolin, 1988). *Drag queens* are a culturally specific, institutionalized gay male role that is based on performance with an emphasis on glamour, parody and exaggeration (Garber, 1992) with *female impersonators* being an even smaller subset, entertainers who perform convincingly as certain female icons such as Marilyn Monroe or Jacqueline Kennedy Onassis.

Not all who transgress the boundaries of gender intend to cross, nor do they necessarily think of themselves in terms of the opposite sex. *Transgender* is a newer term to describe such people (Israel & Tarver, 1997), although it has also come to be used as a catchall to describe the entire community of gender-transgressors. Several participants in this study noted that, given the cultural bias towards the binary, the word has come to take on the implication of gender-crossing, which they felt rendered them even more invisible than they already were. In general, and in this study, the term was used either when participants identified themselves as such, and/or to imply significant or primarily cross-gendered appearance, behavior and identity without completely crossing.

Other forms of blurring gender have an established history within the gay and lesbian community. In particular, lesbian *butch* identity, which describes women who are (relatively) comfortable with their femaleness yet carry significantly masculine traits, has a history as a subcultural form, although the meaning has changed and evolved from a survival adaptation (Faderman, 1991; Kennedy & Davis, 1993) to a thoughtful expression of inner identity (Inness & Lloyd, 1996). *Butch* and its counterpart *femme* are used differently–as adjectives describing relative amounts of masculinity or femininity in the gay male community. "*Queen*" is a gay male adjective that originally designated femininity in gay men, although the term has come to have broader uses that can include mixed gender metaphors such as "muscle queen" to describe gay male bodybuilders where the identity is clearly masculine but feminine possibility is implied.

METHODS

In order to allow for the fullest investigation of this phenomenon, which, while not entirely new, is still novel as a research topic, a qualitative method–semi-structured interviews, combined with qualitative content analysis–was chosen. Interviewing provides access to the meanings people attribute to their experiences and offers the means to explore the participants' point of view while respecting their ability to speak for themselves. Open-ended questions honor respondents' expertise on their own lives (Miller & Glassner, 1997).

Data were analyzed using qualitative thematic analysis methods, which are especially suited to exploring complex, multidimensional phenomena, such as this study of the inner and outer dimensions of alternative gender identities (Boyatzis, 1998). Strategies drawn from grounded theory, which is especially suited for rigorous investigation of unrecognized phenomena and marginalized populations (Charmaz, 1995), included drawing analytic categories directly from the data, rather than from preconceived hypotheses, as well as incorporating emergent themes and applying them retroactively (which sometimes necessitated re-contacting the respondent for further inquiry) to already completed interviews.

An interview schedule and written demographic questionnaire were developed by the researcher and tested on three pilot participants who matched the study criteria, as well as on two controls, a heterosexual female of nontraditional but established femininity and a transsexual woman whose experience of gender intermediacy only described her transition from male to female, rather than her ongoing sense of gender identity. Pilot participants' responses were often qualitatively different from controls. They also provided feedback on the relevance of the question to their lives.

Questions explored life histories, experiences with others in relation to their gender, development of gendered self-concepts, and relationship to others. Given the culturally attributed importance of bodies to determining gender, participants were asked about their attitudes towards their bodies and their attitudes towards making physical changes, both in themselves and in others. Several questions were designed to inquire whether any of the traits that mark people in third-gendered roles in non-Western cultures–such things as artistic abilities, mediating roles and healing abilities–might correlate with gender intermediacy here as well. In keeping with the literature on non-Western third-gendered roles, participants were questioned about evidence of paranormal abilities or any significant transcendent spiritual experiences (near-death, out-of-body, or other nonordinary experience) they might have undergone.

Participants

The individuals in this study were chosen specifically because they live an identity that is in-between. Some identified as well with one or more of the Western gender alternatives enumerated above. Others did not. The distinguishing characteristic of those studied is that they identify as neither man nor woman, or clearly both, AND are visibly recognized by others as such in some way. They frequently encounter questioning along the lines of "Are you a boy or a girl, or what?"

Participants ranged in age from 29 to 77, with a median age of 41. They came from a wide geographic range, including 37% from California, 30% from the Northeast, 17% from the Southeast, 13% from the Northwest (including one participant from Canada) and one from the Midwest. Racially, 26 participants (87%) identified themselves as Caucasian, three (10%) as Native American, two (7%) as Latina, and one each as Asian and African-American (numbers add up to more than 100% due to several participants' multiracial identities).

Sixty percent were born and raised as girls, 40% were born and raised as boys. Some still identified, at least in part, with the gender corresponding to their birth sex; others did not. Some were living or "passing" as the sex opposite to their birth sex; many others simply went about their business as they were, and allowed others to draw their own conclusions. Eight out of the 30 had used hormones and/or surgery to make some changes to their bodies, although they were clear that their intentions were not to "go all the way" and change sex, but rather to highlight characteristics that they felt most represented who they were. Several others were adamantly opposed to the idea of bodily alteration, feeling that it rendered people like them even more invisible than they already were.

Procedure

Participants were recruited through flyers distributed through LGBT (lesbian, gay, bisexual and transgendered) organizations, publications and Internet listservs, as well as snowball sampling among the researcher's personal and professional networks. Candidates were sought who specifically identify with and live a form of gender-*intermediacy*, as opposed to a clear cross-gender identification. Those for whom the integration of masculine and feminine traits was seen as an inner accomplishment alone were ruled out, as were those for whom intermediacy was a stage on the way towards transitioning from one sex and/or gender to another.

Interviews were conducted primarily in person, or over the telephone when interviewing was not feasible, and lasted an average of one and a half hours. They were taped and transcribed by the researcher herself, both due to economic constraints, as well as to increase contact with the data to enhance coding during data analysis. Brief sections of the almost-completed dissertation were sent to selected participants for member validation to verify the researcher's understanding of participants' lives, an important consideration when, as in this case, the researcher is not a part of the group under study (Bloor, 1983).

RESULTS AND DISCUSSION

Nearly all (27, or 90%) were aware of being different from their peers in terms of gender from an early age, on average, by age 5. With a clear sense of who they were, they were able to distinguish between what felt authentically their own from traits that others tried to impose on them. As one participant put it, "I am who I am because I can't not be."

Female-born participants invariably were tomboys as children and were not particularly bothered by others for their gender presentations until puberty. On the other hand, male-born participants were usually made aware quite young that something was "not right" about their presentations through the angry, dismayed or mocking responses of peers and adults.

Participants had employed a variety of coping methods to deal with the ostracism, pressure to conform, and lack of mirroring they experienced: deliberately spending a lot of time alone, assuming leadership roles in order to preempt teasing or being overpowered, cultivating a tough and angry exterior presentation, developing abilities in the creative arts, and excelling in school. One-third had experienced problems with substance abuse, although at the time of the study, all but one of them had been in recovery for at least two years.

As adults, pressure to conform to gender norms carried according to how well each "passed" as one or the other gender. Those with the most ambiguous appearances reported the greatest amount of difficulties in navigating the world. Problems included harassment, threats, stares, and verbal hostility directly related to their appearance. Most female-born participants also reported frequently being intensely scrutinized or even chased out of women's restrooms. Only one female-born participant is regularly read as female. In contrast, all of the male-born participants are read as male nearly all of the time. Three who are physically transitioning report that others evidence confusion but still read them as male, and interpret their appearance as signs that they are gay. (In fact, two are not.)

Even without the sort of mentoring and tracking that accompanies third-gendered roles in non-Western cultures, participants in this study showed a number of parallels to their non-Western counterparts. Nearly half were healers: 13 work in the health and helping professions. Most were highly creative and artistic. Seven were writers, 4 musicians, 3 performing artists (one a drag queen, another an actor, and the third a performance poet). Of these, five earned all or a substantial portion of their incomes from their art. Three others were employed in other creative fields, including a landscape architect, a fashion designer, and a graphic artist. Nearly all felt that some form of artistic expression was important to their lives.

Most found that they naturally served in mediating functions. Twenty-three of the 30 reported being called upon to mediate between men and women, being seen by both as carrying a wider perspective that could encompass both sides. Many also mediated between other groups, such as between different races, different age groups, different cultures, or different subcultures such as between the disability community and the well, or between the gay or lesbian and the transgendered communities.

Most strikingly, 28 out of the 30, or 93%, reported having experienced transcendent spiritual events and/or having unusual "paranormal"-type abilities. Joshua, a gay man, describes a sense common among many participants:

> By the time I was 4, I knew that I was very different . . . I was just very conscious of the fact that I came in with a whole host of memories of–I don't know if they are other lives or not, but I just know that at 2 or 3 . . . I just had all of these experiences of seeing other beings and hearing voices and doing other things that at first I didn't know that everyone didn't do . . . by the time I was 4, I knew that I had a whole reality that I could not talk about with my parents.

Often, the signs of unusual abilities appeared early in life, as Billy related:

> When I was young, I used to play chess with my brother all the time. And every . . . with the white pawn in one hand and the black pawn in the other, he would put it behind his back and mix it up. And every single time I could look at his hand and see black or see white, and every single time I would pick the white one so I could go first.

For others, experiences were more connected to religious practices. Guye, a divinity student, gave an example:

> It was the first Jewish service that I had ever been to, and I had a transcendental experience. I mean, I could speak Hebrew, I sung Hebrew songs, the women next to me didn't believe that I had never sung Hebrew before. I sung one we didn't have the words to. I felt like I met God in that group.

Fred, currently an actor, noted earlier experiences in his life:

> I've had that sort of thing, but I can't describe it. St. Theresa goes into that in some detail, but there are some things you just cannot describe. The best language is the language we also use for sex . . . I know that in my teens I had some experiences like that, but I at-

> tribute them partly to glandular changes that go on in your early teens. . . . But when you're in a monastery, which is a quiet setting, and something happens, then I think you get closer to something you take seriously.

Some were able to put their gifts to use helping others, as Jan related a recent incident:

> I can tell you a quick little thing I had the other day. This guy [George] died . . . we go to a party for his son, who's now 2 years old. I walk into the house and go, "Oh, George is here." I never met him, but I felt him everywhere. So I sat down, and we're all having cake and everything and I hear him say, "Ask Sheila if she has any connection to 'Bubba.'" . . . So I said "Anybody here"–I wouldn't even put it directly to her–"Anybody here got any connection to 'Bubba'?" . . . And she said, "That's what they used to call George when he was a little boy." And I said, "Well, he's here. And he wants you to know that he loves you. And he misses his son terribly."

The number of participants in this study–93%–who described experiences of this sort is notable in comparison with population surveys that report 40%-50% reporting spiritual experiences of *any* intensity (Haraldson & Houtkooper, 1991; Palmer, 1979; Thomas & Cooper, 1980). It is particularly notable that in the Thomas and Cooper (1980) study, which involved more detailed investigation than the tabulation of surveys in other studies, only 9% of the respondents experienced the sorts of profound and/or repeated "psychic" or "mystical" experiences reported by 57% of the sample in this study, with another 16% in the Thomas and Cooper study reporting "moving incidents involving faith," which compares with the remaining 36% of this sample reporting milder or single transcendent experiences in this study.

These findings suggest that there may be elements of third gender identity that are transcultural and inherent to gender intermediacy. Gender is not an inevitable byproduct of biological sex. Perhaps, as non-Western cultures recognize, there is indeed an element of spirit or "calling" involved in our being men, women, or mediators between.

Over 30 years ago, Sidney Jourard wrote about the limitations of conventional psychology:

> The possibility arises that our psychology is a faithful report of human beings who have complied with social pressures and have reduced their experience of themselves and their world in order to "play it safe" and conform. (Jourard, 1966, p. 351)

Thus, as psychologists interested in the full range of human potential, we would do well to look openly, rather than fearfully, at those among us with the gift of bridging gender polarities, as they point the way to a much broader understanding of human possibility, one that includes integrating opposites, holding paradox, the courage of authenticity even in the face of fierce opposition, and ease with transpersonal dimensions.

REFERENCES

American Psychiatric Association. (1994). Diagnostic and statistical manual of mental disorders (4th ed.). Washington, DC: Author.

Besnier, N. (1993). Polynesian gender liminality through time and space. In G. Herdt, (Ed.), *Third sex, third gender: Beyond sexual dimorphism in culture and history*. (pp. 285-328). New York: Zone.

Bloor, M. (1983). Notes on member validation. In R. Emerson, *Contemporary field research: A collection of readings* (pp. 156-172). Boston: Little, Brown.

Bolin, A. (1988). *In search of Eve: Transsexual rites of passage*. South Hadley, MA: Bergin & Garvey.

Boyatzis, R.E. (1998). *Transforming qualitative information: Thematic analysis and code development*. Thousand Oaks, CA: Sage.

Bradford, N. (1983). Transgenderism and the cult of Yellama: Heat, sex and sickness in south Indian ritual. *Journal of Anthropological Research*, *39*(3), 307-322.

Burke, P. (1996). *Gender shock: Exploding the myths of male and female*. New York: Doubleday.

Carrier, J., & Murray, S.O. (1998). Woman-woman marriage in Africa. In S.O. Murray & W. Roscoe (Eds.), *Boy-wives and female husbands: Studies of African homosexualities* (pp. 255-266). New York: St. Martin's.

Charmaz, K. (1995). Grounded theory. In J. Smith, R. Harre & L.V. Langenhove (Eds.), *Rethinking methods in psychology* (pp. 27-49). London: Sage.

Chase, C. (1998). Hermaphrodites with attitude: Mapping the emergence of intersex political activism. In S. Stryker (Ed.), *The transgender issue [Special issue]. GLQ: A Journal of Lesbian and Gay Studies, 4(2)*, 189-211.

Coleman, E., Colgan, P., & Gooren, L. (1992). Male cross-gender behavior in Myanmar (Burma): A description of the acault. *Archives of Sexual Behavior*, *21*(3), 313-321.

Collier, J., & Yanagisako, S. (1987). Toward a unified analysis of gender and kinship. In J. Collier & S. Yanagisako (Eds.), *Gender and kinship: Essays toward a unified analysis* (pp. 14-50). Stanford, CA: Stanford University.

Cromwell, J. (1999). *Transmen and FTMs: Identities, bodies, genders and sexualities.* Urbana, IL: University of Chicago Press.

Devor, H. (1997). *FTM: Female-to-male transsexuals in society.* Bloomington, IN: Indiana University.

Eliade, M. (1964). *Shamanism: Archaic techniques of ecstasy.* New York: Bollingen.

Elliston, D.A. (1999). Negotiating transnational sexual economies: Female Mahu and same-sex sexuality in Tahiti and her islands. In E. Blackwood & S.E. Wieringa (Eds.), *Same-sex relations and female desires: Transgender practices across cultures.* New York: Columbia University Press.

Faderman, L. (1991). *Odd girls and twilight lovers: A history of lesbian life in twentieth-century America.* New York: Penguin.

Fausto-Sterling, A. (1993). The five sexes: Why male and female are not enough. *Sciences, 33*(2), 20-26.

Garber, M. (1992). Vested interests: *Cross-dressing and cultural anxiety.* New York: Routledge.

Grémaux, R. (1993). Woman becomes man in the Balkans. In G. Herdt (Ed.), *Third sex, third gender: Beyond sexual dimorphism in culture and history* (pp. 241-281). New York: Zone.

Halberstam, J. (1998). *Female masculinity.* Durham, NC: Duke University.

Haraldson, E., & Houtkooper, J.M. (1991). Psychic experiences in the multinational human value study: Who reports them? *Journal of the American Society for Psychical Research, 85,* 145-165.

Herdt, G. (1993). Introduction: Third sexes and third genders. In G. Herdt (Ed.), *Third sex, third gender: Beyond sexual dimorphism in culture and history* (pp. 21-81). New York: Zone.

Inness, S.A., & Lloyd, M.E. (1996). G.I. Joes in Barbie land: Recontextualizing butch in twentieth-century lesbian culture. In B. Beemyn & M. Eliason (Eds.), *Queer studies: A lesbian, gay, bisexual and transgender anthology* (pp. 9-34). New York: New York University.

Israel, G., & Tarver, D. (1997). *Transgender care: Recommended guidelines, practical information and personal accounts.* Philadelphia: Temple University.

Jacobs, S.E., & Cromwell, J. (1992). Visions and revisions of reality: Reflections on sex, sexuality, gender and gender variance. *Journal of Homosexuality, 23*(4), 43-69.

Jacobs, S.E., Thomas, W., & Lang, S. (1997). *Two-spirit people: Native American gender identity, sexuality, and spirituality.* Urbana, IL: University of Illinois.

Jourard, S.M. (1966). Toward a psychology of transcendent behavior. In H.A. Otto (Ed.), *Explorations in human potentialities* (pp. 349-377). Springfield, IL: Charles C. Thomas.

Kennedy, E.L., & Davis, M.D. (1993). *Boots of leather, slippers of gold: The history of a lesbian community.* New York: Penguin.

Kessler, S., & McKenna, W. (1978). *Gender: An ethnomethodological approach.* New York: Wiley.

Laqueur, T. (1990). *Making sex: Body and gender from the Greeks to Freud.* Cambridge, MA: Harvard University.

Layton, L. (1998). *Who's that girl? Who's that boy? Clinical practice meets postmodern gender theory.* Northvale, NJ: Jason Aronson.

Miller, J., & Glassner, B. (1997). The 'inside' and the 'outside': Finding realities in interviews. In D. Silverman (Ed.), *Qualitative research: Theory, method and practice* (pp. 99-111). London: Sage.
Money, J., & Ehrhardt, A. (1972). *Man and woman, boy and girl*. Baltimore: Johns Hopkins University.
Murray, S., & Roscoe, W. (1998). *Boy-wives and female husbands: Studies of African homosexualities* (pp. 255-266). New York: St. Martin's.
Nanda, S. (1986). The Hijras of India: Cultural and individual dimensions of an institutionalized third gender role. [Special issue] *Anthropology and Homosexual Behavior: Journal of Homosexuality, 11*, 35-54.
Nanda, S. (1993). Hijras: An alternative sex and gender role in India. In G. Herdt (Ed.), *Third sex, third gender: Beyond sexual dimorphism in culture and history* (pp. 373-417). New York: Zone.
Oboler, R. (1980). Is the female husband a man? Woman/woman marriage among the Nandi of Kenya. *Ethnology, 19*(1), 69-88.
O'Brien, D. (1977). Female husbands in Southern Bantu societies. In A. Schlegel (Ed.), *Sexual stratification: A cross-cultural view* (pp. 109-126). New York: Columbia University Press.
Palmer, J. (1979). A community mail survey of psychic experiences. *Journal of the American Society for Psychical Research, 73*, 221-251.
Rado, S. (1965). A critical examination of the concept of bisexuality. In J. Marmor (Ed.), *Sexual inversion* (pp. 175-189). New York: Basic.
Roscoe, W. (Ed.) & Gay American Indians. (1988). *Living the spirit: A gay American Indian anthology*. New York: St. Martin's.
Roscoe, W. (1991). *The Zuni man-woman*. Albuquerque, NM: University of New Mexico.
Roscoe, W. (1993). How to become a berdache: Toward a unified analysis of gender diversity. In G. Herdt (Ed.), *Third sex, third gender: Beyond sexual dimorphism in culture and history* (pp. 329-372). New York: Zone.
Roscoe, W. (1998). *Changing ones: Third and fourth genders in Native North America*. New York: St. Martin's.
Tafoya, T. (1992). Native gay and lesbian issues: The two-spirited. In B. Berzon (Ed.), *Positively gay* (pp. 253-259). Berkeley: Celestial Arts.
Tannahill, R. (1992). *Sex in history*. Briar Cliff Manor, NY: Stein & Day (Original work published 1980).
Thomas, L.E., & Cooper, P.E. (1980). Incidence and psychological correlates of intense spiritual experiences. *Journal of Transpersonal Psychology, 12*, 75-85.
Williams, W. (1992). *The spirit and the flesh: Sexual diversity in American Indian culture*. Boston: Beacon.
Wilson, A. (1996). How we find ourselves: Identity development and two-spirit people. *Harvard Educational Review, 66*(2), 303-317.
Young, A. (2000). *Women who become men: Albanian sworn virgins*. New York: Berg.

Of Saints and Rogues: A Dialogue of Opposites and Their Attractions

Robert B. Marchesani
E. Mark Stern

KEYWORDS. Angels, the Buddha, Christ, Shiva, children, abuse, innocence, human aggression, da Vinci, twins and twinships, male and female representations

Robert Marchesani: We deal with all sorts of ideals about ourselves and each other that span the gamut of possible existences. Are we saint-makers? Do we aspire to a kind of sainthood ourselves? And how does the temptation to become a rogue of sorts seduce or threaten the therapist and patient?

Robert B. Marchesani, MSSc, is a psychotherapist in private practice in New York and Philadelphia. He currently is a senior candidate at The Philadelphia School of Psychoanalysis and teaches "The Internet and the New Self" in The New School's cyberspace program (www.dialnsa.edu).

E. Mark Stern, EdD, ABPP, is a Fellow of the American Psychological Association, the American Psychological Society, and the Academy of Clinical Psychology. Dr. Stern is Professor Emeritus, Graduate Faculty of Arts and Sciences at Iona College in New Rochelle, New York. He maintains a private practice in psychotherapy in New York City and in Dutchess County in upstate New York.

[Haworth co-indexing entry note]: "Of Saints and Rogues: A Dialogue of Opposites and Their Attractions." Marchesani, Robert B., and E. Mark Stern. Co-published simultaneously in *The Psychotherapy Patient* (The Haworth Press, Inc.) Vol. 13, No. 1/2, 2004, pp. 147-154; and: *Saints and Rogues: Conflicts and Convergence in Psychotherapy* (ed: Robert B. Marchesani, and E. Mark Stern) The Haworth Press, Inc., 2004, pp. 147-154. Single or multiple copies of this article are available for a fee from The Haworth Document Delivery Service [1-800-HAWORTH, 9:00 a.m. - 5:00 p.m. (EST). E-mail address: docdelivery@haworthpress.com].

http://www.haworthpress.com/web/TPP

Digital Object Identifier: 10.1300/J358v13n01_07

E. Mark Stern: Saints are no angels, yet some angels are saints. Likely the vast numbers of saints are cunning rogues. No matter how my patients see me, I need to be a rogue in sheep's clothing. Without my rogue sensibility, I would be some strange cross of a Buddhist seer and a super reasonable cognitive therapist. I think of myself as neither.

RM: I've noticed that sons are often thought to be angels by their mothers, and yet their own experience of themselves is much more roguish.

EMS: The only formula for any son, straight, gay or indifferent, to insure the comparative safety is to play angelic. Even the prodigal son eventually returns home as an archangel, much to the chagrin of his jealously angelic brother. The prevailing myth I grew up with was that you really were no angel until you died. You simply had to act the role of angel. But I think, despite my angelic pretensions, I was seen by my parents as an irascible rogue. And since we're onto offspring, how about daughters? Are there female rogues? I've heard talk of female angels, but they are either rare or nonexistent in angelic literature. A case made for the ladies was in that great piano bar Cole Porter number "That's Why the Lady Is a Tramp." The kind of woman that would hang tight with Dionysius. I think we need to make a case for rogues who resist all temptation to "angelize" themselves.

RM: What is this profession of psychotherapy but a call to some kind of healing relationship? And yet it seems so often to bring about a feeling of devilishness as we try to navigate the barriers and obstacles that seem hurled at us, if not just something to trip over.

EMS: You mean you need to be a saint to put up with the deterrents that call for some high level of sainthood? Hum. Come to think of it, saints may be mutated rogues. To be less than a rogue would somehow not allow for the reciprocity that psychological trickery demands. The patient as rogue; the therapist as rogue. Helps me know that the psychotherapy process is something like drinking out of a common cup. Yet each player is unique in his/her roguishness.

RM: I was leaving my office the day before Independence Day when I came to a corner and stopped for the light. One of the vehicles was a small yellow school bus, one of those extended van types. And through the window I could see a boy's face and head immobilized by a tray. Two young women tended him. Were they his angels? He was quadriplegic. And I was left wondering about so many complaints I hear of freedoms people want. Then there's this little child who can move only his eyes. He cannot decide what to wear, where to sit. He hasn't the ability to exert control over a single limb. Wow! Here was a little Buddha; a little Christ. Here was Shiva it seemed to me, hiding within this child who beckoned a new consciousness of freedom. I was blown away.

EMS: "Blown away" is aerie and saintly. Rogues shake their fists at the prevailing winds, and in the end see it all "like it is." I think less like a rogue when I get blown away. Everything feels less malleable, perhaps destined with sadness. I think that the best of gods move into numerous states. The great Sufi theosophist, Ibn Arabi, tries to image what humankind would be as it truly reflects Allah's many names. That immense field of red clay over there represents a vast stock, but it takes just a small handful to create Adam. Adam has the potential to expand into all the pieces of humanity. We are, each one, in and all about us, that individualized mass that took form with the Big Bang. And probably before what we so cavalierly dub creation. The gods are as small and smaller than the gluon that flows into microscopic infinity. Deformity has nothing, if it refuses to personalize the dynamics of the gods. Your little quadriplegic boy dances like Shiva, and can be valued as no less than the music that propels his microscopic movements. Here enters the saint. It is the saint, the wee lad, who provides the music by which the dance becomes possible. The saints propel the gods. In those rare saintly moments, we look to our patients, and whether in our manner or in our lack of manners, the music begins and the dance happens.

RM: Children may be the saints of the first instance, but fast become rogues. They suffer the wills of parents and other self-proclaimed authorities. In the Canadian film *The Boys of St. Vincent* (1992), the priest takes one of the young boys from the residence one night and puts him on his lap. We hear the priest talking to the boy as though he is his mother. He strokes the boy as he falls into some perverse reverie. The next day the boy is black and blue. This was not what Christ meant when he said, "Suffer the children unto me." Yet it is telling of the twisting that occurs in the creation or destruction of souls and bodies that come under such attack in intimate terrorism–a phrase used to describe domestic violence in which we often see one party serving another. The typical abused wife as portrayed in the British film *East Is East* (2000) is devoted to her husband no matter how he attacks her.

Human aggression was not analyzed or drugged away, or even exorcised away, in the twentieth century. Now that we are in the twenty-first century, we may have to resort to gene therapy to root out our evils.

How does one transform the mind and will of a Bin Laden? Or a George W. Bush? Does the world gather together in deep prayer, meditation, conscious thought and attempt to reverse the power mania in destructive thinking? Is reversal possible when a leader is acting as a cleansing agent in a holy war that the leader has identified as a holy war? Does the new century allow capitalism and all of its assumed entitlements and boundless acquisitions to run rampant? Will we, still wounded from 9/11, but no less self-righteous, ever stop to hear what the rogue may be trying to say? Will the West be merely satisfied to build and rebuild what ultimately amounts to its Towers of Babel? And will this rogue who lives in the rogue state that we have mocked for what we consider its barren lifestyle, will he listen to another way of seeing the world, the freedom of women and children?

EMS: Rogues tend to be onlookers as the would-be holy build their Babels. In their necessary helplessness, they watch, hoping to move on to more humane building sites. Rogues do not have an ingrown strength. They are weak-kneed as they look at the cunning strength of the predators of youth and other waywards.

Yet no rogue, regardless of the shameless trickery he or she may use to focus on the evil doings masked in wet nursing the innocent child, is empowered to exorcise the evil. First, the rogue must decide that there must be an intercession so powerful as to signal a clarion call. Here the rogue decides on martyrdom, if need be, to help in helplessness, to invoke the forces to nudge the social agenda. Psychotherapists have no great powers. Yet they may well offer to witness evil and call it for what it is. Judge not that ye not be judged. Though never forget that to invoke the words that justice is being failed requires a greater reverence and a more expansive loyalty to more than just one's patient. We therapists declared the predators well-fed, even as they were ravaged in their gluttony. The priest abusing the small child; the husband trouncing his ever-forgiving wife: these gluttoned upon, each instance and more and more, requires that the rogue therapist be no saint, but that he or she become a just witness to the crime and see the victims' needs are witnessed as well. I have no formulas. I believe in therapeutic confidentiality. And as well, I believe that we must see more than the patient as THE patient and learn how to move what little expertise we have into more of the cast of the red clay. And behold the patient is as much that melancholic Middle-Eastern starving cave-dweller; that shameful priest; that afflicted visionless national leader; the heavy-handed husband; the angelic faced but since dimmed to assuredness choirboy; the frantic wife. All my patients if even one comes all calling.

RM: In the basement of my grandmother's house, I came across an old worn three-dimensional wooden plaque of the *Last Supper*, on the back of which is written a legend on brittle brown paper. The story goes something like this: Leonardo da Vinci strolled through the city streets in search of models for painting his masterpiece for the monks on the walls of the refectory in the Abbey of Santa Maria delle Gracie in Milan. He had no trouble finding them for all but two of his subjects: Jesus and Judas. He searched for a face that reflected the human and spiritual beauty of the Christus. He stopped into a church in Milan for benediction one day when he beheld the object of his dreams in the sanctuary, swinging the thurible. He visited the sacristy following the service and found the young seminarian Pietro Biandinnelli, and the artist's heart was happy. Da Vinci returned to his masterpiece. Years passed, but the scaffold in the refectory had not been removed. Leonardo almost despaired of ever finding a countenance that bore the traces of the former beauty of the faithful disciple marred by the later marks of vices of the traitor. One day, when his hopes had almost left him, he beheld the face of crime in the myriad of criminal faces of the slums. He fast took out his pencil and pad and began his sketch. "At last I have found my Judas," he cried. A spark of recognition came into the face of the outcast. "I know you Leonardo da Vinci. Before I threw aside my vocation for the priesthood and left God to follow pleasure, I sat as a model for Christ in your *Last Supper*." The legend has it: The same model sat for the face of the Savior and that of the traitor, Judas.

This story makes me wonder if we don't split our "shadow" darkness off and find our opposite to inhabit it. I've often wondered why it was that Adam and Eve were expelled from the garden rather than the serpent. God keeps the serpent in the Garden of Eden. Why God even put the serpent there or allowed the serpent to remain there is another story.

EMS: Opposites inhabit/inhibit. When I was a graduate student, Carny Landis, then a research professor at the New York State Psychiatric Institute, Columbia University, introduced the longitudinal developmental accounts of several sets of twins. Some had been separated at birth and raised by different parents. Those who turned out to have bipolar personalities appeared to follow a pattern of depression and manic excitability in tandem with one another. Mind you, the separated twins had not known each other, yet each appeared to reflect the other's mood swings. The story moves into a later period of my career. At a point in time when Gestalt Therapy was coming into increasing prominence, I sought out a combination of personal therapy and supervision from a prominent Fellow of the New York Institute of Gestalt Therapy. He had been an identical twin, and had not too long before I met him, learned that his twin, who lived on the West Coast, was killed while driving while intoxicated. My mentor was learning what it meant to be a surviving twin and to, perhaps, avoid the depression that led to his twin's drinking and driving. Long after our professional relationship ceased and he became a friend and colleague, I began to notice that he was suffering with deep bouts of depression. He tried repeatedly to commit suicide and finally succumbed under still mysterious circumstances. It was not simply that each of the two was fated, but that the rabble-rousing twin, very much the rogue, set off a pattern which released itself into the surviving twin. The man was a saint in many people's eyes. He was a magnificent therapist and an unusually good and critical teacher. Yet the two lives meshed in the creation of a double tragedy, much in the spirit of da Vinci's fabled twin soul. Christ himself was reported to have had a twin brother Thomas Judas (Thomas is a name with roots in twinship). Jesus was to have had a divine Father and Thomas a human one. Yet they were, according to some recently discovered non-synoptic apocryphal accounts, identical in all but their divinity and non-divinity. You wonder why the serpent remains in the garden. The serpent is that umbilicus that joins all opposites: Adam and Eve; Jacob and Esau, Jesus and Thomas Judas. In doing psychotherapy, I have found that each person reflects and, yes, manifests, much of the common life of the others who I also see and have seen. Patients in therapy and people who have never seen a therapist, nevertheless, become significant, each to the other in ways that I continue to awe at. In ways, people redeem one another, even as they fall prey to the others' wounds. Saints twin well with rogues once the relationship has been witnessed.

RM: I wonder about those moments in psychotherapy when we hear ourselves say one thing only to find the opposite thought take over. And all within a short period of time. You can say you feel one way about a person, only to find yourself feeling the opposite in what appears as no time at all. You hear yourself say you do something for one reason, only to find the motivation elsewhere. One moment, someone may aspire to sainthood and a life of simplicity, the next to wealth and riches. In the play *Rose*, Olympia Dukakis says "The Jews gave us, *On the other hand* . . ." I think that relationships bear a change, some kind of current, and that indeed our own thoughts contain the opposite and sometimes oppositional characteristics. Love and hate sometimes make good marriages.

EMS: Ambivalence, perhaps the choicest jewel construct that Freud endowed his psychoanalysis with, nevertheless, lets the patient scot-free by being able to declare innocence and guilt as one and the same. Then there is James Joyce's "here comes everybody" taking on all contending and contentious thoughts in support of some universal crowd consciousness/unconsciousness. Of course we are each our own opposite. I know that I am not the same person when my alarm clock wakes me into the morning rituals as I am when I bed down after a hectic day. Two persons: one being. How to solve the riddle of the infamous scoundrel and the sanctified martyr?

Psychotherapy patients say what they say "as if" it were all that was said. I've never believed in a notion central to the workings of psychoanalysis and other related forms of therapy. There is no such operational principle that is truly "self-disclosure." The self needs to hide its potentialities even as it brags about its conquests. Indeed self reconstructs the past as it speaks of the present and an as yet fictionalized future. We resemble, i.e., build contrasting modes in order to have even a poke at saying "Now I know." The Jews may have given us "On the one hand, and on the other," even as Jesus cautioned the right hand from knowing what the left may be doing, and even as the Zen Buddhist folk wonder about the sound of even one of those hands clapping. Each side is both sides. Each saint, a rogue. Rogues are shy about owning up to their saintliness. One of my favorite psychoanalysts, who happens also to be a good novelist somewhere in his late 80s or early 90s, Allen Wheelis, in his 1999 *The Listener* sums the sum up quite nicely. For him opposites are ways of trying to pretend that its opposite exists in the first place. He writes: "Maybe there is no meaning but only life; and in art, no meaning but only the illusion of life. Maybe that's the whole thing . . . to search it out so carefully, with so much love, that it comes alive."

RM: What you refer to as some sort of continuous revisioning of one's past, one's history, one's experience of life may be precisely what gives us pause before stories like the da Vinci legend and autobiographical fictions such as Wheelis's.

It may be that the idea that we are not who we think we are, at least until we settle into an acceptance of our ability to act as many others; maybe all the others we've ever loved or been loved by have shown us ourselves, echoed ourselves and muted ourselves, perhaps even called us to new selves. We become other than we thought we were in the face of difference. We respond in kind. We speak of people bringing out the worst in us and people bringing out the best in us. Some provoke, others evoke. But maybe it's not such a bad thing to see our cards being put on the table one by one over the course of our lives. Like a Tarot deck, some are portents, others are great hope. Or like any deck of playing cards, some are the ones we are looking for, the ones we need in the moment depending on where we are in the game. Others we put behind the rest may be the very ones we seek out later in the game.

EMS: And to cap it, nobody ever knows, for sure, what the *me* is all about. Curse the day that forces curtail my vision–your vision–our vision. Curse the day when a person coming to either of us thinks that his or her patienthood is his or hers alone. The rogue informs the would-be saint, even as he speaks these words to himself. The saint pays no mind to the sacrifices she has been called on to make as long as they are on behalf of the rogue. Angels, I said earlier, are rarely portrayed as female. And here we end with angels of mercy, women seeking as much a kinship with all other angels, who by this time move beyond the specifics of any role definition, be it male or female, lover or whore, rogue or saint. We are, as some subatomic physicists have observed of the tinniest of things that be, the expression of "muons": elusive, flitting in and out of vacuum chambers as in and out and in again in existence. These muons are our true essence–seen and unseen, whirling in a dance with an as yet to be revealed partner at about 229,074 times per second. We are in supersymmetry, predicting in our course of existence every known particle of life and being, alive and muted in organic life as we know it, and with so many facets of existence yet to be detected, but certainly hosting who we are and are about to be. Jesus is reputed to have assured his flock that at the time of his rising, that all are equal unto angels (Luke 20:36).

Index

www.ingramcontent.com/pod-product-compliance
Ingram Content Group UK Ltd.
Pitfield, Milton Keynes, MK11 3LW, UK
UKHW022202190926
475702UK00003B/153
* 9 7 8 0 7 8 9 0 2 5 5 2 4 *